NORTHERN IRELAND'S GREATS

First published in hardback in 2005 by
Appletree Press Ltd
The Old Potato Station
14 Howard Street South
Belfast
BT7 1AP

Tel: +44 (0) 28 9024 3074
Fax: +44 (0) 28 9024 6756
E-mail: reception@appletree.ie
Web Site: www.appletree.ie

A catalogue record of this book is available from the British Library.

Northern Ireland's Greats: 100 Top Football Heroes

ISBN: 0 86281 979 2

Desk & Marketing Editor: Jean Brown
Editorial Assistance: Jim Black
Designer: Stuart Wilkinson
Additional Design: Ten Point Design
Production Manager: Paul McAvoy

9 8 7 6 5 4 3 2 1

AP3292

NORTHERN IRELAND'S GREATS

100 Top Football Heroes

DEAN HAYES

Appletree Press

This publication is dedicated to the members of the Northern Ireland team who were the sensation of the 1958 World Cup finals.

Contents

Introduction

Soccer was slower to make its impact in Ireland than in mainland Britain. Rugby and other interests impeded its progress, although the first recorded soccer match played by two Scottish teams in Belfast, was sponsored by Ulster rugby clubs.

With its strong Scottish influence, Belfast was the centre of the Irish FA and Irish League, even before the country was split, Cliftonville and Linfield following the traditions of Queen's Park and Glasgow Rangers.

After the country was divided, Linfield became the dominant club but the national team was based on exiles who moved to the English and less frequently, Scottish Leagues, Belfast offering a rich vein of talent for the scouts.

From the days of Bill McCracken, the master of the offside trap, a steady stream of outstanding Irish players enhanced the Football League. There were rarely enough before the war to create a powerful international side but the 1950s saw a sudden flowering of talent, giving manager Peter Doherty, one of the country's greatest players, some compensation for his own fruitless struggles with little support.

Seven years after the Irish had first played foreign opposition in France in May 1951, Danny Blanchflower, an inspiring captain, Jimmy McIlroy almost his equal as a scheming midfield general, a heroic goalkeeper in Harry Gregg and two excellent wingers in Billy Bingham and Peter McParland were the sensation of the 1958 World Cup, beating Italy to qualify and twice upsetting the powerful Czechoslovakia side to reach the quarter-finals.

They then went into decline as if the effort had exhausted them to leave players of the quality of George Best and Derek Dougan to play out their international careers in a morass of mediocrity but the appointment of Bingham as manager at the end of the seventies heralded a new, equally successful era.

With the peerless Pat Jennings in goal behind such solid defenders as John McClelland, Chris Nicholl, Jimmy Nicholl and Mal Donaghy and inspired midfield leadership from Martin O'Neill and Sammy McIlroy supported by the tireless David McCreery, the side was always hard to beat. They lacked goals however, for all the work of Gerry Armstrong, until the arrival of Norman Whiteside. Two British Championships were won, the side reached the quarter-finals of the World Cup in 1982 before going down again to France and in 1986 again qualified for the finals. As impressive was their ability to conjure unexpected results, beating the powerful Germans twice in the 1984 European Championship qualifiers and winning in Romania to reach the 1986 World Cup.

Since then, Northern Ireland have struggled to make much impact but under new manager Lawrie Sanchez and new leading scorer David Healy, Irish eyes are again beginning to smile. This book profiles 100 of Northern Ireland's best footballers since the Second World War and to those I have not included in my 100, I would say it is their omission that will generate the biggest debate among readers of this book.

In the statistics section at the head of each player's entry, match dates are listed according to the years that marked the end of the season in which the game was played (eg November 1956 is shown under 1957). For each player I have aimed to provide the following information: full name, recognised position, period as a Northern Ireland player, date and place of birth, career details, breakdown of appearances and goals scored for Northern Ireland and biography.

This book is a collection of statistics, biographies and games won and lost. But I hope it's more than that: it is a celebration of the great game.

Dean P. Hayes
Pembrokeshire
May 2005

Bud Aherne

One of the four players selected who played predominantly for the Republic of Ireland, Thomas Aherne, known to everyone as 'Bud', began his soccer career in the League of Ireland with his home-town club Limerick before moving north to join Belfast Celtic in 1945. He figured prominently in the closing chapters of the great Belfast side, winning an Irish League Championship medal in 1947-48 to add to the Irish Cup winners' medal he'd won the previous season.

During his time in Belfast, Bud was a regular in the Irish League representative side. He was also one of only a handful of players to represent both Irelands. He made four appearances for Northern Ireland, all at left-back between September 1946 and March 1950, at a time when the North could choose players from the South for Home International fixtures.

He made his debut for the Republic of Ireland in their first post-war international against Portugal and was a member of the side which inflicted England's first home defeat by an overseas side at Goodison Park in 1949.

He was also a member of the Belfast Celtic team, which the same year achieved an even more unexpected victory over Scotland. The Scots were Home International champions but when they met in America's Triboro Stadium, the result was an astounding 2-0 victory to the Belfastmen.

In March 1949, Bud Aherne was signed by Luton Town after they had seen his outstanding display for Northern Ireland against Wales. Signed for just £6,000, it proved to be a shrewd piece of business for the Hatters. He claimed a first team place immediately and over the next decade at Kenilworth Road he became a cult figure. The Luton faithful admired his tough tackling and his intelligent use of the ball from defence.

Luton was Aherne's only Football League club. He made a total of 267 League appearances and in 1954-55 helped them win promotion to the First Division for the first time in their history. He left Luton in 1961 to become coach to London Spartan League club Vauxhall Motors.

Personal File

Position: Full-back
Born: Thomas Aherne,
Limerick
26 January 1919
Died: January 2000
Clubs: Limerick,
Belfast Celtic,
Luton Town

NI Caps: 4

Games

Year	Opponent	Result	Score	G
1947	England	lost	2-7	
1948	Scotland	won	2-0	
1949	Wales	lost	0-2	
1950	Wales	drew	0-0	

Trevor Anderson

A utility forward of slight build, Trevor Anderson was spotted by Manchester United scout Rob Bishop when playing for Portadown.

He signed for United in October 1972 and made his debut as a substitute in a 2-0 win at Southampton the following March, laying on both goals for Charlton and Holton. After just two appearances for United's first team, he won the first of 22 full caps for Northern Ireland, scoring twice in a 3-0 win over Cyprus.

Anderson had appeared in 19 games for the Red Devils when in November 1974, Swindon Town manager Danny Williams paid £25,000 to take him to the County Ground.

His first game in Swindon's colours was against Chesterfield when he scored the game's only goal. Though he only scored one more goal in his 25 League appearances that season, his goalscoring touch returned in 1975-76 when he was the Robins' top-scorer with 15 goals. Included in that total was a hat-trick of penalties in the 5-1 home win over Walsall on 24 April 1976. He was joint-top scorer with Dave Moss the following season but in December 1977 after scoring 35 goals in 131 League outings, he was allowed to leave the County Ground to join Peterborough United.

He netted six goals in 49 games for 'The Posh' before returning to Ireland in the summer of 1979 to see out his career with Linfield. Later appointed that club's manager, he swept the board – winning the League Championship, Irish Cup, League Cup and Budweiser Cup in 1993-94.

Personal File

Position: Winger
Born: Trevor Anderson,
Belfast
3 March 1951
Clubs: Portadown,
Manchester United,
Swindon Town,
Petersborough United,
Linfield

NI Caps: 22
NI Goals: 4

Games

Year	Opponent	Result	Score	G	Year	Opponent	Result	Score	G
1973	Cyprus	won	3-0	2	1977	England	lost	1-2	
	England	lost	1-2			Scotland	lost	0-3	
	Scotland	won	2-1	1		Wales	drew	1-1	
	Wales	won	1-0			Iceland	lost	0-1	
1974	Bulgaria	drew	0-0		1978	Iceland	won	2-0	
	Portugal	drew	1-1			Holland	lost	0-1	
1975	Scotland	lost	0-3			Belgium	won	3-0	
1976	Israel	drew	1-1			Scotland	drew	1-1	
1977	Holland	drew	2-2			England	lost	0-1	
	Belgium	lost	0-2			Wales	lost	0-1	
	West Germany	lost	0-5		1979	Denmark	won	2-1	1

Gerry Armstrong

Gerry Armstrong's courage, endurance and striking power helped Northern Ireland win the respect they deserved in the 1982 World Cup finals.

He gave up his job as a senior clerical officer with the Northern Ireland Housing Executive in order to seek fame and fortune on the football field. He had started with the local junior clubs St Paul's Swifts and Cromac United before joining Bangor as a part-timer and making the move to Spurs.

He spent the 1975-76 season quite successfully in the club's reserves scoring 10 goals in 24 Football Combination matches and made his first team debut in a testimonial match for Joe Kinnear when he went on as a substitute and scored. Continuing to net goals in friendly and tour matches, the barrel-chested Armstrong was given his chance in the full senior eleven and although he did not retain his place, by the end of the season he was the regular centre-forward. However, the season was a disaster for Spurs – the club being relegated for the first time since promotion in 1950.

For the next three seasons he vied for one of the central striking positions with Colin Lee, John Duncan, Ian Moores and Chris Jones without ever really establishing himself as first choice and even played as an emergency centre-half! With the arrival of Steve Archibald and Garth Crooks in the summer of 1980 it was no surprise that Spurs were prepared to release Armstrong for £250,000 when Watford made an approach.

His style based on never-ending hard work and direct running was perhaps more suited to the Watford way but he still found it hard to establish himself and it was therefore somewhat surprising that such an upturn in his career should come on the international scene.

Having made his debut for Northern Ireland in April 1977 and won 27 caps as a Spurs player, he was already an established member of the province's team when they travelled to Spain for the 1982 World Cup.

Northern Ireland took their place at these finals rated among the no-hopers by almost every international expert. At the end of the tournament they had earned respect throughout the game for their spirit, tenacity and skill. They had been drawn in a formidable first round group alongside Yugoslavia, host-nation Spain and the unpredictable Hondurans. After Honduras drew 1-1 with Spain in the first match, Northern Ireland surprised their critics by holding Yugoslavia to a 1-1 draw. In the match against Honduras, Gerry Armstrong scored after only nine minutes but his team failed to hold onto their lead and the game ended all-square at 1-1. That meant that Northern Ireland almost certainly had to beat Spain to qualify for the next round. Victory for Spain and Billy Bingham's boys were on the next plane home. The 49,000 Spanish fans that packed the Luis Casanova stadium in Valencia expected to see an easy victory. But once again, Armstrong saw his country right, teaming his ball skills with the speed and control of Billy Hamilton to

Personal File

Position: Striker
Born: Gerald Joseph Armstrong, Belfast 23 May 1954
Clubs: Bangor City, Tottenham Hotspur, Watford, Real Mallorca, West Bromwich Albion, Chesterfield, Brighton and Hove Albion, Millwall, Crawley Town, Southwick, Worthington

NI Caps: 63
NI Goals: 12

Games

Year	Opponent	Result	Score	G	Year	Opponent	Result	Score	G
1977	West Germany	lost	0-5		1982	Scotland	drew		
	England	lost	1-2			Israel	won	1-0	1
	Wales	drew	1-1			England	lost	0-4	
	Iceland	lost	0-1			France	lost	0-4	
1978	Belgium	won	3-0	2		Wales	lost	0-3	
	Scotland	drew	1-1			Yugoslavia	drew	0-0	
	England	lost	0-1			Honduras	drew	1-1	1
	Wales	lost	0-1			Spain	won	1-0	1
1979	Republic of Ireland	drew	0-0			Austria	drew	2-2	
	Denmark	won	2-1			France	lost	1-4	1
	Bulgaria	won	2-0	1	1983	Austria	lost	0-2	
	England	lost	0-4			Turkey	won	2-1	
	Bulgaria	won	2-0	1		Albania	won	1-0	
	England	lost	0-2			Scotland	drew	0-0	
	Scotland	lost	0-1			England	drew	0-0	
	Wales	drew	1-1			Wales	lost	0-1	
1980	England	lost	1-5		1984	Austria	won	3-1	
	Republic of Ireland	won	1-0	1		West Germany	won	1-0	
	Israel	drew	0-0			England	lost	0-1	
	Scotland	won	1-0			Wales	drew	1-1	1
	England	drew	1-1			Finland	lost	0-1	
	Wales	won	1-0		1985	Romania	won	3-2	
	Australia	won	2-1			Finland	won	2-1	1
	Australia	drew	1-1			England	lost	0-1	
	Australia	won	2-1			Spain	drew	0-0	
1981	Sweden	won	3-0		1986	Turkey	drew	0-0	
	Portugal	lost	0-1			Romania	won	1-0	
	Scotland	drew	1-1			England	drew	0-0	
	Portugal	won	1-0	1		France	drew	0-0	
	Scotland	lost	0-2			Denmark	drew	1-1	
	Sweden	lost	0-1			Brazil	lost	0-3	

Gerry Armstrong

crack in a superb goal. Armstrong started the move in midfield. Confronted by three defenders, he passed a wide ball to Hamilton on his right. Hamilton set off like a greyhound, dogged by Spain's Tendillo all the way down the wing. When he hammered in a low centre, Spanish goalkeeper and captain Luis Arconarda could only palm the ball out into the path of Armstrong, who came charging through in support. Armstrong seized the chance to fire home the winner, despite the efforts of the diving Spanish defenders.

His whole-hearted commitment and non-stop battling qualities were one of the principal reasons for the unexpected success of the Irish and Gerry left such an impression with the host nation's clubs that a year later he was transferred to Real Mallorca.

He spent two years in Spain before returning to the Football League with West Bromwich Albion. He only stayed at the Hawthorns a short time before joining Chesterfield, initially on loan but the contract was cancelled and at the end of the season he signed for Brighton and Hove Albion. The 1986-87 season saw Brighton relegated to the Third Division but Armstrong remained with the south coast club as youth development officer though still registered as a player. His League career came to a sad end in February 1989 when he left the Goldstone Ground after being convicted of assaulting a fan and then joined Crawley Town.

In March 1990 he resigned after a dispute with the manager before becoming player-manager of Worthing. After a spell as coach to the Sussex FA, he is now assistant-manager to the Northern Ireland team managed by Lawrie Sanchez.

"The best I played with was George Best. The greatest player I played against was Maradonna, even though he only had one 'foot' it was a very special left foot."

- Gerry Armstrong

George Best

Millions of words have been written about George Best, the unknown from Belfast who became a soccer superstar. He didn't make the Irish schoolboy team because he wasn't strong or big enough but Manchester United's Northern Ireland scout Rob Bishop rated him highly and signed him up for Old Trafford. However, the 15-year-old Best was homesick and he and Eric McMordie caught the night ferry back to Belfast. Upon his return, he settled down under the paternal influence of Matt Busby and even worked afternoons for the Manchester Ship Canal Company just in case football didn't work out! Among the first to marvel at his talents at Old Trafford was a fellow Ulsterman, Harry Gregg, then Northern Ireland's goalkeeper. Gregg had been injured and took part in a practice game with the juniors. 'Well this kid from Belfast came at me with the ball,' he has said. 'I went out to meet him; and he done me! In those days I could usually dictate what League players should do, never mind youngsters. But with this boy, I'd gone one way and the ball the other. For the sake of my ego, I tried to believe that I'd sold myself, but it happened again shortly afterwards.'

He made his League debut in September 1963, replacing Ian Moir for the game against West Bromwich Albion. After only 15 League games, Northern Ireland gave him his first cap in the match against Wales at Swansea's Vetch Field.

Best initially played wide on the left but soon began to play in a free attacking role, scoring some of the most stunning goals ever seen at Old Trafford. He won a League Championship medal in 1964-65 and again in 1966-67 but as things began to go wrong, his frustration began to show as he retaliated against harsh treatment to earn himself a reputation for indiscipline, while his taste for wine and women began to undermine his consistency on the field.

No player in the history of British football had until David Beckham been such a centre of attraction as Best and had to cope with so much attention and publicity. With his long black hair, his beard, the fashionable clothes he wore, models and endorsements, his expensive sports cars, the house he had built for himself outside Manchester, the reputed £30,000 a year in earnings from many sources, he was essentially the product and emblem of the years which followed the abolition of soccer's maximum wage in 1961. He himself was described by his mother as a home-loving boy who would often sit quietly for hours in the house. But there was still the paradox of Best's frenetic social life, where he so often appeared as the still centre of whirling activity, not happy to be there, but not able to tear himself away, to be without it.

The peak of Best's career came in 1968 when his team won the European Cup at Wembley, beating Benfica 4-1 after extra-time. One of those goals was a superb effort by Best, who rounded goalkeeper Henrique before coolly rolling the ball into an empty net. It was a euphoric night for Manchester United and for Best, the pinnacle of achievement in a season that saw him gain the titles of English and European Footballer of the Year.

Personal File

Position: Forward
Born: George Best, Belfast 22 May 1946
Clubs: Manchester United, Stockport County (loan), Los Angeles Aztecs, Fulham, Cork, San Diego Sockers, Fort Lauderdale Strikers, San Jose Earthquakes, Hibernian, Motherwell, Glentoran, Bournemouth
NI Caps: 37
NI Goals: 9

Games

Year	Opponent	Result	Score	G	Year	Opponent	Result	Score	G
1964	Wales	won	3-2		1970	USSR	drew	0-0	
	Uruguay	won	3-0			Scotland	lost	0-1	
1965	England	lost	3-4			England	lost	1-3	1
	Switzerland	won	1-0			Wales	lost	0-1	
	Switzerland	lost	1-2	1	1971	Spain	lost	0-3	
	Scotland	lost	2-3	1		Cyprus	won	3-0	1
	Holland	won	2-1			Cyprus	won	5-0	3
	Holland	drew	0-0			England	lost	0-1	
	Albania	won	4-1			Scotland	won	1-0	1
1966	Scotland	won	3-2			Wales	won	1-0	
	Scotland	lost	1-2		1972	USSR	lost	0-1	
	Albania	drew	1-1			Spain	drew	1-1	
1967	England	lost	0-2		1973	Bulgaria	lost	0-3	
1968	Scotland	won	1-0		1974	Portugal	drew	1-1	
1969	Turkey	won	4-1	1	1977	Holland	drew	2-2	
	England	lost	1-3			Belgium	lost	0-2	
	Scotland	drew	1-1			West Germany	lost	0-5	
	Wales	drew	0-0		1978	Iceland	won	2-0	
						Holland	lost	0-1	

"In 1971 I was sent off for arguing with one of my own team-mates!"

-George Best

George Best

George Best had great natural ability – one of the most gifted footballers you could wish to see. He had great speed and awareness, coupled with fantastic dribbling ability. Strong and brave, he was the complete all-round forward, netting a hat-trick for Northern Ireland in a 5-0 defeat of Cyprus.

He was however, becoming increasingly difficult to manage – missing training and failing to turn up for a match. Just before 1972, United sacked their manager Frank O'Farrell and issued a statement that George Best would remain on the transfer list and would not be selected for Manchester United again. A letter from George Best announcing his retirement crossed with this. He walked out on United several times and played his last game for them on New Year's Day 1974. Four days later he failed to turn up for training yet again and his days at Old Trafford were over.

In November 1975 he joined Stockport County on loan, playing three games for them – his drawing power trebled the County side's home attendance. A spell in the States playing for Los Angeles Aztecs followed before he joined Fulham in September 1976. He later played for Cork before returning to America to play for San Diego Sockers, Fort Lauderdale Strikers and San Jose Earthquakes in the NASL. In 1980-81 he played Scottish League football with Hibernian, returning two seasons later to play for Motherwell. He also turned out for Glentoran, Bournemouth and several non-League clubs.

After a succession of glamorous girlfriends, a drink problem and several skirmishes with the law, Best served a prison sentence in 1985. George Best, who recently had a liver transplant, was a footballing genius and has gone down in history as one of world football's all-time greats.

"We had our problems with the wee feller but I prefer to remember the genius."

- Sir Matt Busby

Billy Bingham

Billy Bingham holds the record for the longest-serving British international manager, having been in charge of Northern Ireland for a total of 15 years including a spell of 13 years from 1980 to 1993. A master tactician he is also his country's most successful manager by a mile, appearing in two World Cup tournaments in 1982 and 1986. His greatest moment was when Northern Ireland beat hosts Spain 1-0 on 25th June 1982 (thanks to a Gerry Armstrong goal) to qualify for the second round of the competition.

As a player, Bingham achieved success with Northern Ireland on the pitch as well. A tricky winger, he was part of the team which reached the quarter-finals of the competition in 1958 and in all, he won a total of 56 caps.

Billy Bingham started his illustrious career with Glentoran and after starring in a representative game for the Irish League XI in 1951, Sunderland paid a large fee to take him to Roker Park. Within two years of his arrival in the north-east, he was a permanent member of the Northern Ireland team.

For a winger, Billy Bingham was unusually combative in the air, as he showed on numerous occasions, although more of his goals came from long distance. When shooting, he tended to favour his right foot and on the rare occasions he hit the target with his left, he would endure merciless ribbing from his team-mates. He had scored 47 goals in 227 games for the Wearsiders when on his return from the World Cup, he joined Luton Town for a fee of £15,000. In his first season with the Hatters, he netted 14 goals including the winner in the FA Cup semi-final replay against Norwich City at St Andrew's. Though the club lost their top flight status the following season, Bingham was the Hatters' leading scorer with 16 goals.

In October 1960, Bingham left Kenilworth Road to join Everton. Though in his 30th year, he was still supremely fit and his penetrating style on the right flank became a key ingredient in the club's 1962-63 League Championship-winning side. Quick, direct and always capable of the unexpected – though a distinctive habit of patting the ball from foot to foot often offered a clue that an explosive burst was imminent – the Ulsterman was capable of 'skinning' any full-back on his day and could cross the ball with precision. In addition he was brave and possessed a pugnacious streak behind his charm and ebullience. After losing his place to Scottish international Alex Scott, he left to join Port Vale where a broken leg brought his playing days to an end.

He became manager of Southport, leading them to promotion for the first time in their history. After spells at Plymouth and Linfield when he was also manager of Northern Ireland, he took charge of the Greek national side before rejoining Everton as manager in the summer of 1973.

He inherited a team in need of major reconstruction and so smashed the British transfer record when he signed Bob Latchford from Birmingham City for £350,000. Outsiders were misled by his genial character into believing he

Personal File

Position: Outside Right
Born: William Laurence Bingham, Belfast 5 August 1931
Clubs: Glentoran, Sunderland, Luton Town, Everton, Port Vale

NI Caps: 56
NI Goals: 10

Games

Year	Opponent	Result	Score	G	Year	Opponent	Result	Score	G
1951	France	drew	2-2		1958	West			
1952	Scotland	lost	0-2			Germany	drew	2-2	
	England	lost	0-2			Czechoslovakia	won	2-1	
	Wales	lost	0-3			France	lost	0-4	
1953	England	drew	2-2		1959	England	drew	3-3	
	Scotland	drew	1-1			Spain	lost	2-6	
	France	lost	1-3			Scotland	drew	2-2	
	Wales	lost	2-3			Wales	won	4-1	
1954	Scotland	lost	1-3		1960	Scotland	lost	0-4	
	England	lost	1-3			England	lost	1-2	1
	Wales	won	2-1			Wales	lost	2-3	1
1955	England	lost	0-2		1961	England	lost	2-5	
	Scotland	drew	2-2	1		West			
	Wales	lost	2-3			Germany	lost	3-4	
1956	Scotland	won	2-1	1		Scotland	lost	2-5	
	England	lost	0-3			Italy	lost	2-3	
	Wales	drew	1-1			Greece	lost	1-2	
1957	England	drew	1-1			West			
	Scotland	lost	0-1			Germany	lost	1-2	
	Portugal	drew	1-1	1	1962	Greece	won	2-0	
	Wales	drew	0-0			England	drew	1-1	
	Italy	lost	0-1		1963	Poland	won	2-0	
	Portugal	won	3-0	1		England	lost	1-3	
1958	Scotland	drew	1-1	1		Scotland	lost	1-5	1
	England	won	3-2			Poland	won	2-0	1
	Italy	drew	2-2			Spain	drew	1-1	
	Italy	lost	1-2		1964	Scotland	won	2-1	1
	Wales	drew	1-1			Spain	lost	0-1	
	Czechoslovakia	won	1-0			England	lost	3-8	
	Argentina	lost	1-2						

Billy Bingham

was a soft touch but in fact, he worked his players hard. Sometimes they produced entertaining fare and in 1974-75 came fourth in Division One, but although he continued to buy he could not find the right blend and two years after taking over the reins, he was sacked.

Bingham, who was awarded the MBE for his services to football, later had a spell as manager of Mansfield Town before embarking on his long and successful reign as Northern Ireland team manager.

"He was very good at motivating players. He would make you feel 10 feet tall when you went onto the pitch."

- Billy Hamilton on Billy Bingham

Left: (L-R) Luton Town's Billy Bingham tries to cross the ball past Wolverhampton Wanderers' Gerry Harris

Kingsley Black

Kingsley Black made his Luton Town debut in a League Cup tie against Wigan Athletic which the Hatters won 4-2. At the end of his first season, 1987-88, he had won a League Cup winners' medal after Luton had beaten Arsenal 3-2 and came on as a substitute during the Hatters' reversal in the Simod Cup Final.

The Luton-born winger, who had played schoolboy international football for England, won the first of his 30 full caps for Northern Ireland when he came off the bench to replace Robbie Dennison in a goalless draw against France in April 1988.

The following season he missed just one match as Luton again reached the League Cup Final, only to lose 3-1 to Nottingham Forest. Over the next couple of seasons, Black reached double figures in terms of goals scored but in September 1991 after scoring 30 goals in 157 games he was transferred to Nottingham Forest for a fee of £1.5 million.

His early form for Forest was impressive and at the end of his first season, he was among the goalscorers as they beat Southampton 3-2 to win the Zenith Data Systems Final at Wembley. He later went down with a virus and after failing to get his place back from Ian Woan, went on loan to both Sheffield United and Millwall.

In July 1996 Black joined Grimsby Town, the Mariners paying just £25,000 for his services. He won an Autowindscreen Shield winners' medal following Grimsby's victory over Bournemouth at Wembley, having scored the winner. He later switched to the centre of midfield where his displays led to him rekindling his international career. Black went on to make 171 appearances for the Mariners before joining Lincoln City in the summer of 2001. Sadly, he was hampered by injuries and illness during his time at Sincil Bank and his Football League career finally came to an end when he parted company with the club by mutual consent.

Personal File

Position: Left-winger
Born: Kingsley Terence Black,
Luton Town
22 June 1968
Clubs: Luton Town,
Nottingham Forest,
Sheffield United (loan),
Millwall (loan),
Grimsby Town,
Lincoln City

NI Caps: 30
NI Goals: 1

Games

Year	Opponent	Result	Score	G	Year	Opponent	Result	Score	G
1988	France	drew	0-0		1992	Faroe Islands	won	5-0	
	Malta	won	3-0			Austria	won	2-1	1
1989	Republic of					Denmark	lost	1-2	
	Ireland	drew	0-0			Scotland	lost	0-1	
1989	Hungary	lost	0-1			Lithuania	drew	2-2	
	Spain	lost	0-4			Germany	drew	1-1	
	Spain	lost	0-2		1993	Spain	drew	0-0	
	Chile	lost	0-1			Denmark	lost	0-1	
1990	Hungary	lost	1-2			Albania	won	2-1	
	Norway	lost	2-3			Republic of			
	Uruguay	won	1-0			Ireland	lost	0-3	
1991	Yugoslavia	lost	0-2			Spain	lost	1-3	
	Denmark	drew	1-1		1994	Denmark	lost	0-1	
	Austria	drew	0-0			Republic			
	Poland	won	3-1			Of Ireland	drew	1-1	
	Yugoslavia	lost	1-4			Romania	won	2-0	
	Faroe Islands	drew	1-1						

Danny Blanchflower

Danny Blanchflower was a thinker, not just a footballer and a master tactician. He had a knack for spotting weaknesses in the opposition and exploiting them, or to adjust any deficiencies in his own side.

Born with the Christian names Robert Dennis, he somehow became known as Danny to everyone. As a child, Blanchflower was an all-round sportsman who played football for his school sides and the local Boys' Brigade. He studied at Belfast Technical College and was an apprentice engineer for a while.

In 1939 he formed his own club called Bloomfield United and so successful was it that he eventually founded a complete league competition. He and his brother Jackie were coached by their mother who had played for a women's side in Belfast. Scout Sammy Weir of Glentoran spotted Danny playing and signed him on amateur forms for the club as a 16-year-old.

It was wartime by now and Danny volunteered for the RAF. He had won a scholarship to St Andrew's University and was not called up until he had completed his studies in 1944. During Christmas 1945 he returned to Ireland on leave and signed professional forms for Glentoran. He made his first team debut as an inside-forward and in February 1947 he played for the Irish League against the Football League at Goodison Park and impressed many people; this led to a move to Barnsley in April 1949 for a fee of £6,500. Just six months later he made his full international debut against Scotland at Windsor Park but this ended in tears as his side lost 8-2.

Blanchflower was probably too much of an individualist for Barnsley and questioned their outdated training methods and outlook on the game. Things did not improve all that much after his move to Aston Villa in March 1951 for an increased fee of £15,000. His intellectual approach to the game and his passion for trying new ideas met with the same conservative resistance at Villa Park. The critical move in his career came in December 1954 when he joined Spurs for a £30,000 fee.

Danny succeeded Alf Ramsey as captain but after falling out with recently appointed manager Jimmy Anderson, he lost both the captaincy and his place in the team. When Bill Nicholson became manager there was a meeting of minds and he reinstated Blanchflower as captain.

It was not long before Spurs were the supreme team in English football and honours came thick and fast. Blanchflower captained the side to the League and Cup double in 1960-61, the first time it had been achieved that century. He also scored from the penalty-spot in the Cup Final victory over Burnley the following year, sending keeper Blacklaw the wrong way. After the disappointment of their semi-final defeat against Benfica in the European Cup in 1962, Spurs went on to win the European Cup Winners' Cup the following season. In one of the greatest displays, they beat Athletico Madrid

Personal File

Position: Right-half
Born: Robert Dennis Blanchflower, Belfast
10 Febuary 1926
Died: 9 December 1993
Clubs: Glentoran,
Barnsley,
Aston Villa
Tottenham Hotspur

NI Caps: 56
NI Goals: 2

Games

Year	Opponent	Result	Score	G	Year	Opponent	Result	Score	G
1950	Scotland	lost	2-8		1958	Czechoslovakia	won	1-0	
	Wales	drew	0-0			Czechoslovakia	won	2-1	
1951	England	lost	1-4			Argentina	lost	1-3	
	Scotland	lost	1-6			France	lost	0-4	
	France	drew	2-2			West			
1952	Wales	lost	0-3			Germany	drew	2-2	
1953	England	drew	2-2		1959	England	drew	3-3	
	Scotland	drew	1-1			Spain	lost	2-6	
	Wales	lost	2-3			Scotland	drew	2-2	
	France	lost	1-3			Wales	won	4-1	
1954	England	lost	1-3		1960	England	lost	1-2	
	Scotland	lost	1-3			Scotland	lost	0-4	
	Wales	won	2-1			Wales	lost	2-3	1
1955	England	lost	0-2		1961	England	lost	2-5	
	Scotland	drew	2-2			Scotland	lost	2-5	1
	Wales	lost	2-3			Wales	lost	1-5	
1956	England	lost	0-3			West			
	Scotland	won	2-1			Germany	lost	3-4	
	Wales	drew	1-1			West			
1957	England	drew	1-1			Germany	lost	1-2	
	Scotland	lost	0-1		1962	England	drew	1-1	
	Wales	drew	0-0			Scotland	lost	1-6	
	Italy	lost	0-1			Wales	lost	0-4	
	Portugal	drew	1-1			Greece	won	2-0	
	Portugal	won	0-0			Holland	lost	0-4	
1958	England	won	3-2			England	lost	1-3	
	Scotland	drew	1-1			Scotland	lost	1-5	
	Wales	drew	1-1			Poland	won	2-0	
	Italy	drew	2-2			Poland	won	2-0	
	Italy	won	2-1						

Danny Blanchflower

5-1 in Rotterdam. Danny was voted 'Footballer of the Year' in both 1958 and 1961. He struck up a formidable and fruitful relationship with Peter Doherty, the Northern Ireland team manager, who, like Blanchflower, was a supremely talented individual. Together they produced some startling results.

Once in the Irish side, he made the No.4 shirt his own, playing in 56 out of 62 internationals including 41 on the trot. Ireland beat England for the first time in 30 years, this victory coming at Wembley in 1957 by 3-2. They achieved even greater things in the World Cup in 1958 when they reached the quarter-finals. This included a memorable defeat of Czechoslovakia with a team that had been hit by injuries. He did his best to confuse the foreign journalists in Sweden, explaining that the Irish team's tactics were to equalise before the other team had scored!

On hanging up his boots, Blanchflower started a career as a journalist for the *Sunday Express*, gaining a reputation for being outspoken and openly attacking the football establishment. He also created a stir when he refused to appear on the 'This Is Your Life' TV programme, considering it a great invasion of his privacy.

He made a brief excursion into football management in December 1978 when he took charge of Chelsea but resigned after just nine months. He left the *Sunday Express* in 1988 due to ill-health. In May 1990 he received an honour never open to him in his playing days, when Spurs met a Northern Ireland XI in a benefit match. Danny Blanchflower, one of the game's all-time greats, died in December 1993.

"Too many captains did no more than carry the ball and call 'heads'."

- Danny Blanchflower

Left: (L-R) England captain Billy Wright shakes hands with Northern Ireland captain Danny Blanchflower before the match.

Jackie Blanchflower

Brother to the great Spurs player, Danny Blanchflower with whom he played in the Northern Ireland national team, Jackie Blanchflower is best remembered as a centre-half, yet he played only the last 29 League games of his career in that position.

His other appearances for Manchester United were either at wing-half or as a goalscoring inside-right or on one occasion as a centre-forward. Having come through the junior ranks at Old Trafford, Jackie Blanchflower made his League debut at right-half in a goalless draw against Liverpool in November 1951.

Blanchflower's second game was not until April 1953 and he had to wait a further six months before his third appearance. Then he came in as a replacement for Stan Pearson and held the No.8 spot for the remainder of the 1953-54 season. He lost his place in the United side to John Doherty in 1955-56 and did not regain a regular place until the end of the following season when he took over from Mark Jones at centre-half.

He won League Championship medals in 1955-56 and 1956-57 and in this latter season, his performances earned him a place in United's FA Cup Final side against Aston Villa.

However, he spent much of the 2-1 defeat in goal, following an early injury to keeper Ray Wood, who clashed with Villa's Northern Ireland international winger Peter McParland.

Jones regained the centre-half position in December 1957 but Blanchflower, who won 12 caps for Northern Ireland, still went on the ill-fated trip to Belgrade in February 1958. The injuries he received at Munich meant that he never played again.

Blanchflower, who had made 16 appearances for the Red Devils, later ran a shop close to Old Trafford and became an entertaining after-dinner speaker.

"Danny didn't kiss the Blarney Stone – he swallowed it!"

- Jackie Blanchflower on his brother Danny

Personal File

Position: Right-half
Born: John Blanchflower, Belfast 7 March 1933
Died: 2 September 1998
Clubs: Glentoran, Barnley, Aston Villa, Tottenham Hotspur

NI Caps: 56
NI Goals: 2

Games

Year	Opponent	Result	Score	G	Year	Opponent	Result	Score	G
1950	Scotland	lost	2-8		1958	Czechoslovakia	won	1-0	
	Wales	drew	0-0			Czechoslovakia	won	2-1	
1951	England	lost	1-4			Argentina	lost	1-3	
	Scotland	lost	1-6			France	lost	0-4	
	France	drew	2-2			West Germany	drew	2-2	
1952	Wales	lost	0-3		1959	England	drew	3-3	
1953	England	drew	2-2			Spain	lost	2-6	
	Scotland	drew	1-1			Scotland	drew	2-2	
	Wales	lost	2-3			Wales	won	4-1	
	France	lost	1-3		1960	England	lost	1 2	
1954	England	lost	1-3			Scotland	lost	0-4	
	Scotland	lost	1-3			Wales	lost	2-3	1
	Wales	won	2-1		1961	England	lost	2-5	
1955	England	lost	0-2			Scotland	lost	2-5	1
	Scotland	drew	2-2			Wales	lost	1-5)	
	Wales	lost	2-3			West Germany	lost	3-4	
1956	England	lost	0-3			West Germany	lost	1-2	
	Scotland	won	2-1		1962	England	drew	1-1	
	Wales	drew	1-1			Scotland	lost	1-6	
1957	England	drew	1-1			Wales	lost	0-4	
	Scotland	lost	0-1			Greece	won	2-0	
	Wales	drew	0-0			Holland	lost	0-4	
	Italy	lost	0-1			England	lost	1-3	
	Portugal	drew	1-1			Scotland	lost	1-5	
	Portugal	won	3-0			Poland	won	2-0	
1958	England	won	3-2			Poland	won	2-0	
	Scotland	drew	1-1						
	Wales	drew	1-1						
	Italy	drew	2-2						
	Italy	won	2-1						

Noel Brotherston

Noel Brotherston began his career with Tottenham Hotspur but wasn't given much of a chance at White Hart Lane, making only one appearance before being released on a free transfer and joining Blackburn Rovers in the summer of 1977.

After making his debut for the Lancashire club in a 1-1 draw at Notts County on the opening day of the 1977-78 season, the prematurely balding Brotherston proved to be a revelation, ending the campaign as the club's leading scorer with 11 goals.

One of the trickiest wingers outside of the First Division, Brotherston won the first of 27 full international caps for Northern Ireland when he played against Scotland in the Home International Championships – it was his cross that provided the chance for Willie Hamilton to score the game's only goal. On his third appearance for the national side against Wales, Brotherston scored what proved to be the winner and gave Northern Ireland the Home International Championship outright for the first time since 1914. He was a member of Irish squad for the 1982 World Cup Finals in Spain, although the form of Norman Whiteside meant that Brotherston was restricted to substitute appearances during the competition.

A player who relied on skill and trickery, he suffered from a series of injuries and a loss of form towards the end of his career at Ewood Park, so much so that he was absent when Rovers won the Full Members Cup in 1987. He had scored 46 goals, many of them spectacular, in 364 League and Cup games when Don Mackay released him in the summer of 1987.

Brotherston joined Bury and had one good season with the Shakers before going on loan to League newcomers Scarborough and then the Swedish club Motola, prior to ending his career with non-League Chorley.

Brotherston then became a painter and decorator but sadly died of a heart attack aged 38 in 1995.

Personal File

Position: Winger
Born: Noel Brotherston,
Dundonald
18 November 1956
Died: 6 May 1995
Clubs: Tottenham Hotspur,
Blackburn Rovers,
Bury, Scarborough (loan),
Motola (Sweden), Chorley

NI Caps: 27
NI Goals: 3

Games

Year	Opponent	Result	Score	G	Year	Opponent	Result	Score	G
1980	Scotland	won	1-0		1982	Honduras	drew	1-1	
	England	drew	1-1			Austria	drew	2-2	
	Wales	won	1-0	1	1983	Austria	lost	0-2	
	Australia	won	2-1			West			
	Australia	drew	1-1			Germany	won	1-0	
	Australia	won	2-1	1		Albania	drew	0-0	
1981	Sweden	won	3-1	1		Turkey	won	2-1	
	Portugal	lost	0-1			Albania	won	1-0	
1982	Scotland	drew	0-0			Scotland	drew	0-0	
	Israel	won	1-0			England	drew	0-0	
	England	lost	0-4			Wales	lost	0-1	
	France	lost	0-4		1984	Turkey	lost	0-1	
	Scotland	drew	1-1		1985	Israel	won	3-0	
	Wales	lost	0-3			Turkey	won	2-0	

Johnny Carey

Johnny Carey arrived at Old Trafford in 1936 after being spotted by Manchester United's chief scout at the time, Louis Rocca. He'd actually gone to Dublin to watch another player, instead he came back with a recommendation that Carey be signed. Rocca later declared that 'No greater Irish player crossed the water to make a name in English football.' After helping United win promotion to the First Division in 1937-38, he impressed in the top flight the following season before war intervened.

When he linked up with Manchester United after the hostilities, Matt Busby was well off for forwards and converted Carey to full-back and made him captain.

Johnny Carey turned out against England in two international matches within three days and for different countries! He played for Northern Ireland in Belfast on 28 September 1946 and for the Republic of Ireland in Dublin on 30 September. Later in that same season, he played in four countries in eight days. He played at Anfield for Manchester United on 3 May 1947 and then for the Republic of Ireland against Portugal in Dublin the next day. He then played in a Dutch trial match at the Hague on 6 May and for the Rest of Europe against Great Britain at Hampden Park on 10 May.

Carey was a man so versatile that he figured in nine different positions for the Reds, ten if you include the occasion he pulled on the goalkeeper's jersey when Jack Crompton was taken ill at an away match. He was also versatile on the international stage, appearing in seven different positions during his appearances for both Northern Ireland and the Republic.

He led United to victory in the 1948 FA Cup Final over Blackpool and was voted 'Footballer of the Year' in 1949. The following year he was voted 'Sportsman of the Year' and in 1951-52 led the Reds to the League title. When Carey retired after 304 appearances in a United shirt, the directors took the unusual step of inviting him to their boardroom to express their appreciation of his long and loyal service to the club. United were keen to keep him on the staff and offered him a position as coach.

However, Blackburn Rovers offered him a similar position with more prospects of becoming manager at Ewood Park. He took Rovers into the First Division, later managing a number of clubs including Everton, Leyton Orient and Nottingham Forest before rejoining Blackburn as administrative manager. One of the most highly respected men in the game – a superb footballer and inspiring captain – Johnny Carey, who made only seven appearances for Northern Ireland, was undoubtedly one of the all-time greats.

left: Manchester United's John Carey (l) moves across to intercept

Personal File

Position: Full-back
Born: John James Carey,
Dublin
23 February 1919
Died: 27 August 1995
Clubs: St James' Gate,
Manchester United

NI Caps: 7

Games

Year	Opponent	Result	Score	G
1947	England	lost	2-7	
	Scotland	drew	0-0	
	Wales	won	2-1	
1948	England	drew	2-2	
1949	England	lost	2-6	
	Scotland	lost	2-3	
	Wales	lost	0-2	

"By his outstanding personality as a sportsman... he set a shining example to all who follow him."

- Tribute to Manchester United minute book in 1953

Roy Carroll

Goalkeeper Roy Carroll began his Football League career with Hull City, making a terrific Tigers' debut at Swindon Town in January 1996. He retained his place with a series of eye-catching performances, displaying a presence and maturity beyond his years. He attracted many scouts, with Bolton showing a particular interest but at the end of the season, in which he was voted Hull's 'Player of the Year', he was still at Boothferry Park. He got his first full international call-up in October 1996 for Northern Ireland's World Cup qualifier against Armenia.

Towards the end of the 1996-97 season, Carroll was surprisingly sold to Wigan Athletic for a fee of £350,000, helping the Tigers out of a financial dilemma. Despite being the Latics' record signing, he had to wait until November 1997 before replacing Lee Butler at Watford. He went on to become runner-up in Wigan's 'Player of the Year' award. A virtual ever-present in 1998-99, he maintained a high level of consistency between the posts. Though speculation abounded with stories of a move to a Premiership club, Carroll, who won an Autowindscreen Shield winners' medal, was again voted runner-up in the club's 'Player of the Year' awards. Recognised by his fellow professionals with selection for the PFA award-winning Division Two side, he played a large part in the Latics' run of 26 League games without defeat at the start of the 1999-2000 season. An emergency appendix operation saw him miss the last seven games of the season and though speculation continued to link him to one of the top Premiership clubs, he was still at the JJB Stadium for the 2000-01 season. His performances continued to be of the highest class and he went on to keep 13 clean sheets in 34 first team outings, to help the Latics reach the play-offs for the second successive season.

Firmly established as Northern Ireland's first-choice keeper, he eventually left Wigan to join Manchester United for £2.5 million as understudy to Fabian Barthez. He endured something of a baptism of fire when Aston Villa's Darius Vassell beat him after just four minutes of his Premiership debut in September 2001, but his record was impressive throughout the campaign, more than justifying Sir Alex Ferguson's faith in him.

Though he was pushed further down the Old Trafford pecking order following the signing of Spanish goalkeeper Ricardo, it all changed again as the season progressed and he bounced back to relegate the Spaniard to third choice. He again found his way to regular first team football blocked by the signing of Tim Howard but he remained a trusted and patient deputy. When Sir Alex decided to rest Howard following the Reds' exit from the Champions League, Carroll took his chance with relish, inspiring United to their 15th FA Cup Final where they beat Millwall.

Though he shared the goalkeeping duties with Tim Howard in 2004-05, he was in goal for the FA Cup Final against Arsenal when United lost on penalties but was then released by the Old Trafford club in the summer of 2005. He has joined Premiership new boys West Ham United who will be hoping the Northern Ireland keeper's displays will keep them in the top flight.

Personal File

Position: Goalkeeper
Born: Roy Eric Carroll,
        Enniskillen
        30 September 1977
Clubs: Hull City,
        Wigan Athletic,
        Manchester United,
        West Ham United

NI Caps: 17

Games

Year	Opponent	Result	Score	Year	Opponent	Result	Score	G
1997	Thailand	drew	0-0	2002	Liechtenstein	drew	0-0	
1999	Republic				Spain	lost	0-5	
	of Ireland	won	1-0	2003	Finland	lost	0-1	
2000	Luxembourg	won	3-1		Italy	lost	0-2	
	Malta	won	3-0	2004	Serbia &			
2001	Malta	won	1-0		Montenegro	drew	1-1	
	Denmark	drew	1-1	2005	Switzerland	drew	0-0	
	Iceland	lost	0-1		Austria	drew	3-3	
	Czech				Canada	lost	0-1	
	Republic	lost	0-1					
	Bulgaria	lost	3-4					

PEACOCK

THUMB NAIL SKETCHES OF

IRELAND

By MALCOLM BRODIE
Sports Editor,
"Belfast Telegraph."

CASEY

Y GREGG (Doncaster Rovers)
oalkeeper Reckoned now by many shrewd
one of the best goalkeepers in Britain,
succeeded Norman Uprichard (Portsmouth)
ntry's last line defender. A Coleraine boy,
one of many players in the five figure
oulded at Doncaster. 4 caps.

CUNNINGHAM (Leicester City)
Back Cunningham was born in Co.
all his football was confined to Scotland
transferred to Leicester three seasons ago.
well in his first International in 1954,
made an immediate bid for his transfer
en. 9 caps.

MICHAEL (Newcastle United)
k A regular in Ireland teams since
merly with Linfield, began his senior
tonville. Has travelled the world with
untry. 17 caps.

ANCHFLOWER (Tottenham)
Half Joined Glentoran as a centre
sn't long at the Oval before they
osition was right half. Transferred
Aston Villa before moving to White
. Turned down lucrative coaching
n F.A. He now appears regularly
ision as a commentator. 19 caps.

(Glenavon)
Smallest man in the Irish party,
Charles, but is undaunted by the
t wing half and inside forward
ins Glenavon in next Saturday's
st Derry City. Small in stature
houlders above most others in

(Glasgow Celtic)
Danny Blanchflower, Bertie
halves in the four countries.

A Coleraine boy, he loves football—either pla
watching it. In his earlier days he appeared
forwards, but is now the recognised Celtic
mainstay. 15 caps.

BILLY BINGHAM (Sunderland)
Outside Right This Belfast boy
dangerous type of winger. He seldom gives
time to make a studied clearance. He seldom gives
play for the Irish League against the Footb
which persuaded Sunderland manager, Bi
to give Glentoran £8,000 for him. 17 cap

JIMMY McILROY (Burnley)
Inside Right One of the greatest insi
in Britain today, he can manipulate the ball
and split open a defence with accurate,
passes. Joined Burnley from Gentoran.

JIMMY JONES (Glenavon)
Centre Forward Gets his third
leader of the Irish attack. Scored in his
ance against Wales at Cardiff a year
leading scorer in Irish League Football w
55 goals.

TOM CASEY (Newcastle Unite
Inside Left I almost wrote le
his name, as that is the position he ha
for his club and Ireland in recent seas
moved to inside forward as an experim
effort to give punch to the line.
Bangor, he joined Leeds United, ther
before joining Newcastle. Was on tour
F.A. in 1953-54. 4 caps.

PETER McPARLAND (Aston
Outside Left Peter is a native
it was from Dundalk that he mad
Aston Villa, who owe their place i
Final against Manchester United to
efforts. A strong win

Tommy Casey's name appears in a list of Northern Ireland players in the 1950's.

Tommy Casey

A human dynamo on the field, Tommy Casey was a 90-minute man with lots of stamina and endeavour. He started out with Belfast YMCA and East Belfast before joining Bangor. He won youth caps in 1948 and in May 1949 was one of three Bangor youngsters who joined Leeds United.

Unable to make much headway at Elland Road, he joined Bournemouth before two years later being recommended to Newcastle United by former stalwart Bill McCracken.

Tommy Casey spent six seasons in Newcastle United's squad, his best campaigns being 1952-53, 1955-56 and 1956-57. A rival to Charlie Crowe, he stepped into his contemporary's place for the 1955 Wembley showpiece following Crowe's unfortunate injury and played his part in a 3-1 defeat of Manchester City.

Tenacious and full of vigour, Tommy Casey, who won 12 full caps for Northern Ireland, was the iron-man of his country's noted 1958 World Cup line-up that reached the quarter-finals. After parting company with the Magpies, Casey had a brief spell with Portsmouth before joining Bristol City. On leaving the first-class scene, he was player-manager at Gloucester City. Following a spell as Swansea's coach, he was appointed Distillery's manager. He was later coach at both Everton and Coventry City before becoming manager of Grimsby Town. Casey, who was sacked by the Mariners on the day he moved into his newly-purchased house, later managed KR (Reykjavik) and Harstaad before this much-travelled player quit the game to become a self-employed fishmonger in Portbury near Bristol.

Personal File

Position: Wing-half
Born: Thomas Casey,
Comber,
11 March 1930
Clubs: Bangor City,
Leeds United,
Bournemouth,
Newcastle United,
Portsmouth, Bristol City,
Gloucester City

NI Caps: 12
NI Goals: 2

Games

Year	Opponent	Result	Score	G
1955	Wales	lost	2-3	
1956	Wales	drew	1-1	
1957	England	drew	1-1	
	Scotland	lost	0-1	
	Portugal	drew	1-1	
	Wales	drew	0-0	
	Italy	lost	0-1	
	Portugal	won	3-0	1
1958	West Germany	drew	2-2	
	France	lost	0-4	
1959	England	drew	3-3	1
	Spain	lost	2-6	

Tommy Cassidy

A tall, skilful midfield man, Tommy Cassidy joined Newcastle United from Glentoran for a fee of £25,000 in October 1970. Although he appeared in the First Division only occasionally during his first three years at St James Park, he won the first of his 24 full international caps for Northern Ireland, aged only 20, in a 1-0 defeat by England at Windsor Park in May 1971.

His first season as a regular in the Newcastle side was 1973-74 and at the end of it he picked up an FA Cup finalist's medal following the Magpies' Wembley defeat by Liverpool after Burnley had been beaten in the semi-final.

Cassidy was at Wembley again two years later, on the losing side as Newcastle were beaten by Manchester City in the League Cup Final, with Dennis Tueart's overhead masterpiece winning the day.

Tommy Cassidy's swansong as a Newcastle player was a prominent role in Northern Ireland's impressive performance in the Home International Championships of May 1980. Wins against Wales and Scotland and a draw at Wembley against England meant that the Province clinched their first outright win in the tournament for 66 years!

Cassidy signed for Burnley, newly-relegated to the Third Division in the summer of 1980 for a fee of £30,000. While not always an automatic choice during his time at Turf Moor, he helped the Clarets to the Third Division Championship in 1981-82. Following the Lancashire club's relegation from the Second Division, Cassidy was released in May 1983.

He played and coached in Cyprus for a number of years and enjoyed some success with Apoel Nicosia, managing them to the Cypriot League Championship in 1986. He later returned to England and went on to manage Gateshead in the Vauxhall Conference and Glentoran in the Irish League.

Personal File

Position: Midfielder
Born: Thomas Cassidy, Belfast 18 November 1950
Clubs: Glentoran, Newcastle United, Burnley

NI Caps: 24
NI Goals: 1

Games

Year	Opponent	Result	Score	G	Year	Opponent	Result	Score	G
1971	England	lost	0-1		1980	Republic of Ireland	won	1-0	
1972	USSR	drew	1-1			Israel	drew	0-0	
1974	Bulgaria	drew	0-0			Scotland	won	1-0	
	Scotland	won	1-0	1		England	drew	1-1	
	England	lost	0-1			Wales	won	1-0	
	Wales	lost	0-1			Australia	won	2-1	
	Norway	lost	1-2			Australia	drew	1-1	
1976	Scotland	lost	0 3			Australia	won	2-1	
	England	lost	0-4		1981	Sweden	won	3-0	
	Wales	lost	0-1			Portugal	lost	0-1	
1977	West Germany	lost	0-5		1982	Israel	won	1-0	
1980	England	lost	1-5			Spain	won	1-0	

Colin Clarke

The family of much-travelled striker Colin Clarke moved from Newry to Ipswich when he was 12 and so consequently he joined the Portman Road club as an apprentice. He failed to make the grade with Ipswich and joined Peterborough United on a free transfer. After playing in 82 games for the London Road club, he joined Tranmere Rovers, this following a brief loan spell with Gillingham.

At Prenton Park he scored 29 goals in all competitions during the course of the 1984-85 season, a campaign in which the Wirral club just missed out on promotion to Division Three, before moving to the south coast and Bournemouth.

His goalscoring feats at Dean Court led to him winning the first of 38 full international caps for Northern Ireland and the attention of a number of top foreign clubs, including Torino of Italy. His performances for Northern Ireland in the 1986 World Cup Finals convinced Southampton boss Chris Nicholl that Clarke had the ability to succeed in the top flight and in June of that year, he paid £400,000 for his services.

Clarke made immediate history by becoming the first Southampton player to score a hat-trick on his debut in a 5-1 win over Queen's Park Rangers on the opening day of the 1986-87 season. He followed this up with another three goals in the 4-1 home win over Newcastle United in October 1986 and ended the season as the club's top scorer with 20 league goals. He then began to suffer with a series of injuries and had a loan spell back at Bournemouth before joining Queen's Park Rangers.

A season later he signed for Portsmouth for a fee of £415,000 and topped the Fratton Park club's scoring charts with 13 goals including a hat-trick in a 4-1 defeat of Bristol City.

Clarke, who netted a hat-trick for Northern Ireland in the September 1991 encounter against the Faroe Islands at Landskrona in Sweden, held his country's scoring record until it was recently overtaken by David Healy. Sadly, a year later injury forced the blond striker to hang up his boots and carve out a career in catering.

Left: Clarke & Edinho, 1986 World Cup Finals

Personal File

Position: Forward
Born: Colin John Clarke,
Newry
30 October 1962
Clubs: Ipswich Town,
Petersborough United,
Gillingham (loan),
Tranmere Rovers, Bournemouth,
Southampton,
Queen's Park Rangers,
Portsmouth

NI Caps: 38
NI Goals: 13

Games

Year	Opponent	Result	Score	G	Year	Opponent	Result	Score	G
1986	France	drew	0-0		1989	Malta	won	2-0	1
	Denmark	drew	1-1			Chile	lost	0-1	
	Morocco	won	2-1	1	1990	Hungary	lost	1-2	
	Algeria	drew	1-1			Republic of Ireland	lost	0-3	
	Spain	lost	1-2	1		Norway	lost	2-3	
	Brazil	lost	0-3		1991	Yugoslavia	lost	0-2	
1987	England	lost	0-3			Denmark	drew	1-1	1
	Turkey	drew	0-0			Austria	drew	0-0	
	Yugoslavia	lost	1-2	1		Poland	won	3-1	
1988	Yugoslavia	lost	0-3			Yugoslavia	lost	1-4	
	Turkey	won	1-0			Faroe Islands	drew	1-1	1
	Greece	lost	2-3	2	1992	Faroe Islands	won	5-0	3
	Poland	drew	1-1			Austria	won	2-1	
	France	drew	0-0			Denmark	lost	1-2	
	Malta	won	3-0	1		Scotland	lost	0-1	
1989	Republic of Ireland	drew	0-0			Germany	drew	1-1	
	Hungary	lost	0-1		1993	Albania	won	3-0	1
	Spain	lost	0-4			Spain	drew	0-0	
	Spain	lost	0-2			Denmark	lost	0-1	

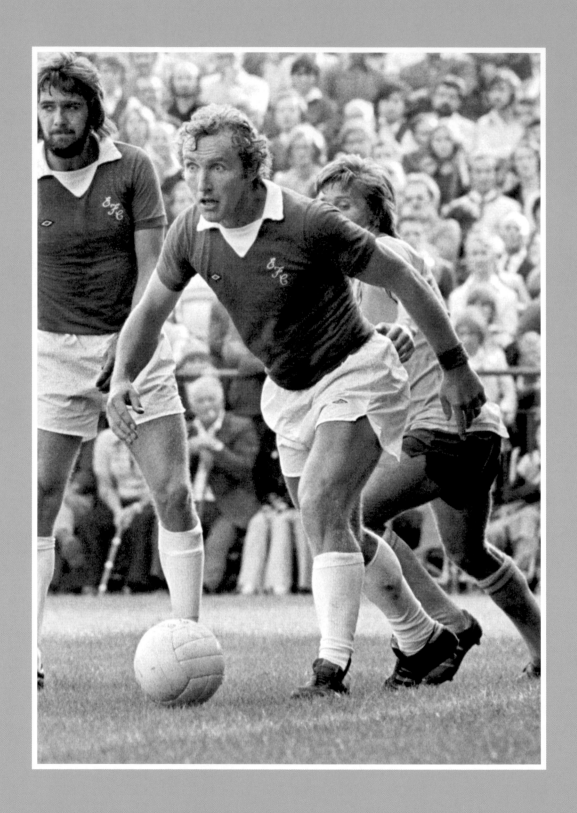

Dave Clements

The blond curly haired Ulsterman played his early football as a winger for Portadown before joining Wolverhampton Wanderers. Unable to make the grade at Molineux, he moved on to Coventry City in the summer of 1964.

After scoring on his Football League debut in a 1-1 draw at Northampton Town in January 1965, Clements went on to score eight goals in his first ten games for the club. Two months after playing his first game, he was given his international debut by Northern Ireland but it wasn't the happiest of debuts as visitors Wales won 5-0 at Windsor Park!

At Highfield Road, Clements was converted into a half-back, the position from which he scored his first international goal in the 1-0 defeat of Scotland in October 1967. After seven seasons with the Sky Blues, Clements, who had scored 30 goals in 257 games, left to join Sheffield Wednesday for a fee of £100,000.

Though this versatile player preferred midfield, Owls' boss Derek Dooley played him at left-back and though he missed very few games in his time at Hillsborough, he eventually became unsettled and asked for a move. Having just played for Wednesday in the opening game of the 1973-74 season, he left the Yorkshire club to sign for Everton for £60,000.

As a character of strength, integrity and intelligence, he earned widespread respect during his sojourn at Goodison Park, though like many other Everton men of his era, he suffered from frequent team changes. Ever a positive influence on the Merseyside club's youngsters, it surprised few when he took over the reins of the Northern Ireland side in March 1975 while still a First Division regular. However, when the opportunity of a transfer to New York Cosmos came up in January 1976, he gave up the early chance of a long-term career in international management to cross the Atlantic.

Personal File

Position: Left-back/Wing-half
Born: David Clements,
Larne
15 Sept 1945
Clubs: Portadown,
Wolverhampton Wanderers,
Coventry City,
Sheffield Wednesday,
Everton, New York Cosmos

NI Caps: 48
NI Goals: 2

Games

Year	Opponent	Result	Score	G	Year	Opponent	Result	Score	G
1965	Wales	lost	0-5		1972	Scotland	lost	0-2	
1966	Mexico	won	4-1			England	won	1-0	
1967	Scotland	lost	1-2			Wales	drew	0-0	
	Wales	drew	0-0		1973	Bulgaria	lost	0-3	
1968	Scotland	won	1-0	1		Cyprus	lost	0-1	
	England	lost	0-2			Portugal	drew	1-1	
1969	Turkey	won	4-1			Cyprus	won	3-0	
	Turkey	won	3-0			England	lost	1-2	1
	England	lost	1-3			Scotland	won	2-1	
	Scotland	drew	1-1			Wales	won	1-0	
	Wales	drew	0-0		1974	Bulgaria	drew	0-0	
1970	USSR	drew	0-0			Portugal	drew	1-1	
	USSR	lost	0-2			Scotland	won	1-0	
	Scotland	lost	0-1			England	lost	0-1	
	England	lost	1-3			Wales	lost	0-1	
	Wales	lost	0-1		1975	Norway	lost	1-2	
1971	Spain	lost	0-3			Yugoslavia	won	1-0	
	Cyprus	won	5-0			England	drew	0-0	
	England	lost	0-1			Scotlan	lost	0-3	
	Scotland	won	1-0			Wales	won	1-0	
	Wales	won	1-0		1976	Sweden	lost	1-2	
1972	USSR	lost	0-1			Yugoslavia	lost	0-1	
	USSR	drew	1-1			England	lost	0-4	
	Spain	drew	1-1			Wales	lost	0-1	

Terry Cochrane

At 23 years of age, Terry Cochrane was a relative late-comer to English League football when Burnley manager Joe Brown paid Coleraine £38,000 for his services in October 1976.

As a labourer and later an electrician, Cochrane's football career in Ireland had been very much part-time, and he seemed to have missed his chance of succeeding in the professional game following earlier unimpressive trials at both Nottingham Forest and Everton.

After helping Coleraine to victory against Linfield in the Irish Cup Final of 1975, Terry Cochrane won his first full cap the following October against Norway in Belfast. By the time he represented his country again, he had crossed the water to Turf Moor to join a Burnley side coming to terms with life after relegation from the top flight.

He scored on his Clarets' debut and in two relatively undistinguished years for Burnley displayed his pace and trickery out on the wing, playing opposite the enigmatic but equally colourful Tony Morley on the other flank.

After four more Irish caps, Terry Cochrane became a target for Middlesbrough boss John Neal. An offer of almost a quarter of a million pounds was too much for the Clarets to resist and soon after the start of the 1978-79 season, the tricky winger was on his way to Ayresome Park.

In five years on Teeside, he continued to be a favourite with the crowds who appreciated his wonderful ball control and dazzling wing play. He became a fixture in the Northern Ireland side, winning a further 19 caps and scoring against England at Wembley but in 1982 he was unable to prevent Boro being relegated back to Division Two. Cochrane was never a regular after that and amid rumours of a rift with Boro manager Malcolm Allison, he moved to Third Division Gillingham in October 1983. By now turned 30, he showed he could still turn on the style and the Gills flirted with promotion in each of his three seasons in Kent.

In 1986 he left for the United States to try indoor football in Dallas. On his return, after the briefest of spells as a non-contract player with Millwall and Hartlepool United, he finally left League football in 1987 to join Billingham Synthonia of the Northern League. At the age of 36, Terry Cochrane finally won his very first English honour when Billingham won the Northern League Championship in 1989.

Cochrane still lives in the Middlesbrough area and after completing his FA coaching badge, he now plays his part in grooming the north-east football stars of tomorrow.

Personal File

Position: Winger
Born: George Terence Cochrane, Killyleagh 23 January 1953
Clubs: Derry City, Linfield, Coleraine, Burnley, Middlesborough, Gillingham, Dallas, Millwall, Hartlepool United, Billingham Synthonia

NI Caps: 26
NI Goals: 1

Games

Year	Opponent	Result	Score	G	Year	Opponent	Result	Score	G
1976	Norway	won	3-0		1980	Australia	won	2-1	
1978	Scotland	drew	1-1			Australia	drew	1-1	
	England	lost	0-1			Australia	won	2-1	
	Wales	lost	0-1		1981	Sweden	won	3-0	
1979	Republic of Ireland	drew	0-0			Portugal	lost	0-1	
	Denmark	lost	0-4			Scotland	drew	1-1	
	Bulgaria	won	2-0			Portugal	won	1-0	
	England	lost	0-4			Scotland	lost	0-2	
	Bulgaria	won	2-0			Sweden	lost	0-1	
	England	lost	0-2		1982	England	lost	0-4	
1980	Israel	drew	0-0			France	lost	1-4	
	England	drew	1-1	1	1984	Scotland	won	2-0	
	Wales	won	1-0			Finland	lost	0-1	

David Craig

Newcastle United has produced many distinguished full-backs over the years but perhaps the finest of them all was David Craig. He gave the Magpies 18 years service, clocking up over 400 games in a black 'n' white shirt and yet missed many more through injury. A one club man, he played football for his local Boys' Brigade team in Ireland and was spotted early by Scunthorpe United. A trial in Lincolnshire followed but being homesick, Craig was on the boat across the Irish Sea within a matter of weeks. Back in Comber, a town a few miles from Belfast, he trained as an apprentice engineer before Newcastle offered him terms.

On the St James Park staff at this time were Irish internationals Dick Keith and Alf McMichael, a great full-back partnership for club and country. For a long time, Craig lacked confidence but Keith took him under his wing and helped his young countryman a great deal and David Craig was to eventually replace his mentor in the Newcastle side. In 1962 Craig was a member of the Magpies side that won the FA Youth Cup and after a season and a half in the club's reserve side, manager Joe Harvey gave him a chance in United's Second Division side against Cardiff City.

During the following campaign, Newcastle won the Second Division Championship and Craig missed only two games at right-back. Alongside was Frank Clark, the two of them being Newcastle's full-back pairing for the next decade.

He won his first representative honours, being picked for the Irish Under 23 side against Wales and two years later was in the full international side, also against the Welsh when he partnered Burnley's Alex Elder. David Craig won 25 caps for Northern Ireland, yet that number should have been 35 or even 40, but for those niggling injuries that disrupted his career during the seventies.

Craig became an accomplished First Division defender and as Newcastle pushed for a European place, he performed at his peak. A regular in the United side, he helped the club win the UEFA Cup in 1969, though a knee ligament problem almost caused him to miss the final. He wasn't as lucky in 1974 when a dislocated elbow caused him to miss the FA Cup Final against Liverpool. Fate was also cruel to him two years later when damaged medial ligaments forced him to miss United's League Cup Final appearance at Wembley.

The following years saw his number of first team appearances dwindle and he played his last football for the club in 1977-78. He had entered the scene on promotion and left it when relegated 412 games later. Craig had played an important part in United's 13 year spell in the top flight.

During the summer of 1978 he joined Blyth Spartans for a brief period before concentrating on other interests. He started a milk distribution business, then managed a couple of newsagents with Alan Thompson, a former Newcastle coach and the man who met Craig off the plane back in 1960.

Personal File

Position: Full-back
Born: David James Craig,
Belfast
8 June 1944
Clubs: Newcastle United,
Blyth Spartans

NI Caps: 25

Games

Year	Opponent	Result	Score	G	Year	Opponent	Result	Score	G
1967	Wales	drew	0-0		1971	Spain	lost	0-3	
1968	Wales	lost	0-2			Scotland	won	1-0	
1969	Turkey	won	4-1		1972	USSR	drew	1-1	
	Turkey	won	3-0			Scotland	lost	0-2	
	England	lost	1-3		1973	Cyprus	lost	0-1	
	Scotland	drew	1-1			Cyprus	won	1-0	
	Wales	drew	0-0			England	lost	1-2	
1970	England	lost	1-3			Scotland	won	2-1	
	Scotland	lost	0-1			Wales	won	1-0	
	Wales	drew	0-0		1974	Bulgaria	drew	0-0	
	USSR	lost	0-2			Portugal	drew	1-1	
1971	Cyprus	won	3-0		1975	Norway	lost	1-2	
	Cyprus	won	5-0						

"He never caused me a problem and was on many occasions the first name I put on the teamsheet."

- Joe Harvey, Newcastle United Manager

Johnny Crossan (on the far left)

Johnny Crossan

Johnny Crossan first hit the headlines whilst an amateur with Irish League club Coleraine, when he was alleged to have been paid!

Peter Doherty brought him to England to sign for Bristol City but when his registration forms were sent to the Football League for approval, they were refused and Crossan was later banned from playing in England.

He then signed for the Dutch League club Sparta Rotterdam before later playing for the Belgian League Champions Standard Liege.

When the Football League ban was eventually lifted, Crossan joined Sunderland in October 1962 for a fee of £26,700. He made his debut in a 6-2 home win over Grimsby Town and though he failed to get on the scoresheet, it wasn't long before he scored the first of two hat-tricks for the club in a 3-2 win at Walsall in March 1963. His second came at the end of the season in a 4-0 home win over Southampton. During the club's promotion-winning season of 1963-64, Crossan, who was ever-present, scored 22 goals including five 'doubles' and another five goals in six FA Cup ties. Also that season he netted two penalties for Northern Ireland in the 3-0 defeat of Uruguay.

Midway through the 1964-65 season, Crossan, who had scored 48 goals in 99 games, left Roker Park to sign for Manchester City for a fee of £40,000.

In one of his first games for Northern Ireland following his transfer to the Maine Road club, he netted a hat-trick in a 4-1 victory over Albania.

Crossan skippered City back to the First Division but after losing his place to Colin Bell, he joined Middlesbrough for £35,000 – Boro's then record fee. Capped 24 times by Northern Ireland, Crossan suffered from insomnia and received hospital treatment during his time at Ayresome Park before leaving to return to Belgium where he ended his playing days with Tongren FC.

Personal File

Position: Inside-forward
Born: John Andrew Crossan, Derry 29 November 1938
Clubs: Coleraine, Sparta Rotterdam, Standard Liege, Sunderland, Manchester City, Middlesbrough, Tongren FC (Belgium)

NI Caps: 24
NI Goals: 10

Games

Year	Opponent	Result	Score	G	Year	Opponent	Result	Score	G
1960	England	lost	1-2		1965	Holland	won	2-1	1
1963	Poland	won	2-0	1		Wales	lost	0-5	
	Wales	lost	1-4			Holland	drew	0-0	
	Spain	drew	1-1			Albania	won	4-1	3
1964	Scotland	won	2-1		1966	Scotland	won	3-2	1
	Spain	lost	0-1			Scotland	lost	1-2	
1964	England	lost	3-8	1		Albania	drew	1-1	
	Wales	won	3-2			West Germany	lost	0-2	
	Uruguay	won	3-0	2	1967	England	lost	0-2	
1965	England	lost	3-4			Scotland	lost	1-2	
	Switzerland	won	1-0	1	1968	Scotland	won	1-0	
	Switzerland	lost	1-2						
	Scotland	lost	2-3						

Willie Cunningham

Able to play in either full-back position, Willie Cunningham learned his football in Scotland, having joined St Mirren from Ardrossan Winton Rovers in the summer of 1948.

His form for St Mirren – he played in the League Cup against Celtic in August 1949 in front of a crowd of 47,438 (still St Mirren's record attendance for a game at Love Street) – led to him winning the first of 30 full international caps for Northern Ireland against Wales in March 1951.

His stylish defensive play led to Leicester City laying out £4,750 for him in November 1954. He settled in well at Filbert Street, initially shuffling between the two full-back berths before being squeezed out by the Stan Milburn/ John Ogilvie partnership which saw City through the 1956-57 promotion-winning season. He returned for three seasons of First Division battling but again ironically, only ever played twice for the Foxes in the centre-half position he held for Northern Ireland throughout the 1958 World Cup. The 23 international appearances he made whilst with Leicester, several of them while in the club's reserves, made Cunningham the club's most-capped player of that time. This was subsequently overtaken by Gordon Banks and more recently by fellow Northern Ireland international John O'Neill with 39 appearances.

In September 1960, Cunningham joined Dunfermline Athletic – a good move for him as he played in the 1961 Scottish Cup victory and was manager when the Pars returned to Hampden Park in 1965, having had a spell coaching under Jock Stein in the interim. He later had further spells of management at Falkirk and St Mirren and in 1971 turned down the Scottish FA's offer of the national team manager's post.

> ## "He played so well in his first International in 1954, that Leicester made an immediate bid for his transfer from St Mirren."

Malcolm Brodie

Left: (L-R) Rangers' Harold Davis pursues Dunfermline Athletic's Willie Cunningham

Personal File

Position: Full-back
Born: William Edward Cunningham, Belfast 20 February 1930
Clubs: Ardrossan Winton Rovers, St Mirren, Leicester City, Dunfermline Athletic

NI Caps: 30

Games

Year	Opponent	Result	Score	G	Year	Opponent	Result	Score	G
1951	Wales	lost	1-2		1958	Czechoslovakia	won	1-0	
1953	England	drew	2-2			Argentina	lost	1-3	
1954	Scotland	lost	1-3			West Germany	drew	2-2	
1955	Scotland	drew	2-2			Czechoslovakia	won	2-1	
1956	Scotland	won	2-1			France	lost	0-4	
	England	lost	0-3		1959	England	drew	3-3	
	Wales	drew	1-1			Scotland	drew	2-2	
1957	England	drew	1-1			Wales	won	4-1	
	Scotland	lost	0-1		1960	Scotland	lost	0-4	
	Portugal	drew	1-1			England	lost	1-2	
	Wales	drew	0-0			Wales	lost	2-3	
	Italy	lost	0-1		1961	Wales	lost	1-5	
	Portugal	won	3-0		1962	Wales	lost	0-4	
1958	Scotland	drew	1-1			Holland	lost	0-4	
	Italy	lost	1-3						
	Wales	drew	1-1						

HARRY GREGG (Don...
...dges find Gregg Reckoned...
Harry has succeeded Norman...
in his country's last line defe...
Gregg is one of many play...
category moulded at Doncaste...

WILLIE CUNNINGHAM (Ne...
Right Back Cunningh...
Antrim, but all his football wa...
before being transferred to Leic...
He played so well in his first...
that Leicester made an immedia...
from St. Mirren. 9 caps.

ALFIE McMICHAEL (Ne...
Left Back A regular in...
1949, Alfie, formerly with Linfi...
career with Cliftonville. Has trav...
his club and country. 17 caps.

DANNY BLANCHFLOWE
Captain. Right Half Joined Gl...
forward, but wasn't long at the...
realised his true position was righ...
to Barnsley, then Aston Villa befor...
Hart Lane in 1954. Turned down...
post with Canadian F.A. He now...
on commercial television as a comm...

BILLY CUSH (Glenavon)
Centre Half Smallest man i...
he faces "Big John" Charles, but is u...
sk. Has appeared at wing half and...
his country. Captains Glenav...
Cup Final against D...
nds head and...
4 c...

Wilbur Cush appears in the International line-up in 1957.

Wilbur Cush

Able to play at both half-back and inside-forward, Wilbur Cush developed with Lurgan Boys' Club and Shankhill YMCA before signing for Glenavon in the summer of 1947. They were one of the 'Cinderella' clubs of Irish football but, inspired by the displays of Cush, they swept to their first-ever Irish League and Cup wins. His form for Glenavon led to him winning the first of 26 full international caps for Northern Ireland when he played in the 4-1 home defeat by England in October 1950.

A regular member of the Irish League XI, Cush won Irish Gold Cup winners' medals in 1954 and 1956, an Ulster Cup winners' medal in 1955, an Irish Cup winners' medal in 1957 and an Irish League Championship medal in 1952.

Cush was Ulster's 'Footballer of the Year' when he was snapped up by Leeds United for just £7,000 in November 1957. Within a month, his form for the national team led to him scoring both Northern Ireland's goals in a 2-2 draw with Italy. Wilbur Cush also scored Northern Ireland's first-ever goal in the finals of the World Cup, heading the only goal of the game against Czechoslovakia on 8 June 1958 in Halmstad. Northern Ireland, who were rank outsiders, reached the quarter-finals before losing 4-0 to France.

On his arrival at Elland Road, Cush was appointed United's captain and over the next three seasons, he appeared in 90 League and Cup games for the Yorkshire club. Following Leeds' relegation to Division Two at the end of the 1959-60 season, Cush moved to Portadown. In November 1966 he rejoined Glenavon and later became their trainer-coach.

"Small in stature he stands head and shoulders above most others in ability."

- Malcolm Brodie on Wilbur Cush

Personal File

Position: Wing-half/Inside-forward
Born: Wilbur Cush,
Lurgan,
10 June 1928
Died: 28 July 1981
Clubs: Glenavon,
Leeds United,
Portadown

NI Caps: 26
NI Goals: 5

Games

Year	Opponent	Result	Score	G	Year	Opponent	Result	Score	G
1951	England	lost	1-4		1958	West Germany	drew	2-2	
	Wales	lost	1-6			Czechoslovakia	won	2-1	
1954	Scotland	lost	1-3			France	lost	0-4	
	England	lost	1-3		1959	England	drew	3-3	1
1957	Portugal	drew	1-1			Spain	lost	2-6	1
	Wales	drew	0-0			Scotland	drew	2-2	
	Italy	lost	0-1			Wales	won	4-1	
	Portugal	won	3-0		1960	Scotland	lost	0-4	
1958	Italy	drew	2-2	2		England	lost	1-2	
	Italy	lost	1-3			Wales	lost	2-3	
	Wales	drew	1-1		1961	West Germany	lost	1-2	
	Czechoslovakia	won	1-0	1		Greece	lost	1-2	
	Argentina	lost	1-3		1962	Greece	won	2-0	

Peter Doherty

The mercurial flame-haired Peter Doherty was one of the outstanding players of his generation, the complete inside-forward and a great crowd favourite.

He was barely 15 when the local Irish League club, Coleraine, watched him playing junior football for Station United and invited him for a trial. What happened that Saturday was a trailer for Doherty's whole turbulent career. The shy red-headed boy was hustled into the dressing-room and told to put on a jersey because the right-winger had missed his train. He did not receive one pass throughout the first-half and nobody spoke to him at half-time, and when the winger did eventually appear, the substitute was ordered to give up his shirt.

After beginning his career with Glentoran, Doherty joined Blackpool in November 1933 for a fee of £1,500. He made his debut in a 2-1 win at Bradford the following month but was a little disappointing in his first season at Bloomfield Road and it was 1934-35 before he won a regular place. Linking well with Bobby Finan and Jimmy Hampson, Doherty scored 13 goals in 35 games as the Seasiders just missed out on promotion, finishing fourth in Division Two. That season his form earned him the first of 16 international caps for Northern Ireland when he played against England at Goodison Park. He had scored 29 goals in 88 games for Blackpool when in February 1936 he was transferred to Manchester City for £10,000. In his first full season at Maine Road, he helped City win the League Championship with 30 goals in 41 games. He was also top-scorer with 23 goals the following relegation season and in all scored 81 goals in 133 games for City.

After the war he linked up with Raich Carter at Derby County to help the Rams win the FA Cup in 1946. He later joined Huddersfield Town before becoming player-manager of Doncaster Rovers whom he helped win the Third Division (North) Championship.

Northern Ireland had never appointed a team manager when Doherty took them over in the late fifties and had certainly never even begun to generate the atmosphere of comradeship and dedication he achieved in taking the country to the quarter-finals of the 1958 World Cup.

Personal File

Position: Inside-forward
Born: Peter Dermot Doherty,
        Magherafelt
        15 June 1913
Died: 6 April 1990
Clubs: Glentoran,
        Blackpool,
        Manchester City,
        Derby County,
        Huddersfield Town,
        Doncaster Rovers

NI Caps: 16
NI Goals: 3

Games

Year	Opponent	Result	Score	G	Year	Opponent	Result	Score	G
1935	England	lost	1-2		1939	England	lost	0-7	
	Wales	lost	1-3			Wales	lost	1-3	
1936	England	lost	1-3		1947	England	lost	2-7	
	Scotland	lost	1-2			Wales	won	2-1	1
1937	England	lost	1-3		1948	England	drew	2-2	1
	Wales	lost	1-4			Wales	lost	0-2	
1938	England	lost	1-5		1949	Scotland	lost	2-3	
	Scotland	drew	1-1	1	1951	Scotland	lost	1-6	

"He was almost a one-man team – and if Ireland had had two Dohertys that day, I shudder to think what might have happened."

- Maurice Edelston commentating on a wartime match between Ireland (4) and the Combined Services (7).

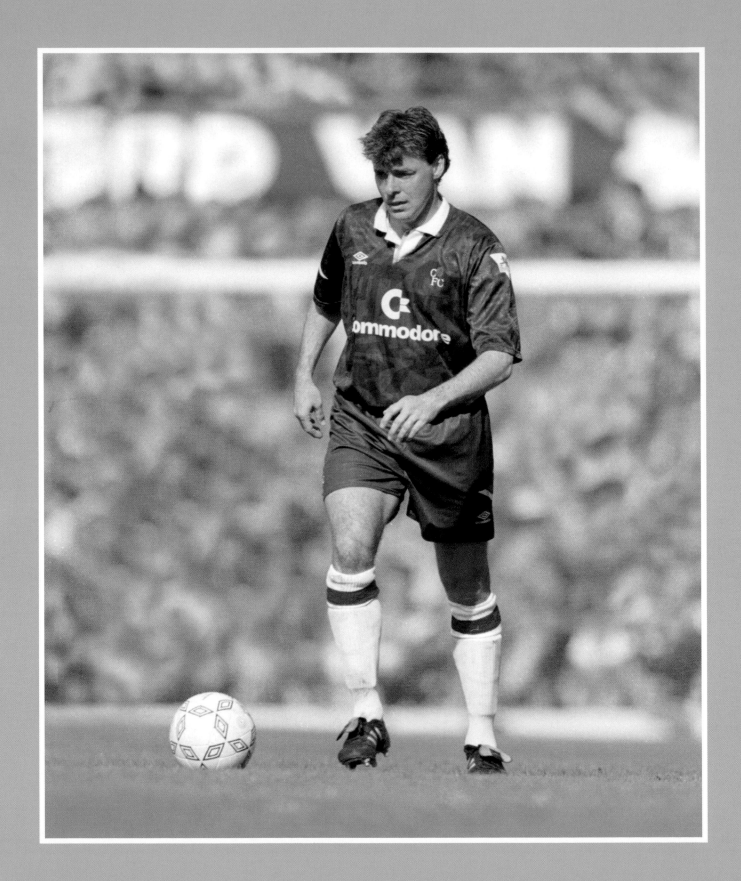

Mal Donaghy

Mal Donaghy joined Luton Town from the Irish League side Larne in the summer of 1978 and made his Football League debut in a 6-1 thrashing of Oldham Athletic at the start of the 1978-79 season. He soon settled into the Luton side as a regular and was ever-present in seasons 1979-80, 1980-81, 1981-82, 1984-85, 1985-86 and 1986-87. During his 10 years at Kenilworth Road he missed only 16 league games, a remarkable record of consistency.

Donaghy won the first of 91 international caps when he played for Northern Ireland against Scotland at Windsor Park in May 1980 and shared the spoils of a 1-0 victory.

Although he wasn't a noted goalscorer, he scored nine in 1981-82 when the Hatters won the Second Division title. Prior to signing for Manchester United, he also won a League Cup winners' medal when Luton beat Arsenal 3-2 in 1988.

At Old Trafford, he initially played alongside Steve Bruce at the centre of defence but on the arrival of Gary Pallister, he was switched to right-back. Following a lay-off through injury he was loaned back to Luton before returning to United. In 1990-91 he wore five different numbered outfield shirts and was on the bench for the European Cup Winners' Cup Final victory over Barcelona. He remained a valuable squad player at Old Trafford and was unlucky not to play in United's League Cup Final victory over Nottingham Forest, as he had played regularly in the preceding weeks.

Donaghy was transferred to Chelsea prior to the start of the 1992-93 season for a fee of £100,000 plus £5,000 per game up to fifty. At today's inflated prices for inferior quality players, he turned out to be one of the bargains of the first Premier League season, where his intelligent reading of the game compensated for his lack of pace. He then appeared in a number of games under new player-manager Glenn Hoddle before leaving the first-class game.

He is currently Development Officer for the Northern Ireland Federation.

"A Rolls Royce player"

- Billy Bingham

Personal File

Position: Defender
Born: Malachy Martin Donaghy, Belfast
13 September 1957
Clubs: Larne Town,
Luton Town,
Manchester United,
Chelsea

NI Caps: 91

Games

Year	Opponent	Result	Score	G	Year	Opponent	Result	Score	G
1980	Scotland	won	1-0		1987	Israel	drew	1-1	
	England	drew	1-1			England	lost	0-2	
	Wales	won	1-0			Yugoslavia	lost	1-2	
1981	Sweden	won	3-0		1988	Yugoslavia	lost	0-3	
	Portugal	lost	0-1			Turkey	won	1-0	
	Scotland	lost	0-2			Greece	lost	2-3	
1982	Scotland	drew	0-0			Poland	drew	1-1	
	Israel	won	1-0			France	drew	0-0	
	England	lost	0-4			Malta	won	3-0	
	France	lost	0-4		1989	Republic of Ireland	drew	0-0	
	Scotland	drew	1-1			Hungary	lost	0-1	
	Wales	lost	0-3			Spain	lost	0-4	
	Yugoslavia	drew	0-0			Spain	lost	0-2	
	Honduras	drew	1-1			Malta	won	2-0	
	Spain	won	1-0			Chile	lost	0-1	
	France	lost	1-4		1990	Republic of Ireland	lost	0-3	
1983	Austria	lost	0-2			Norway	lost	2-3	
	West Germany	won	1-0		1991	Yugoslavia	lost	0-2	
	Albania	drew				Denmark	drew		
	Turkey	won	2-1			Austria	drew	0-0	
	Albania	won	1-0			Poland	won	3-1	
	Scotland	drew	0-0			Yugoslavia	lost	1-4	
	England	drew	0-0			Faroe Islands	drew	1-1	
	Wales	lost	0-1		1992	Faroe Islands	won	5-0	
1984	Austria	won	3-1			Austria	won	2-1	
	Turkey	lost	0-1			Denmark	lost	1-2	
	West Germany	won	1-0			Scotland	lost	0-1	
	Scotland	won	2-0			Lithuania	drew	2-2	
	England	lost	0-1			Germany	drew	1-1	
	Wales	drew	1-1		1993	Albania	won	3-0	
	Finland	lost	0-1			Spain	drew	0-0	
1985	Romania	won	3-2			Denmark	lost	0-1	
	Finland	won	2-1			Albania	won	2-1	
	England	lost	0-1			Republic of Ireland	lost	0-3	
	Spain	drew	0-0			Spain	lost	1-3	
	Turkey	won	2-0			Lithuania	won	1-0	
1986	Turkey	drew	0-0			Latvia	won	2-1	
	Romania	won	1-0		1994	Latvia	won	2-0	
	England	drew	0-0			Denmark	lost	0-1	
	France	drew	0-0			Republic of Ireland	drew	1-1	
	Denmark	drew				Romania	won	2-0	
	Morocco	won	2-1			Liechtenstein	won	4-1	
	Algeria	drew	1-1			Colombia	lost	0-2	
	Spain	lost	1-2			Mexico	lost	0-3	
	Brazil	lost	0-3						
1987	England	lost	0-3						
	Turkey	drew	0-0						

Derek Dougan

Known wherever he played as simply the 'Doog', Derek Dougan began his career with Distillery before signing professional forms for Portsmouth in August 1957. He remained at Fratton Park until March 1959 when he was transferred to Blackburn Rovers for £15,000. A year later, he had scored the two semi-final goals that beat Sheffield Wednesday to take Rovers through to the FA Cup Final against one of his future clubs, Wolverhampton Wanderers. He posted a transfer request on the morning of the Cup Final, which 10-men Rovers lost 3-0.

Following Gerry Hitchens' departure to Inter Milan, Aston Villa splashed out £15,000 for the popular player's services. During his time at Villa Park, Dougan amused many with his adoption of a shaven head and scared more with his propensity for off-field scrapes, but after two years he was on the move again, this time to Peterborough United. Perhaps this spell in the Third Division helped to restore his sense of perspective, or perhaps a renewed burst of media interest in the 'Doog' when Posh met Arsenal in the FA Cup rekindled his ambitions. At any rate, Dougan took a pay cut to join Leicester City, back in the top flight.

Leading City's forward line with his unique flair, he lapped up the crowd's adulation, not least on the occasion when he netted a flamboyant hat-trick against his former club, Aston Villa.

Shortly before the transfer deadline in 1967, Wolves' manager Ronnie Allen moved in and secured Dougan's services for a fee of £50,000. In just over eight seasons at Molineux, Dougan scored 123 goals in 323 League and Cup appearances. He helped the Wanderers clinch promotion from the Second Division in 1966-67 and then collected a League Cup winners' medal in 1974. In between times he played his part in Wolves' UEFA Cup run to the final in 1971-72 and while still an active member of the team, became Chairman of the PFA. Capped 43 times by Northern Ireland, Derek Dougan was one of the game's great characters. Forever involved with officialdom, he was sent-off at least half-a-dozen times in his colourful career. A stimulating and entertaining TV pundit, he surprised few when he later moved into management, albeit with Kettering Town. He later returned to Wolves as chief executive before becoming involved in raising money for various charities.

Personal File

Position: Centre-Forward
Born: Alexander Derek Dougan, Belfast 20 January 1938
Clubs: Distillery, Portsmouth, Blackburn Rovers, Aston Villa, Peterborough United, Leicester City, Wolverhampton Wanderers

NI Caps: 43
NI Goals: 8

Games

Year	Opponent	Result	Score	G	Year	Opponent	Result	Score	G
1958	Czechoslovakia	won	1-0		1969	Turkey	won	4-1	1
1960	Scotland	lost	0-4			Turkey	won	3-0	
1961	England	lost	2-5			England	lost	1-3	
	Wales	lost	1-5	1		Scotland	drew	1-1	
	Italy	lost	2-3	1		Wales	drew	0-0	
	Greece	lost	1-2		1970	USSR	drew	0-0	
1963	Poland	won	2-0	1		USSR	lost	0-2	
	Scotland	lost	1-5			Scotland	lost	0-1	
	Poland	won	2-0			England	lost	1-3	
1966	Scotland	won	3-2	1	1971	Spain	lost	0-3	
	Scotland	lost	1-2			Cyprus	won	3-0	1
	Albania	drew	1-1			Cyprus	won	5-0	1
	Wales	won	4-1			England	lost	0-1	
	West Germany	lost	0-2			Scotland	won	1-0	
	Mexico	won	4-1			Wales	won	1-0	
1967	England	lost	0-2		1972	USSR	lost	0-1	
	Scotland	lost	1-2			USSR	drew	1-1	
	Wales	drew	0-0			Scotland	lost	0-2	
1968	Scotland	won	1-0			England	won	1-0	
	Wales	lost	0-2			Wales	drew	0-0	
1969	Israel	won	3-2	1	1973	Bulgaria	lost	0-3	
						Cyprus	lost	0-1	

Iain Dowie

Iain Dowie was a relatively late starter in League football. At 24 years old the former Hendon player, who had also turned out for St Albans and Wealdstone made his first class debut as a substitute for Luton Town in January 1989. After Roy Wegerle departed for Queen's Park Rangers, Dowie won a regular place in the Luton side and impressed by scoring 15 First Division goals in 53 starts.

He was transferred to West Ham United in March 1991 for a fee of £480,000 as the Hammers aimed to bolster their top flight prospects. Promotion was attained with Dowie playing in the last 12 matches and scoring four goals. Five months later, he was surprisingly sold to Southampton for £500,000.

While he never truly set the world on fire at The Dell, he was admired for his bravery and wholehearted commitment to the Saints' cause in troubled times. The perfect foil for the blossoming Alan Shearer, he went on to score some crucial goals as the Saints fought some desperate battles to avoid the drop.

In January 1995 he joined Crystal Palace but his stay at Selhurst Park was short, and in September of that year he returned to Upton Park. Initially forming a good partnership with Tony Cottee, Dowie then began to look out of place amongst the host of foreign imports that Harry Redknapp brought to Upton Park.

However, he did enjoy more success with Northern Ireland, being appointed captain for the game against Albania in 1997. He celebrated the honour with two goals!

In January 1998, Dowie moved to Queen's Park Rangers and while still playing for the Loftus Road club, embarked on a coaching career. Dowie, who scored 12 goals in 59 games for Northern Ireland, then had a brief spell working in the media before becoming assistant-manager of Oldham Athletic. He took over the reins and enjoyed a successful debut season at Boundary Park as the Latics reached the play-offs. In December 2003 he became manager of Crystal Palace and led the Eagles into the Premiership via the play-offs.

"Football is all about passion and playing for the shirt."

- Iain Dowie

Personal File

Position: Forward
Born: Iain Dowie,
Hatfield
9 January 1965
Clubs: St Albans,
Wealdstone,
Hendon, Luton Town,
Fulham (loan),
West Ham United,
Southampton,
Crystal Palace,
Queen's Park Rangers

NI Caps: 59
NI Goals: 12

Games

Year	Opponent	Result	Score	G	Year	Opponent	Result	Score	G
1990	Norway	lost	2-3			Latvia	won	1-0	1
	Uruguay	won	1-0			Canada	lost	0-2	
1991	Yugoslavia	lost	0-2			Chile	lost	1-2	1
	Denmark	drew	1-1			Latvia	lost	1-2	1
	Austria	drew	0-0		1996	Portugal	drew	1-1	
	Yugoslavia	lost	1-4			Austria	won	5-3	1
	Faroe Islands	drew	1-1			Norway	lost	0-2	
1992	Faroe Islands	won	5-0			Germany	drew	1-1	
	Austria	won	2-1	1	1997	Ukraine	lost	0-1	
	Denmark	lost	1-2			Armenia	drew	1-1	
	Scotland	lost	0-1			Germany	drew	1-1	
	Lithuania	drew	2-2			Albania	won	2-0	2
1993	Albania	won	3-0			Portugal	drew	0-0	
	Albania	won	2-1			Ukraine	lost	1-2	1
	Republic of Ireland	lost	0-3			Armenia	drew	0-0	
	Spain	lost	1-3			Thailand	drew	0-0	
	Lithuania	won	1-0	1	1998	Albania	lost	0-1	
	Latvia	won	2-1			Portugal	lost	0-1	
1994	Latvia	won	2-0			Slovakia	won	1-0	
	Denmark	lost	0-1			Switzerland	won	1-0	
	Republic of Ireland	drew	1-1			Spain	lost	1-4	
	Romania	won	2-0		1999	Turkey	lost	0-3	
	Liechtenstein	won	4-1	1		Finland	won	1-0	
	Colombia	lost	0-2			Moldova	drew	2-2	1
	Mexico	lost	0-3			Germany	lost	0-3	
1995	Austria	won	2-1			Moldova	drew	0-0	
	Republic of Ireland	lost	0-4			Canada	drew	1-1	
	Republic of Ireland	drew	1-1	1		Republic of Ireland	won	1-0	
					2000	France	lost	0-1	
						Turkey	lost	0-3	
						Germany	lost	0-4	

Tommy Eglington (centre) playing for Everton

Tommy Eglington

One of Everton's greatest-ever servants, Tommy Eglington also stands out as one of the early giants of Irish football. Like many of his contemporaries, he excelled at hurling and Gaelic football during his schooldays, but it was as one of the finest match-winning left-wingers in the game of football that he came to be remembered.

Eglington joined Everton in the summer of 1946 in a double transfer deal involving the Blues' other immediate post-war great Peter Farrell. The double deal which cost everyone £10,000 has often been described as the best piece of business in the club's history.

Elegant and unruffled, with an explosive burst of pace and a thundering shot, Eglington had been with Shamrock Rovers for one full season, 1945-46, ending the campaign as the Hoops' top-scorer with 11 goals before he departed for Goodison Park.

Eglington made his League debut for Everton in a 3-2 home win over Arsenal in September 1946, going on to claim a regular place almost immediately. He kept his place for the next 11 seasons, all but three of which were spent in the top flight. Following the Blues' relegation in the 1950-51 season, they were promoted back to Division One at the end of 1953-54 having finished as runners-up to Leicester City on goal difference.

During his spell at the lower level, Eglington guaranteed himself a place in the pages of Everton's history when on 27 September 1952 he almost single-handedly demolished Doncaster Rovers at Goodison Park by scoring five Toffee goals in a 7-1 win. He ended that season as the club's leading scorer with 14 goals.

One of only a handful of players who have appeared for both Northern Ireland and the Republic, Eglington was a member of the Republic side which recorded an historic 2-0 victory over England at Goodison Park in 1949. He made six appearances for Northern Ireland and was the Republic's regular outside-right for a decade in the immediate post-war years.

A player with intricate close control and stunning shooting power, Eglington left Everton for Tranmere Rovers in the summer of 1957 after scoring 76 goals in 394 League games.

For three seasons he gave the Birkenhead club the same wholehearted service that he had given the Blues, scoring 36 goals in 172 outings in Division Three (North).

When he finally hung up his boots, Eglington returned to his native Dublin where he ran a butcher's shop.

Personal File

Position: Striker
Born: Thomas Joseph Eglington, Dublin
15 January 1923
Died: 18 February 2004
Clubs: Shamrock Rovers, Everton, Tranmere Rovers

NI Caps: 6

Games

Year	Opponent	Result	Score	G
1947	Scotland	drew	0-0	
	Wales	won	2-1	
1948	Scotland	won	2-0	
	England	drew	2-2	
	Wales	lost	0-2	
1949	England	lost	2-6	

Alex Elder (left) of Stoke City F.C. slides in to make a tackle during a game against Tottenham Hotspur, November 1968.
(© Central Press / Hulton Archive / Getty Images)

Alex Elder

When 17-year-old Alex Elder was signed by Burnley manager Harry Potts from Glentoran in January 1959, he was to become the last piece in the jigsaw which made up the Clarets' League Championship-winning side of 1959-60. He made his Burnley debut in a testing game at Preston North End, marking the mercurial Tom Finney. Although the Clarets lost 1-0, he had done more than enough to make the left-back position his own for the rest of that epic season – and for the foreseeable future. His hard solid tackling and accurate passing became trademarks of his game as did his barnstorming runs at opposition defences. He missed only one game that season to enable him to win his first full international cap in a 3-2 defeat of Wales at Wrexham in April 1960. He was still only 18 and went on to become virtually a fixture in the national side for almost a decade.

At Turf Moor, he forged a formidable full-back partnership with John Angus - the two were inseparable until Elder broke an ankle in pre-season training in August 1963. Once fit he returned to the side and took over from Brian Miller as club captain in the summer of 1965. He led the Clarets to a European Fairs Cup place at the end of the season. The third place finish could have been even better but for a bizarre own-goal by the skipper in the last home match of the season in May 1966. From the most acute of angles, Elder contrived to lob the ball over the advancing Adam Blacklaw for the only goal of the game against Leeds, ensuring that the Yorkshire club clinched the runners-up position to Liverpool at Burnley's expense.

He was still only 26 when he was transferred to Stoke City in August 1967 for a fee of £50,000. He was injured in pre-season training at the Victoria Ground and suffered persistent knee problems during his time in the Potteries.

His only season as a regular was 1968-69 when the Potters just hung on to their top flight status. Released in May 1973 he had a brief spell playing non-League football for Leek Town before working as a sales representative for a brewery.

"One of the finest full backs in the Football League."

-W H McClatchey

Personal File

Position: Left-back
Born: Alexander Russell Elder,
Lisburn
25 April 1941
Clubs: Altona FC,
Glentoran,
Burnley,
Stoke City,
Leek Town

NI Caps: 40
NI Goals: 1

Games

Year	Opponent	Result	Score	G	Year	Opponent	Result	Score	G
1960	Wales	lost	2-3		1965	Scotland	lost	2-3	
1961	Scotland	lost	2-5			Wales	lost	0-5	
	England	lost	2-5			Switzerland	won	1-0	
	Wales	lost	1-5			Switzerland	lost	1-2	
	West Germany	lost	3-4			Holland	won	2-1	
	West Germany	lost	1-2			Holland	drew	0-0	
	Greece	lost	1-2			Albania	won	4-1	
1962	England	drew	1-1		1966	England	lost	1-2	
	Scotland	lost	1-6			Scotland	won	3-2	
	Greece	won	2-0			Wales	won	4-1	
1963	England	lost	1-3			Mexico	won	4-1	1
	Scotland	lost	1-5			Albania	drew	1-1	
	Wales	lost	1-4		1967	England	lost	0-2	
	Poland	won	2-0			Scotland	lost	1-2	
	Poland	won	2-0			Wales	drew	0-0	
	Spain	drew	1-1		1968	England	lost	0-2	
1964	Wales	won	3-2			Wales	won	2-0	
	Uruguay	won	3-0		1969	England	lost	1-3	
1965	England	lost	3-4			Scotland	drew	1-1	
						Wales	drew	0-0	
					1970	USSR	lost	0-2	

Stuart Elliott

Stuart Elliott began his career with Glentoran, helping them win the Irish League Championship in 1998-99 and the Irish Cup in 1999-2000. His form for Glentoran led to Motherwell paying £100,000 for his services in the summer of 2000.

In his first season at Fir Park, Elliott ended the campaign as The Well's top scorer with 10 goals including 'doubles' in the matches against Kilmarnock and Dunfermline Athletic, as well as one of the season's quickest goals in the 2-1 win at Dundee. He led the way again in 2001-02, netting 11 goals but in the close season, having netted 23 goals in 75 games he was transferred to Hull City for £230,000.

Elliott won the first of 25 international caps for Northern Ireland against Malta in September 2000. A left-sided attacking midfield player, who can also play as a striker, he settled in well with the Tigers.

At his best when running at defenders and delivering quality crosses, he also poses a potent threat in the air and was the club's leading scorer, this in spite of missing six weeks with knee ligament damage.

A man of strong religious beliefs, he pledged to repay the faith shown in him by his Hull colleagues and supporters and reinstated his commitment to a three-year contract. In 2003-04 he again reached double figures for Hull despite being hampered by a mystery virus throughout the first three months of the season. Now a regular in the Northern Ireland side, he headed the Coca Cola League One scoring charts with Bristol City's Leroy Lita with 29 goals, helping the Tigers win promotion to the Championship. It just remains to be seen how long the Yorkshire club can hold on to this hot talent.

"I don't care who I am playing against – I am always confident I can get the goals."

- Stuart Elliott

Personal File

Position: Striker
Born: Stuart Elliott,
Belfast
23 July 1978
Clubs: Glentoran,
Motherwell,
Hull City

NI Caps: 25
NI Goals: 3

Games

Year	Opponent	Result	Score	G	Year	Opponent	Result	Score	G
2001	Malta	won	1-0		2002	Spain	lost	0-5	
	Denmark	drew	1-1		2003	Finland	lost	0-1	
	Iceland	lost	0-1			Armenia	lost	0-1	
	Norway	lost	0-4			Italy	lost	0-2	
	Czech				2004	Greece	lost	0-1	
	Republic	lost	0-1			Barbados	drew	1-1	
	Bulgaria	lost	3-4	1		St Kitts	won	2-0	
	Bulgaria	lost	0-1			Trinidad			
	Czech					and Tobago	won	3-0	1
	Republic	lost	1-3		2005	Switzerland	drew	0-0	
2002	Denmark	drew	1-1			Poland	lost	0-3	
	Malta	won	1-0			Azerbaijan	drew	0-0	
	Poland	lost	1-4			Austria	drew	3-3	1
	Liechtenstein	drew	0-0			England	lost	0-4	

Peter Farrell

Peter Farrell's career coincided with that of his Everton team-mate Tommy Eglington, for after playing with Shamrock Rovers as a schoolboy, the two of them joined Everton in a combined deal which cost the Blues £10,000 spread over two years. Like his close friend Eglington, Farrell enjoyed 11 seasons with Everton, during which time he became something of a living legend on Merseyside, being one of the few footballers to have a street named after him – Farrell Close.

His debut for Everton was postponed until late November 1946 because of an injury he sustained while playing tennis. After that, he was a virtual ever-present in the Everton side, though on 22 September 1956 for the match against Sunderland which the Blues won 2-1, the club decided to give Farrell a well-earned rest. This afforded one reporter the opportunity to pay tribute to "one of the most loyal servants the Goodison Park club has ever seen in its long history…Personally I think his inspiration and experience will be missed…as captain, there have been few as good and none better, always giving his last ounce to the cause."

On the international front, Farrell appeared at left-half for Northern Ireland in seven internationals between September 1946 and March 1949, while he was a regular member in the Republic of Ireland side from 1946 to 1957. He also scored one of the goals in the Republic's epic 2-0 defeat of England at Goodison Park in September 1949. Farrell also achieved the unusual honour of captaining the Republic in his first international for them. Farrell was the Everton captain when the Blues dropped down to Division Two in 1950-51 for only the second time in their history. However their fall from grace was short-lived; three seasons later they found their way back into the top flight. An inspiration to all around him and very popular on the field, Farrell was also something of a hero off it, mixing freely with the club's supporters in a down-to-earth manner.

In October 1957, less than six months after Eglington left Everton for Tranmere Rovers, Peter Farrell embarked on the same short journey across the River Mersey to link up yet again with his close friend and colleague. He was immediately appointed captain at Prenton Park and although his three seasons on the Wirral were not the happiest of his career, he continued to play as enthusiastically as ever, more than justifying Tranmere's £2,500 investment in a player heading towards the end of his career.

Farrell left Tranmere at the end of 1960 to join Welsh non-League side Hdyhist Town as player-manager, later returning to Ireland to continue in management before working in broadcasting with RTÉ in Dublin.

Left: Peter Farrell (right)

Personal File

Position: Wing-half
Born: Peter Desmond Farrell,
Dublin
16 August 1923
Died: 16 March 1999
Clubs: Shamrock Rovers,
Everton,
Tranmere Rovers,
Hdyhist Town

NI Caps: 7

Games

Year	Opponent	Result	Score	G
1947	Scotland	drew	0-0	
	Wales	won	2-1	
1948	Scotland	won	2-0	
	England	drew	2-2	
	Wales	lost	0-2	
1949	England	lost	2-6	
	Wales	lost	0-2	

"One of the most loyal servants the Goodison Park club has ever seen."

- Sports Reporter

Alan Fettis

Having started out with Ards, goalkeeper Alan Fettis joined Hull City in the summer of 1991 and soon established himself as one of the long-lost of outstanding Hull keepers. An excellent shot-stopper, he soon won full international honours, making his debut for Northern Ireland against Denmark in November 1991.

Over the seasons at Boothferry Park, Fettis, a possessor of superb reflexes, began to grow in both strength and confidence, but a nagging thumb injury in 1994-95 gave the likeable keeper an early autumn and winter period. However, this did give him a permanent place in the game's record books. Having been asked to appear as an outfield substitute, he promptly scored in the defeat of leaders Oxford United amid unprecedented scenes at Boothferry Park, and eclipsed that with another goal at Blackpool with the last kick of the season! He started the following season in dispute with the Yorkshire club and later after a loan spell with West Bromwich Albion, was transferred to Nottingham Forest for £250,000 as understudy to Mark Crossley.

Having sat on the bench for most of his time at the City Ground, he eventually made his Forest debut in difficult circumstances when coming on as a substitute for Crossley at Chesterfield in the FA Cup, after the former had been sent-off. Thus, the first shot he had to face was the resultant penalty, which proved to be the match-winner. After slipping to fourth choice at Forest, Fettis joined Blackburn Rovers for £300,000 but made only a few appearances due to the fine form of Tim Flowers and John Filan. The lack of senior football cost him his place with Northern Ireland and he moved to York City to team up with his former Hull boss, Terry Doolan.

His form for the Bootham Crescent club was outstanding, helping them avoid the drop into the Conference and winning Fettis the 'Clubman of the Year' award in both seasons 2000-01 and 2001-02. York's financial troubles saw him return to his former club Hull City, where his form not only won him a place in the PFA award-winning side but a recall to the Northern Ireland squad after an absence of five years. After suffering a knee injury, he had loan spells with Sheffield United and Grimsby Town. He returned to take to 178 his total of first team appearances for Hull City.

Personal File

Position: Goalkeeper
Born: Alan William Fettis,
Belfast
1 February 1971
Clubs: Ards,
Hull City,
West Bromwich Albion (loan),
Nottingham Forest,
Blackburn Rovers,
York City,
Sheffield United (loan)
Grimsby Town, Hull City

NI Caps: 25

Games

Year	Opponent	Result	Score	G	Year	Opponent	Result	Score	G
1992	Denmark	lost	1-2		1996	Austria	won	5-3	
	Lithuania	drew	2-2			Norway	lost	0-2	
1993	Denmark	lost	0-1			Germany	drew	1-1	
1994	Mexico	lost	0-3		1997	Ukraine	lost	0-1	
1995	Portugal	lost	1-2			Armenia	drew	1-1	
	Republic of Ireland	drew	1-1			Armenia	drew	0-0	
	Latvia	won	1-0		1998	Portugal	lost	0-1	
	Canada	lost	0-2			Slovakia	won	1-0	
	Chile	lost	1-2			Switzerland	won	1-0	
	Latvia	lost	1-2			Spain	lost	1-4	
1996	Portugal	drew	1-1		1999	Turkey	lost	0-3	
	Liechtenstein	won	4-0			Finland	won	1-0	
						Moldova	drew	2-2	

"I expect to be judged on my performance on the International stage."

- Alan Fettis

Tom Finney

Following a trial with Manchester United, Finney was invited back the following year but could not go as he had started work for Belfast Gas. He began his career with Distillery before switching to Crusaders and in the 1972-73 season, was part of the team that gained their first-ever League title. In August 1973 he joined Luton Town and in his first full League game scored twice as the Hatters raced into a 6-0 half-time lead over Carlisle United. He also scored in the next three games and was already being compared to the ex-Luton legend Malcolm Macdonald. Finney then hit a barren spell and suffered a knee injury which kept him out of the side for three months. As Luton faced bankruptcy they were forced to sell players and Finney was transferred to Sunderland for £50,000.

His chances were instantly curtailed by the almost simultaneous signing of Bryan 'Pop' Robson. Although Finney had played in enough games the following season to help the Wearsiders win the Second Division Championship, he was offloaded to Cambridge United for £15,000. Finney soon struck up a scintillating partnership with Alan Biley that ripped apart Fourth Division defences wherever they went. Finney scored 16 League goals in that 1976-77 season including consecutive home hat-tricks against Southport and Brentford as United won the Fourth Division title. The duo continued to weave their magic spell in the Third Division and by the end of that promotion-winning campaign, had totted up 64 goals between them. Finney remained at the Abbey throughout Cambridge's Second Division days, winning the 'Player of the Year' award in 1979-80. His natural aggression also manifested itself with a fearful temper on the pitch and he earned himself five sendings-off in his United career.

Finney won the first of his 14 caps in September 1974, just before making his Sunderland debut, scoring in the 2-1 defeat by Norway. He also scored against Wales but was then frozen out for four years until his exploits with Cambridge won him another chance.

After a spell with Brentford, Finney rejoined Cambridge, taking his total of League and Cup goals to 65 in 352 appearances, later managing Ely City, March Town and Histon Town before becoming Cambridge City's assistant-manager.

Personal File

Position: Midfielder
Born: Thomas Finney, Belfast 6 November 1952
Clubs: Distillery, Crusaders, Luton Town, Sunderland, Cambridge United, Brentford

NI Caps: 14
NI Goals: 2

Games

Year	Opponent	Result	Score	G	Year	Opponent	Result	Score	G
1975	Norway	lost	1-2	1	1980	England	lost	1-5	
	England	drew	0-0			Israel	drew	0-0	
	Scotland	lost	0-3			Scotland	won	1-0	
	Wales	won	1-0	1		England	drew	1-1	
1976	Norway	won	3-0			Wales	won	1-0	
	Yugoslavia	lost	0-1			Australia	won	2-1	
	Scotland	lost	0-3			Australia	drew	1-1	

"If I'd still been playing today I would have been suspended from September to February."

- Tom Finney on himself

Gary Fleming

After working his way up through the ranks at the City Ground, full-back Gary Fleming made his Nottingham Forest debut in a 1-1 draw at Arsenal in April 1985. Midway through the following campaign he won a regular place in the Forest side. Over the next few seasons he was outstanding in the Reds' defence, winning the first of 31 full caps for Northern Ireland in a 3-0 defeat by England at Wembley in October 1986.

In 1987-88 he was a member of the Forest side that finished third in Division One, but then missed the entire following season through injury and illness.

In the summer of 1989, Fleming joined Manchester City for a fee of £150,000 but was unable to hold down a regular place at Maine Road and went on loan to Notts County.

In March 1990, Barnsley manager Mel Machin paid £85,000 for his services. During his time at Oakwell, Fleming was a regular selection for Northern Ireland and though he was one of the Yorkshire club's better players, the club hovered around the First Division mid-table placings. In 1994-95, Fleming was ever-present as the Tykes finished sixth, just missing out on the play-offs – this after he had been moved to play in a sweeper role.

Fleming developed into a class player in that position; his ability to read the game meant he dealt with situations before they developed. Having started the following season in fine style, Fleming had played in 271 games for Barnsley when he suffered a serious knee injury that not only ended his campaign but sadly, also his career.

Fleming has recently had a spell as physiotherapist to the Northern Ireland national side.

Personal File

Position: Full-back
Born: Gary James Fleming, Belfast
17 February 1967
Clubs: Nottingham Forest, Manchester City, Notts County (loan), Barnsley

NI Caps: 31

Games

Year	Opponent	Result	Score	G	Year	Opponent	Result	Score	G
1987	England	lost	0-3		1993	Denmark	lost	0-1	
	Israel	drew	1-1			Albania	won	2-1	
	England	lost	0-2			Spain	lost	1-3	
	Yugoslavia	lost	1-2			Lithuania	won	1-0	
1988	Turkey	won	1-0			Latvia	won	2-1	
	Greece	lost	2-3		1994	Latvia	won	2-0	
	Poland	drew	1-1			Denmark	lost	0-1	
1989	Malta	won	2-0			Republic of Ireland	drew	1-1	
	Chile	lost	0-1			Romania	won	2-0	
1990	Hungary	lost	1-2			Liechtenstein	won	4-1	
	Republic of Ireland	lost	0-3			Colombia	lost	0-2	
						Mexico	lost	0-3	
1991	Yugoslavia	lost	1-4		1995	Portugal	lost	1-2	
1992	Lithuania	drew	2-2			Austria	won	2-1	
	Germany	drew	1-1			Republic of Ireland	lost	0-4	
1993	Albania	won	3-0						
	Spain	drew	0-0						

Keith Gillespie

A key member of the successful Manchester United youth side that reached the FA Youth Cup Final two years running, winning it the first time round, Keith Gillespie made an early and astonishing first team debut in a third round FA Cup tie against Bury, creating the first goal and scoring the second in a 2-0 win. However, he was unable to win a regular place in the United side and in September 1993 he joined Wigan Athletic on loan. In an eight-match spell, he scored four goals including two brilliant solo efforts from the halfway line in a 6-3 defeat of Chester City.

On his return to Old Trafford, he continued to play mainly reserve team football until in January 1995 he joined Newcastle United practically unnoticed, being valued at £1 million in the deal that took Andy Cole to Manchester United. The young Northern Ireland international proved that he had the ability to become a huge name in his own right. Gillespie possessed balance and control on the ball and searing pace running at defenders, qualities that could destroy the opposition. However, it was only 1997-98, following the appointment of Kenny Dalglish that Gillespie won a regular place in the Magpies' side. It was during this campaign that he destroyed the Barcelona defence, enabling Tino Asprilla to net a memorable hat-trick. Unfortunately his season ended on a sad note when a bad ankle injury caused him to miss the FA Cup Final.

Despite remaining a regular in the Northern Ireland team, he found it difficult to find a starting place in Ruud Gullit's team and in December 1998 he was transferred to Blackburn Rovers for £2.25 million. Still troubled by ankle and hamstring problems, he missed as many games as he played and in December 2000 he rejoined Wigan on loan. In his second spell with the club he showed that he had lost none of his pace and created a number of goalscoring opportunities for the Latics' strikers but just when it seemed that a permanent deal could be arranged, he returned to Ewood Park, won back his first team place and helped Rovers win promotion to the Premiership.

He then emerged from being written out of Blackburn's plans to become an integral member of the side, though he did remain as enigmatic as ever! Remaining a regular in the Northern Ireland side, he found himself on the bench for many of Blackburn's matches and in the summer of 2003 he joined Leicester City in their unsuccessful fight against relegation from the top flight.

Despite some outstanding performances in the Championship, he has recently been released by Leicester City and is now looking for his sixth League club.

Personal File

Position: Winger
Born: Keith Robert Gillespie,
Bangor
18 February 1975
Clubs: Manchester United,
Wigan Athletic,
Newcastle United,
Blackburn Rovers,
Leicester City

NI Caps: 60
NI Goals: 1

Games

Year	Opponent	Result	Score	G	Year	Opponent	Result	Score	G
1995	Portugal	lost	1-2		2001	Czech			
	Austria	won	2-1	1		Republic	lost	0-1	
	Republic					Bulgaria	lost	3-4	
	of Ireland	lost	0-4			Bulgaria	lost	0-1	
	Republic				2002	Denmark	drew	1-1	
	of Ireland	drew	1-1			Iceland	won	3-0	
	Latvia	won	1-0			Poland	lost	1-4	
	Canada	lost	0-2			Liechtenstein	drew	0-0	
	Chile	lost	1-2			Spain	lost	0-5	
	Latvia	lost	1-2		2003	Cyprus	drew	0-0	
1996	Portugal	drew	1-1			Spain	lost	0-3	
	Austria	won	5-3			Ukraine	drew	0-0	
	Norway	lost	0-2			Finland	lost	0-1	
	Germany	drew	1-1			Armenia	lost	0-1	
1997	Ukraine	lost	0-1			Greece	lost	0-2	
	Armenia	drew	1-1		2004	Ukraine	drew	0-0	
	Belgium	won	3-0			Armenia	lost	0-1	
	Portugal	drew	0-0			Greece	lost	0-1	
	Ukraine	lost	1-2			Norway	lost	1-4	
1998	Germany	lost	1-3			Serbia &			
	Albania	lost	0-1			Montenegro	drew	1-1	
	Slovakia	won	1-0			Barbados	drew	1-1	
	Switzerland	won	1-0			St Kitts &			
1999	Turkey	lost	0-3			Nevis	won	2-0	
	Moldova	drew	0-0			Trinidad &			
2000	France	lost	0-1			Tobago	won	3-0	
	Turkey	lost	0-3		2005	Switzerland	drew	0-0	
	Germany	lost	0-4			Azerbaijan	drew	0-0	
	Luxembourg	won	3-1			Austria	drew	3-3	
	Malta	won	3-0			Canada	lost	0-1	
	Hungary	lost	0-1			England	lost	0-4	
2001	Yugoslavia	lost	1-2						

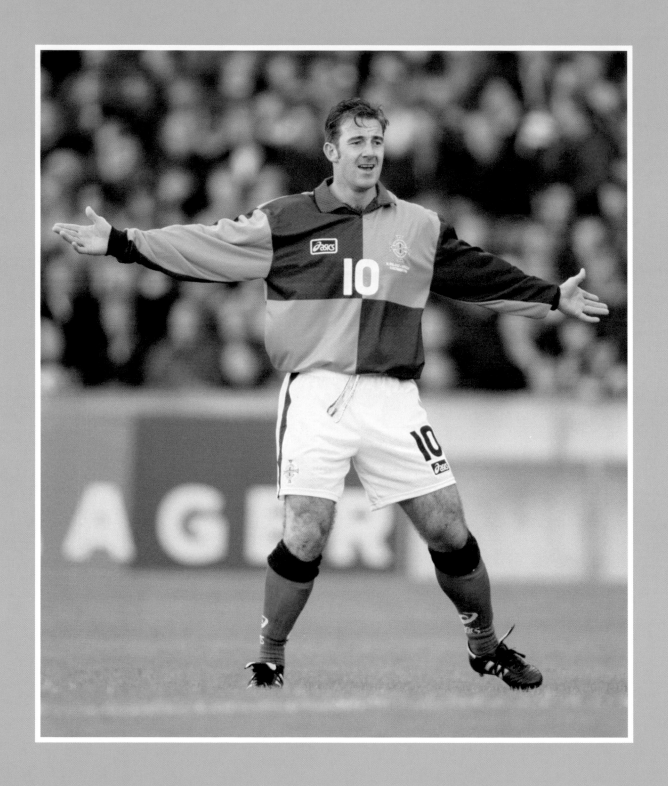

Phil Gray

Strong-running striker Phil Gray began his Football League career with Tottenham Hotspur and made his debut in the virtual reserve team that fulfilled a fixture at Everton five days before the 1987 FA Cup Final. After that he failed to make much of an impact, mainly due to numerous injury problems that sidelined him for lengthy spells. He was loaned out to Barnsley and Fulham before being allowed to join Luton Town for £275,000 in August 1991. Within a month of his arrival at Kenilworth Road, Gray had been elevated to Northern Ireland's full international squad, though he had to wait until 1993 before winning the first of 26 caps. Gray again suffered from injuries whilst with the Hatters and though he topped the club's scoring charts in 1992-93 with 19 goals, he was transferred to Sunderland in the close season for £800,000.

In his first two seasons on Wearside, Gray was the Black Cats' leading scorer but in 1995-96 he was injured during February and missed out on the title run-in. However, he thoroughly deserved his First Division Championship medal for before his injury, he had scored nine goals including a 35-yard piledriver in the 4-0 defeat of Grimsby Town.

At the end of that season, Gray, who had scored 41 goals in 132 games became a free agent and joined French club Nancy. He later played for Fortuna Sittard before rejoining Luton Town for £400,000 in September 1997.

Injuries then began to impair his performances but he went on to score 53 goals in 161 games in his two spells with the club before leaving to join Burnley. After an impressive start, he lost his place and moved on to Oxford United, still retaining his place in the Northern Ireland side. After initially displaying his predatory instincts, he was used only sparingly and after a loan spell with Conference outfit Boston United, he went to play for Chelmsford City.

Personal File

Position: Forward
Born: Philip Gray,
Belfast
2 October 1968
Clubs: Tottenham Hotspur,
Barnsley (loan),
Fullham (loan), Luton Town,
Sunderland, Nancy (France),
Fortuna Sittard (Holland),
Burnley, Oxford United,
Boston United,
Chelmsford City

NI Caps: 26
NI Goals: 6

Games

Year	Opponent	Result	Score	G	Year	Opponent	Result	Score	G
1993	Denmark	lost	0-1		1995	Canada	lost	0-2	
	Albania	won	2-1			Chile	lost	1-2	
	Republic				1996	Portugal	drew	1-1	
	of Ireland	lost	0-3			Liechtenstein	won	4-0	1
	Spain	lost	1-3			Austria	won	5-3	1
1994	Latvia	won	2-0	1	1997	Ukraine	lost	0-1	
	Denmark	lost	0-1			Armenia	drew	1-1	
	Republic					Germany	drew	1-1	
	of Ireland	drew	1-1		1999	Moldova	drew	2-2	
	Romania	won	2-0	1	2001	Malta	won	1-0	1
	Liechtenstein	won	4-1			Denmark	drew	1-1	
1995	Portugal	lost	1-2			Iceland	lost	0-1	
	Austria	won	2-1	1		Norway	lost	0-4	
	Republic					Czech			
	of Ireland	lost	0-4			Republic	lost	0-1	

Northern Ireland goalkeeper Harry Gregg (l) jumps high to take a cross under pressure from England's Don Revie (r)

Harry Gregg

Harry Gregg began his footballing career with Dundalk and was a part-timer with Linfield and Coleraine, earning £1 a week as a joiner before he was snapped up by Doncaster Rovers in the summer of 1951. He had appeared in 93 games for the Belle Vue club when in December 1957, Manchester United manager Matt Busby signed him for what was then a record fee for a goalkeeper of £23,000.

The New Year began well for Gregg and Manchester United. A 3-2 home win over Red Star Belgrade in the European Cup was followed by a 3-3 draw in Belgrade. The Irishman was in superb form, saving shot after shot that by rights should have seen United out of the competition. However, his form was such that United won a place in the European Cup semi-finals. The day after United's thrilling 3-3 draw in Belgrade, tragedy struck. The plane that was carrying home the victorious United team crashed on the runway at Munich Airport, killing many of the players. Harry Gregg crawled virtually unscathed from the wreckage and as the plane's crew shouted for people to get away from the aircraft for fear of fire, he returned to the plane and helped some of the passengers to safety including a 22-month old baby girl.

Remarkably three weeks later, Gregg played in the 3-0 win over Sheffield Wednesday in the FA Cup and three months later in the final against Bolton Wanderers. He had a great contest with Bolton and England centre-forward Nat Lofthouse, but there was to be no fairy tale ending as Bolton ran out winners 2-0. Gregg was the victim of the controversial challenge made by Lofthouse, who bundled both Gregg and the ball over the line.

Despite his disappointments at Wembley, Gregg had a superb year at international level as Northern Ireland qualified for the World Cup Finals. The bulk of the Irish party flew to Sweden but Gregg, with the Munich disaster fresh in his mind, sailed separately by ferry. In the last group match, Ireland needed at least one point from their match against West Germany, the reigning world champions. Surprisingly with about 10 minutes left, the Irish led 2-1, though Gregg was injured and playing virtually on one leg. He was diving all over the penalty area, though a late equaliser from Uwe Seeler meant that Ireland had to meet Czechoslovakia in a play-off match. Gregg wasn't fit but Northern Ireland qualified. Unfortunately the injury-hit side were beaten 4-0 by France in the quarter-final.

Gregg continued his superb displays for United and Northern Ireland until December 1966 when he joined Stoke City on a permanent basis after a loan period at the Victoria Ground.

In 1967 he became manager of Shrewsbury Town, later taking over the reins of both Swansea and Crewe Alexandra. In 1984 he was appointed assistant to Lou Macari at Swindon Town but departed less than a year later after the two former United stars ended up not speaking to each other!

Personal File

Position: Goalkeeper
Born: Henry Gregg,
        Derry
        27 October 1932
Clubs: Dundalk,
        Linfield,
        Coleraine,
        Doncaster Rovers,
        Manchester United,
        Stoke City

NI Caps: 25

Games

Year	Opponent	Result	Score	G	Year	Opponent	Result	Score	G
1954	Wales	won	2-1		1958	West			
1957	England	drew	1-1			Germany	drew	2-2	
	Scotland	lost	0-1			France	lost	0-4	
	Portugal	drew	1-1		1959	England	drew	3-3	
	Wales	drew	0-0			Wales	won	4-1	
	Italy	lost	0-1		1960	Scotland	lost	0-4	
	Portugal	won	3-0			England	lost	1-2	
1958	England	won	3-2			Wales	lost	2-3	
	Italy	drew	2-2		1961	England	lost	2-5	
	Wales	drew	1-1			Scotland	lost	2-5	
	Czechoslovakia	won	1-0		1962	Scotland	lost	1-6	
	Argentina	lost	1-3			Greece	won	2-0	
					1964	Scotland	won	2-1	
						England	lost	3-8	

"Five people in the snow in the distance were shouting, 'Run! Run! Run!' I heard a child crying. It's as simple as that, no big John Wayne stuff! I shouted, 'Come back here, there's people alive...'"

- Harry Gregg on the Munich disaster

Danny Griffin

Central defender Danny Griffin began his career with Scottish League St Johnstone, whom he joined from St Andrew's Boys' Club in February 1994. After some impressive displays for the club's junior sides, he made his first team debut in a 1-0 home win over Clydebank in April 1995. The following season he was an important member of the St Johnstone side that won the Scottish First Division Championship, scoring his first goal in a 4-0 win at Partick Thistle. Towards the end of that season, Griffin won the first of 29 full caps when he wore the No.2 shirt in a 1-1 home draw against Germany.

Over the next few seasons at McDiarmid Park, Griffin was an integral member of the Saints' side, with probably his best displays coming in 1998-99 when the club finished third in the Premier League. His only goal that season secured the points in a 1-0 win at Dundee United.

In fact, it was the Tannadice club who paid £600,000 for Griffin's services in the summer of 2000 and though he was a regular member of their side, the club struggled in the top flight.

During the early part of the 2003-04 season, Griffin fell out of favour with the Terrors' manager Ian McCall and was allowed to move south of the border to join Stockport County on a free transfer.

He linked up with his former Northern Ireland team boss Sammy McIlroy and made a huge impact at Edgeley Park before being stretchered off at Blackpool in March 2004 with an Achilles injury, which ruled him out of action for the rest of the campaign.

"Super, Super Dan, Super Danny Griffin!"

- Northern Ireland Supporters' Song

Personal File

Position: Central defender
Born: Daniel Joseph Griffin,
Belfast
19 August 1977
Clubs: St Andrew's BC,
St Johnstone,
Dundee United,
Stockport County

NI Caps: 29
NI Goals: 1

Games

Year	Opponent	Result	Score	G	Year	Opponent	Result	Score	G
1996	Germany	drew	1-1		2001	Bulgaria	lost	3-4	
1997	Ukraine	lost	0-1			Bulgaria	lost	0-1	
	Italy	lost	0-2			Czech Republic	lost	1-3	
	Belgium	won	3-0						
	Thailand	drew	0-0		2002	Denmark	drew	1-1	
1998	Germany	lost	1-3			Iceland	won	2-0	
	Albania	lost	0-1			Malta	won	1-0	
1999	Moldova	drew	2-2			Poland	lost	1-4	
	Republic of Ireland	won	1-0	1	2003	Cyprus	drew	0-0	
2000	Luxembourg	won	3-1			Italy	lost	0-2	
	Malta	won	3-0			Spain	drew	0-0	
	Hungary	lost	0-1		2004	Ukraine	drew	0-0	
2001	Yugoslavia	lost	1-2			Armenia	lost	0-1	
	Norway	lost	0-4			Greece	lost	0-1	
	Czech Republic	lost	0-1			Norway	lost	1-4	

Billy Hamilton

Billy Hamilton was first signed by Linfield as a 16-year-old and after becoming a first team regular, played in the historic Irish League and Cup double winning team of 1977-78. He also won his first international honour in March of that season when he was selected for Northern Ireland's Under 21 side against the Republic in Dublin.

It was inevitable that English clubs would come calling and it was Queen's Park Rangers who paid Linfield £25,000 for Hamilton's services in April 1978. Before he had even kicked a ball for Rangers, he had collected his first full cap, appearing as a substitute in his country's 1-1 draw with Scotland at Hampden Park in May 1978.

With Clive Allen scoring goals from every angle, Queen's Park Rangers felt they could afford to let Billy Hamilton go, and in November 1979 he joined Burnley with the Turf Moor club paying £38,000 for his signature. In a disappointing first season for the Clarets, Hamilton top-scored, albeit with seven goals. The signing of Steve Taylor the following summer was an important factor in Hamilton's development and the two formed a fine understanding. In 1981-82, Hamilton again top-scored, helping the Clarets to win the Third Division Championship.

Hamilton, who was Burnley's 'Player of the Year', headed off to Spain for the World Cup Finals, where he was one of Northern Ireland's stars. He made Gerry Armstrong's famous winner against the host country in the first series of group matches, then took centre stage, scoring both goals in the gripping 2-2 draw with Austria in the Vicente Calderon Stadium, Madrid in the quarter-final.

Hamilton continued to top score for Burnley over the coming seasons and in 1983-84 he produced the best return of his career with 18 goals. At the end of that season, Hamilton, who had scored 77 goals in 252 games, was sold to ambitious Oxford United, newly promoted from the Third Division as champions. He was an immediate hit with the Oxford fans and played a vital role in United's rampage through Division Two, emerging as Champions to reach the top flight for the first time ever in 1985.

He was injured during that successful campaign and as a result, played only occasionally during the following historic First Division season. He also missed Oxford's memorable League Cup run and victory in the Wembley final over his first club, Queen's Park Rangers. After succumbing to the inevitability of retirement from top-class football, Hamilton teamed up with Brian Flynn at Limerick in the League of Ireland as player-manager and in 1988-89 was the League's leading scorer with 21 goals.

He later moved to Northern Ireland as player-manager of Distillery before hanging up his boots and concentrating on management. He later opened a sports shop in Bangor.

Personal File

Position: Forward
Born: William Robert Hamilton, Belfast 9 May 1957
Clubs: Linfield, Queen's Park Rangers, Burnley, Oxford United, Limerick, Distillery

NI Caps: 41
NI Goals: 5

Games

Year	Opponent	Result	Score	G	Year	Opponent	Result	Score	G
1978	Scotland	drew	1-1		1983	Austria	lost	0-2	
1980	Scotland	won	1-0	1		West Germany	won	1-0	
	England	drew	1-1			Albania	drew	0-0	
	Wales	won	1-0			Albania	won	1-0	
	Australia	won	2-1			Scotland	drew	0-0	
	Australia	drew	1-1			England	drew	0-0	
1981	Sweden	won	3-0			Wales	lost	0-1	
	Portugal	lost	0-1		1984	Austria	won	3-1	1
	Scotland	drew	1-1	1		Turkey	lost	0-1	
	Portugal	won	1-0			West Germany	won	1-0	
	Scotland	lost	0-2			Scotland	won	2-0	
	Sweden	lost	0-1			England	lost	0-1	
1982	Scotland	drew	0-0			Wales	drew	1-1	
	Israel	won	1-0			Finland	lost	0-1	
	England	lost	0-4			Romania	won	3-2	
	Wales	lost	0-3		1985	Spain	drew	0-0	
	Yugoslavia	drew	0-0		1986	Morocco	won	2-1	
	Honduras	drew	1-1			Algeria	drew	1-1	
	Spain	won	1-0			Spain	lost	1-2	
	Austria	drew	2-2	2		Brazil	lost	0-3	
	France	lost	1-4						

"We fought very hard as team and for each other."

- Billy Hamilton during BBC interview

Bryan Hamilton

Bryan Hamilton started his playing career with Distillery and earned the first of his 50 Northern Ireland caps while starring for Linfield, before Ipswich Town won the race for his signature in August 1971.

It was at Portman Road that Hamilton enjoyed his best moments as a player under Bobby Robson in a talented Ipswich side. Although he only played in a handful of matches in 1971-72 he was ever-present and joint-top scorer with 11 League goals in 1972-73. The following season he was the club's leading scorer with 16 goals in 41 games as Town finished fourth in Division One. He netted his only hat-trick for the club in March 1975 as Newcastle United were beaten 5-4 at Portman Road. Hamilton had scored 56 goals in 199 games when he left Ipswich to join Everton for £40,000.

Though Hamilton wasn't a prolific scorer at international level, he had the happy knack of scoring vital goals; three of his four goals for Northern Ireland came in 1-0 wins over Wales (twice) and Yugoslavia.

He played for the Goodison club in the League Cup Final of 1977, although he will always be remembered on Merseyside for scoring the "goal that never was". In the FA Cup semi-final against Liverpool, the game stood at 2-2 when with just seconds remaining, Bryan Hamilton's thigh deflected a Duncan McKenzie flick into the Liverpool net. Everyone in Maine Road thought the Irish midfielder had put Everton into the 1977 FA Cup Final. It was to become an infamous slice of Blues folklore that referee Clive Thomas disallowed the effort for alleged handball; the score remained at 2-2 and the Reds marched on to win the replay. Recollections of that bitter incident will dominate any discussion on the short Goodison sojourn of the chunky, dark-haired link-man without doing justice to his ability.

Though his goalscoring tally on Merseyside slumped, he compensated by precise passing and mature reading of the game as well as formidable eagerness and lung-power. He lost his place in the Everton side midway through the 1976-77 season and moved to Millwall for £25,000 that summer. Hamilton later played for Swindon Town before joining Tranmere Rovers as player-manager.

Working on the proverbial shoestring, Bryan Hamilton saw several crises through at Prenton Park before leaving to take up the manager's role at Wigan Athletic.

A Freight Rover Trophy win at Wembley in May 1985 was the highlight of his time at Springfield Park and in June 1986 after impressing on a World Cup TV panel with his easy manner and analytical shrewdness, he was appointed manager of Leicester City. After a promising start, the Foxes were relegated in 1986-87 and unable to halt a slide, which threatened to lead to Third Division football, Hamilton was sacked in December 1987. Shortly afterwards he returned to Wigan as Chief Executive and later re-assumed control of team matters.

Personal File

Position: Midfielder
Born: Bryan Hamilton,
Belfast
21 December 1946
Clubs: Distillery, Linfield,
Ipswich Town,
Everton, Millwall,
Swindon Town,
Tranmere Rovers

NI Caps: 50
NI Goals: 4

Games

Year	Opponent	Result	Score	G	Year	Opponent	Result	Score	G
1969	Turkey	won	3-0		1976	Yugoslavia	lost	0-1	
1971	Cyprus	won	3-0			Israel	drew	1-1	
	Cyprus	won	5-0			Scotland	lost	0-3	
	England	lost	0-1			England	lost	0-4	
	Scotland	won	1-0			Wales	lost	0-1	
	Wales	won	1-0	1	1977	Holland	drew	2-2	
1972	USSR	lost	0-1			Belgium	lost	0-2	
	USSR	drew	1-1			West			
	Spain	drew	1-1			Germany	lost	0-5	
1973	Bulgaria	lost	0-3			England	lost	1-2	
	Cyprus	lost	0-1			Scotland	lost	0-3	
	Portugal	drew	1-1			Wales	drew	1-1	
	Cyprus	won	3-0			Iceland	lost	0-1	
	England	lost	1-2		1978	Scotland	drew	1-1	
	Scotland	won	2-1			England	lost	0-1	
	Wales	won	1-0	1		Wales	lost	0-1	
1974	Bulgaria	drew	0-0		1979	Republic			
	Scotland	won	1-0			of Ireland	drew	0-0	
	England	lost	0-1			Bulgaria	won	2-0	
	Wales	lost	0-1			Bulgaria	won	2-0	
1975	Norway	lost	1-2			England	lost	0-2	
	Sweden	won	2-0			Scotland	lost	0-1	
	Yugoslavia	won	1-0	1		Wales	drew	1-1	
	England	drew	0-0			Denmark	lost	0-4	
1976	Sweden	lost	1-2		1980	Australia	won	2-1	
	Norway	won	3-0	1		Australia	won	2-1	

Bryan Hamilton

On leaving Wigan a second time, Bryan Hamilton became a surprise choice to succeed Billy Bingham as Northern Ireland's national manager. He got off to a flying start, as his side pulled off a surprise 2-0 win over Romania. His first major challenge was to lead Northern Ireland to qualification for Euro '96. He failed but his team put up a respectable performance and only just lost out to their neighbours the Republic of Ireland for a play-off place. Highlights of that campaign included a memorable double over Austria (including a 5-3 home win) and a draw with group winners Portugal in Lisbon.

Since leaving his post with the national side, Hamilton has twice been called in to add his experience to the Ipswich backroom staff and had a spell in charge of Norwich City.

Left: Everton substitute Bryan Hamilton (Centre) raises his arms in celebration after beating Liverpool goalkeeper Ray Clemence. The goal was disallowed for offside, and the match ended in a 2-2 draw.

Martin Harvey

Martin Harvey was a stylish and constructive wing-half, strong in the tackle and an excellent all-round player.

He worked his way up through the ranks at Sunderland to make his League debut for the Wearsiders in a goalless draw at Plymouth Argyle in October 1959. Over the next four seasons, Harvey only appeared in 23 League games but did score his first goal for the club in a 2-1 defeat of Luton Town in April 1962.

Though not a regular in the Sunderland side, Harvey, who had won honours for Northern Ireland at schoolboy, Under 23 and 'B' international level, won full international honours when he played against Italy in Bologna in April 1961. He went on to win 34 caps for Northern Ireland, after replacing the great Danny Blanchflower in the No.4 shirt, scoring all his three international goals against Wales! One of these was the winner in a 3-2 victory at Swansea's Vetch Field in the game following the 8-3 defeat by England.

After establishing himself in Sunderland's midfield during the club's Second Division promotion-winning season of 1963-64, replacing Stan Anderson, he went on to be a virtual ever-present for the next nine seasons. He had appeared in 361 League and Cup games for the north-east club when in 1972 he left Roker Park to become assistant-manager of Carlisle United.

He later took over from Bobby Moncur as the Brunton Park club's manager and as results improved, the club eventually finished sixth in 1979-80. However, after a bad start the following season Harvey resigned, becoming the shortest-ever serving manager of the Cumbrian club.

After a spell coaching Plymouth Argyle, he worked alongside fellow Northern Ireland international Jimmy Nicholl at Millwall.

Personal File

Position: Wing-half
Born: Martin Harvey,
Belfast
19 September 1941
Clubs: Sunderland

NI Caps: 34
NI Goals: 3

Games

Year	Opponent	Result	Score	G	Year	Opponent	Result	Score	G
1961	Italy	lost	2-3		1966	Scotland	won	3-2	
1962	Holland	lost	0-4			Scotland	lost	1-2	
1963	Wales	lost	1-4	1		Albania	drew	1-1	
	Spain	drew	1-1			Wales	won	4-1	1
1964	Scotland	won	2-1			West			
	Spain	lost	0-1			Germany	lost	0-2	
	England	lost	3-8			Mexico	won	4-1	
	Wales	won	3-2	1	1967	England	lost	0-2	
	Uruguay	won	3-0			Scotland	lost	1-2	
1965	England	lost	3-4		1968	England	lost	0-2	
	Switzerland	won	1-0			Wales	lost	0-2	
	Switzerland	lost	1-2			Israel	won	3-2	
	Scotland	lost	2-3		1969	Turkey	won	4-1	
	Holland	won	2-1			Turkey	won	3-0	
	Wales	lost	0-5			England	lost	1-3	
	Holland	drew	0-0		1970	USSR	lost	0-2	
	Albania	won	4-1		1971	Cyprus	won	5-0	
						Wales	won	1-0	

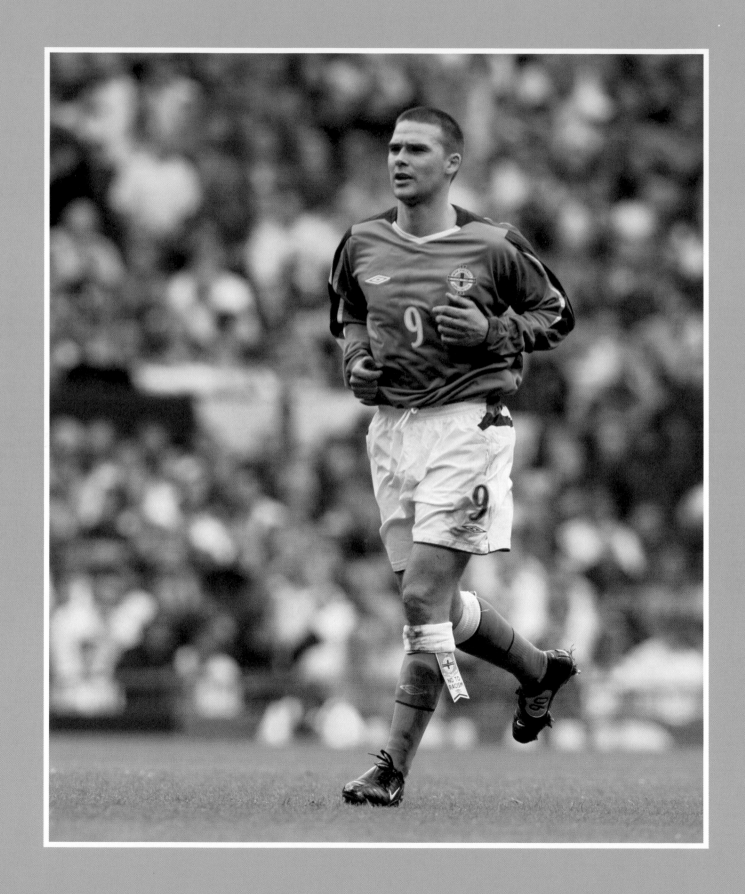

David Healy

David Healy made the national headlines when he broke Northern Ireland's goalscoring drought against Norway, and in the summer of 2004 he established a new career record of goals for the national team.

Beginning his career with Manchester United where he had a penchant for scoring goals, David Healy had a disappointing introduction to first team action when the Reds were beaten by Aston Villa in the Worthington Cup competition of 1999-2000.

However, he really came to the fore when he made his international debut for Northern Ireland, scoring twice in a 3-1 win over Luxembourg. He also netted in his next international against Malta, as the Irish triumphed 3-0.

At club level, he went on loan to Port Vale but despite netting twice in his first four games, he couldn't prevent the Valiants' relegation to Division Two. On his return to Old Trafford he signed a four-year contract with United. Although he continued to impress on the international front he made little headway in United's first team squad.

In December 2000, Healy joined Preston for a North End club record fee of £1.5 million. He provided an immediate return on the club's investment by scoring after just four minutes of his debut against Sheffield United. Possessing an eye for goal, the nippy striker continued to find the net for Northern Ireland before netting his first senior hat-trick in a 6-0 win over Stockport County.

At international level, manager Sammy McIlroy used him as a lone striker – his pace leading to several goalscoring opportunities.

During the early part of the 2002-03 season, Healy found himself on the bench unable to displace either Ricardo Fuller or Richard Cresswell, and spent a couple of loan spells with Norwich City where he seemed to rediscover some of his confidence.

At international level he remained a regular in the Northern Ireland side, though they failed to score in a record number of games! In 2003-04, Healy got back on track and took his tally of goals for North End to 39 in 128 League games before leaving Deepdale to join fellow Championship club, Leeds United.

Last season in the World Cup qualifier against Wales, Healy had mixed fortunes, for after scoring Northern Ireland's second goal, he received his marching orders.

Personal File

Position: Striker
Born: David Johnathan Healy,
Downpatrick
5 August 1979
Clubs: Manchester United,
Port Vale (loan),
Preston North End,
Norwich City (loan),
Leeds United

NI Caps: 41
NI Goals: 16

Games

Year	Opponent	Result	Score	G	Year	Opponent	Result	Score	G
2000	Luxembourg	won	3-1	2	2003	Finland	lost	0-1	
	Malta	won	3-0	1		Armenia	lost	0-1	
	Hungary	lost	0-1			Greece	lost	0-2	
2001	Yugoslavia	lost	1-2	1		Italy	lost	0-2	
	Malta	won	1-0			Spain	drew	0-0	
	Denmark	drew	1-1	1	2004	Ukraine	drew	0-0	
	Iceland	lost	0-1			Armenia	lost	0-1	
	Norway	lost	0-3			Greece	lost	0-1	
	Czech Republic	lost	0-1			Norway	lost	1-4	1
	Bulgaria	lost	3-4	1		Estonia	won	1-0	1
	Bulgaria	lost	0-1			Serbia & Montenegro	drew	1-1	
	Czech Republic	lost	1-3			Barbados	drew	1-1	1
2002	Denmark	drew	1-1			St Kitts & Nevis	won	2-0	1
	Iceland	won	3-0	1		Trinidad and Tobago	won	3-0	2
	Malta	won	1-0	1	2005	Switzerland	drew	0-0	
	Poland	lost	1-4			Poland	lost	0-3	
	Liechtenstein	drew	0-0			Wales	drew	2-2	1
	Spain	lost	0-5			Austria	drew	3-3	1
2003	Cyprus	drew	0-0			Canada	lost	0-1	
	Spain	lost	0-3			England	lost	0-4	
	Ukraine	drew	0-0						

Danny Hegan

Danny Hegan was a player with loads of skill but he allowed his social activities to rule his life, and though the Coatbridge-born midfielder won seven full caps for Northern Ireland, through parentage, he was never the outstanding player he should have been.

He began his career with Albion Rovers before moving into the Football League with Sunderland. Unable to break into the first team at Roker Park, he joined Ipswich Town in September 1963. He didn't have the best of debuts as Town were thrashed 6-0 by Bolton Wanderers at Burnden Park. Over the next six seasons, Danny Hegan was a virtual ever-present in the Ipswich side and in 1967-68 missed just one game as the club won the Second Division Championship. It was during the 1968-69 season when the club were back in the top flight that he began to feel he was getting into a rut, but Hegan, who had an Irish father, gave a series of displays that brought him very close to full international honours for Northern Ireland.

He was on the transfer list for a number of months until the 1969 close season, when he was allowed to join West Bromwich Albion in exchange for Ian Collard, who was valued at £60,000 and a cheque for £30,000.

Hegan, who had scored 38 goals in 234 League and Cup games for Ipswich, won the first of seven international caps for Northern Ireland while at the Hawthorns, when he played against the USSR in October 1969.

He later joined Albion's rivals, Wolverhampton Wanderers, collecting a runners-up medal in the 1972 UEFA Cup Final defeat by Spurs.

After ending his Football League career with his first club Sunderland, Hegan played in South Africa before hanging up his boots to become a soccer coach at Butlin's Holiday Camp, Clacton in January 1982.

Danny Hegan was later sued for libel by Billy Bremner and the former Leeds United and Scotland skipper was duly awarded £100,000 damages!

Personal File

Position: Midfielder
Born: Daniel Hegan, Coatbridge 14 June 1943
Clubs: Albion Rovers, Sunderland, Ipswich Town, West Bromwich Albion, Wolverhampton Wanderers

NI Caps: 7

Games

Year	Opponent	Result	Score	G
1970	USSR	lost	0-2	
1972	USSR	lost	0-1	
	Scotland	lost	0-2	
	England	won	1-0	
	Wales	drew	0-0	
1973	Bulgaria	lost	0-3	
	Cyprus	lost	0-1	

Colin Hill

Colin Hill is a fine example of how you can resurrect your career even when having the misfortune of being discarded as a youngster.

He was a prolific scorer in junior football with Hillingdon when signing schoolboy forms for Arsenal in December 1977. A champion sprinter and javelin thrower as a schoolboy, he eventually turned professional and in doing so, turned from a striker to a defender, becoming a more than capable full- or centre-back. A regular in the Gunners' side in 1983-84, he lost his place following the signing of Viv Anderson and eventually he was given a free transfer. He joined CS Maritimo of Madeira who play in the Portuguese League.

Hill spent 15 months in Portugal before returning to England to play for Colchester United in October 1987. His fine form for the Layer Road club over two seasons earned him considerable recognition and Dave Bassett, the Sheffield United manager paid £85,000 for his signature in the summer of 1989.

In his first season at Bramall Lane, he helped the club win promotion to Division One, winning the first of 27 full caps for Northern Ireland when playing against Norway in March 1990. Hill, whose only goal at international level came a year later in the 4-1 defeat by Yugoslavia, then joined Leicester City on loan before the move was made permanent.

In fact, he played for the Foxes in the Wembley defeat by Blackburn Rovers before the following season being voted the club's 'Player of the Year'. He was then sidelined by injury from collecting a hat-trick of successive play-off final appearances in 1994. Appointed Leicester's captain, he was oddly overlooked at international level by Billy Bingham and even when Bryan Hamilton took over the Irish reins, Colin Hill seemed fated – his first three call-ups were negated by injury.

Sadly injuries and illness hampered his progress at Filbert Street, and in the summer of 1997 after making 175 first team appearances, he left Leicester on a free transfer to play for Swedish club Trelleborg.

In November 1997 he joined Northampton Town, becoming the club's first player for 30 years to win an international cap while still on the club's books. Sent-off in the opening game of the 1998-99 season following one of the best one-handed saves seen at Sixfields, he retired at the end of the campaign.

Personal File

Position:	Central defender
Born:	Colin Frederick Hill, Uxbridge 12 November 1963
Clubs:	Arsenal, CS Maritimo (Portugal), Colchester United, Sheffield United, Leicester City, Trelleborg (Sweden), Northampton Town

NI Caps: 27
NI Goals: 1

Games

Year	Opponent	Result	Score	G	Year	Opponent	Result	Score	G
1990	Norway	lost	2-3		1996	Germany	drew	1-1	
	Uruguay	won	1-0		1997	Ukraine	lost	0-1	
1991	Poland	won	3-1			Armenia	drew	1-1	
	Yugoslavia	lost	1-4	1		Germany	drew	1-1	
1992	Austria	won	2-1			Albania	won	2-0	
	Denmark	lost	1-2			Portugal	drew	0-0	
1995	Republic of Ireland	drew	1-1			Ukraine	lost	1-2	
	Latvia	won	1-0			Armenia	drew	0-0	
1996	Portugal	drew	1-1			Thailand	drew	0-0	
	Liechtenstein	won	4-0		1998	Germany	lost	1-3	
	Austria	won	5-3			Albania	lost	0-1	
	Norway	lost	0-2			Portugal	lost	0-1	
	Sweden	lost	1-2			Slovakia	won	1-0	
					1999	Turkey	lost	0-3	

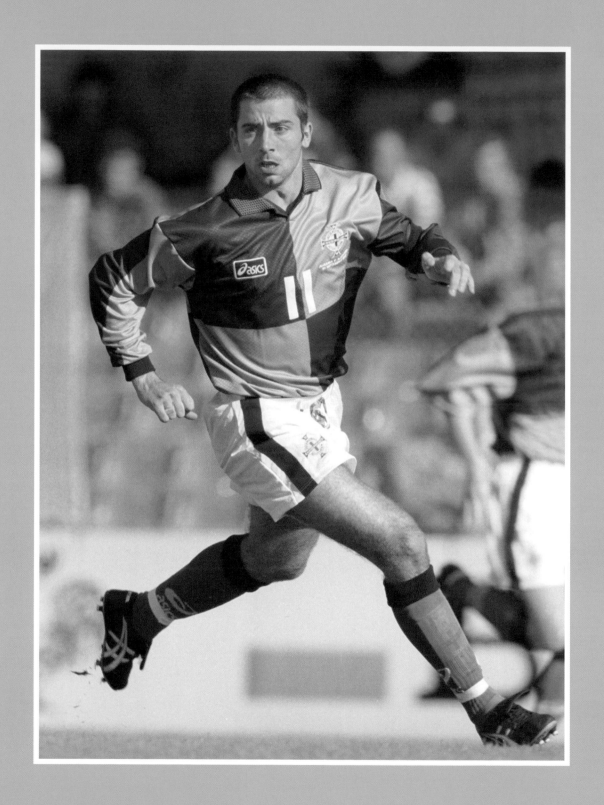

Kevin Horlock

With opportunities scarce and with no first team games under his belt, Kevin Horlock was transferred from West Ham United to Swindon Town at the start of the 1992-93 season.

Not expected to feature quickly in first team action, an injury crisis pitched him into service and in only his third appearance he helped the Robins beat his former team at Upton Park. Equally at home in midfield or at left-back, Horlock soon became a regular member of the Swindon side. His consistency following the arrival of player-manager Steve McMahon culminated in his selection for a full Northern Ireland cap against Latvia in April 1995.

The following season was a remarkable one for Horlock. Having missed the opening game after undergoing a knee operation, he appeared in each of Swindon's subsequent 58 games en-route to a Second Division Championship medal. Also that season, Horlock scored a hat-trick at Bristol Rovers!

He had scored 26 goals in 192 League and Cup games when Manchester City paid £1.25 million for his services.

By now a regular in the Northern Ireland side, he was rewarded with the club captaincy at Maine Road. Although not an aggressive player, he began to pick up more than his fair share of yellow and red cards. In 1999-2000 he scored a number of vital goals and passed his personal goal tally from the previous season. He demonstrated his willingness to follow up his own forward passes to get into goalscoring positions to receive a lay-off from the strikers. Horlock had just begun to get to grips with life in the Premiership when in the game against Charlton Athletic, he fractured an ankle.

The 2001-02 season was probably Horlock's best in a City shirt: playing in a midfield 'holding' role he helped his side equal their record for goals in one season, as they won the First Division Championship.

After losing his place to Joey Barton, Horlock, capped 32 times by Northern Ireland, joined West Ham United, to make his long-awaited first team debut!

Personal File

Position: Midfielder
Born: Kevin Horlock,
Erith
1 November 1972
Clubs: West Ham United,
Swindon Town,
Manchester City,
West Ham United

NI Caps: 32

Games

Year	Opponent	Result	Score	G	Year	Opponent	Result	Score	G
1995	Latvia	won	1-0		1999	Canada	drew	1-1	
	Canada	lost	0-2		2000	France	lost	0-1	
1997	Germany	drew	1-1			Turkey	lost	0-3	
	Albania	won	2-0			Germany	lost	0-4	
	Italy	lost	0-2			Malta	won	3-0	
	Belgium	won	3-0		2001	Yugoslavia	lost	1-2	
	Ukraine	lost	1-2			Malta	won	1-0	
	Armenia	drew	0-0			Denmark	drew	1-1	
	Thailand	drew	0-0			Iceland	lost	0-1	
1998	Germany	lost	1-3		2002	Denmark	drew	1-1	
	Albania	lost	0-1			Iceland	won	3-0	
	Portugal	lost	0-1			Malta	won	1-0	
1999	Turkey	lost	0-3			Spain	lost	0-5	
	Finland	won	1-0		2003	Cyprus	drew	0-0	
	Germany	lost	0-3			Spain	lost	0-3	
	Moldova	drew	0-0			Ukraine	drew	0-0	

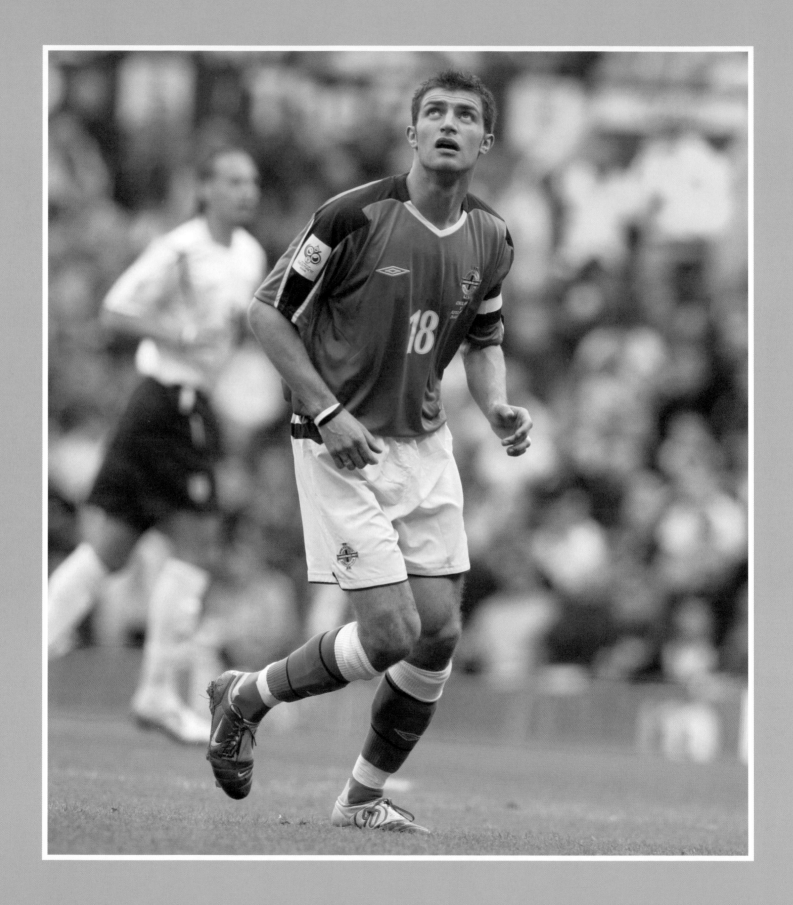

Aaron Hughes

Having joined Newcastle United as a 15-year-old, Hughes was given his initial taste of first team football in the pre-1997-98 season Irish International Tournament and after performing well, established himself in the senior squad. He had a testing introduction to competitive football in that he made his debut as a substitute in the Champions League match against Barcelona in the Nou Camp.

Although primarily a central defender, Hughes demonstrated his flexibility by playing at full-back and as a man-to-man marker and was clearly a young man with a bright future. He made his full international debut at the age of 18 in a 1-0 defeat of Slovakia in March 1998.

Though he continued to be a regular in the Northern Ireland side, he found it difficult in 1998-99 to hold down a first team place at St James Park, though he did become the Magpies' youngest-ever Premiership player, and came off the bench in the FA Cup semi-final against Spurs to help his side reach Wembley.

The following season he became the club's youngest-ever Premiership scorer, as he started to take opportunities to add an attacking element to his game.

He finally established himself as a Newcastle regular in 2000-01 when after switching to right-back, he made the position his own. The emergence of Andy Griffin plus Hughes' versatility saw him switch to the opposite flank where calm and composed, he read the game well and was comfortable and rarely hurried on the ball.

Hughes had appeared in almost 300 games for the Magpies when he was transferred to Aston Villa. He continues to be a regular in the Northern Ireland side and was recently honoured with the captaincy of his country.

"I always get a buzz pulling on the Northern Ireland jersey. It's a huge honour to captain your country."

- Aaron Hughes

Personal File

Position: Defender
Born: Aaron William Hughes, Cookstown 8 November 1979
Clubs: Newcastle United, Aston Villa

NI Caps: 42

Games

Year	Opponent	Result	Score	G	Year	Opponent	Result	Score	G
1998	Slovakia	won	1-0		2002	Denmark	drew	1-1	
	Switzerland	won	1-0			Iceland	won	3-0	
	Spain	lost	1-4			Poland	lost	1-4	
1999	Turkey	lost	0-3			Spain	lost	0-5	
	Finland	won	1-0		2003	Spain	lost	0-3	
	Moldova	drew	0-0			Ukraine	drew	0-0	
	Canada	drew	1-1			Finland	lost	0-1	
	Republic of Ireland	won	1-0			Armenia	lost	0-1	
2000	France	lost	0-1			Greece	lost	0-2	
	Turkey	lost	0-3			Italy	lost	0-2	
	Luxembourg	won	3-1			Spain	drew	0-0	
	Hungary	lost	0-1		2004	Ukraine	drew	0-0	
	Yugoslavia	lost	1-2			Armenia	lost	0-1	
	Malta	won	1-0			Greece	lost	0-1	
	Denmark	drew	1-1			Norway	lost	1-4	
	Iceland	lost	0-1		2005	Switzerland	drew	0-0	
	Norway	lost	0-4			Poland	lost	0-3	
	Czech Republic	lost	0-1			Wales	drew	2-2	
	Bulgaria	lost	0-1			Azerbaijan	drew	0-0	
	Czech Republic	lost	1-3			Austria	drew	3-3	
						Canada	lost	0-1	
						England	lost	0-4	

Michael Hughes

Winger Michael Hughes started his Football League career with Manchester City, whom he joined from Carrick Rangers. He had played in only 33 first team games for the then Maine Road club when in the summer of 1992 he left to play for French club RS Strasbourg.

He arrived at Upton Park on loan in November 1994 but in spite of performing well, he returned to Strasbourg, before rejoining the Hammers for a second loan spell in October 1995. Equally at home on either flank, Hughes provided some excellent crosses for fellow Northern Ireland international Iain Dowie to feed off.

Eventually the Hammers made the move permanent but in September 1997 after appearing in a total of 97 games, he was surprisingly transferred across London to Wimbledon for a fee of £1.6 million.

He ended his first campaign as the Dons supporters' 'Player of the Year', having been instrumental in the club's survival. Over the next couple of seasons, he continued to produce some excellent performances.

Towards the end of the 1999-2000 season and shortly after winning his 50th Northern Ireland cap against Germany, Hughes had the misfortune to break his leg. He spent much of the following season recuperating before returning to action shortly before the end of the 2000-01 season.

Loaned out to Birmingham City, he impressed with some neat clever passing before a stress fracture of the ankle put him on the sidelines. After missing out on the whole of the 2002-03 campaign due to contractual problems, Hughes, who has won 71 caps for Northern Ireland, signed for Crystal Palace.

The diminutive hardworking midfielder helped Palace win promotion to the Premiership, the high point being the winning penalty in the shoot-out that decided the play-off semi-final against Sunderland.

Unable to prevent the Eagles from being relegated back to the Championship after just one season of top flight football, Hughes was also sent-off in the game against Wales at the Millennium Stadium.

Personal File

Position: Midfielder
Born: Michael Eamonn Hughes, Larne 2 August 1971
Clubs: Carrick Rangers, Manchester City, RS Strasbourg (France), West Ham United, Wimbledon, Birmingham City (loan), Crystal Palace

NI Caps: 71
NI Goals: 5

Games

Year	Opponent	Result	Score	G	Year	Opponent	Result	Score	G
1992	Denmark	lost	1-2		1997	Italy	lost	0-2	
	Scotland	lost	0-1			Ukraine	lost	1-2	
	Lithuania	drew	2-2		1998	Germany	lost	1-3	1
	Germany	drew	1-1	1		Portugal	lost	0-1	
1993	Albania	won	3-0			Slovakia	won	1-0	
	Spain	drew	0-0			Switzerland	won	1-0	
	Denmark	lost	0-1			Spain	lost	1-4	
	Republic of Ireland	lost	0-3		1999	Turkey	lost	0-3	
	Spain	lost	1-3			Finland	won	1-0	
	Lithuania	won	1-0			Moldova	drew	2-2	
	Latvia	won	2-1			Germany	lost	0-3	
1994	Latvia	won	2-0			Moldova	drew	0-0	
	Denmark	lost	0-1		2000	France	lost	0-1	
	Republic of Ireland	drew	1-1			Turkey	lost	0-3	
	Romania	won	2-0			Germany	lost	0-4	
	Liechtenstein	won	4-1			Finland	lost	1-4	
	Colombia	lost	0-2			Luxembourg	won	3-1	
	Mexico	lost	0-3			Malta	won	3-0	1
1995	Portugal	lost	1-2			Hungary	lost	0-1	
	Austria	won	2-1		2001	Czech Republic	lost	0-1	
	Republic of Ireland	lost	0-4			Bulgaria	lost	3-4	
	Republic of Ireland	drew	1-1			Bulgaria	lost	0-1	
	Latvia	won	1-0			Czech Republic	lost	1-3	
	Canada	lost	0-2		2002	Denmark	drew	1-1	
	Chile	lost	1-2			Iceland	won	3-0	1
	Latvia	lost	1-2			Malta	won	1-0	
1996	Portugal	drew	1-1	1		Poland	lost	1-4	
	Liechtenstein	won	4-0			Liechtenstein	drew	0-0	
	Austria	won	5-3		2003	Spain	lost	0-3	
	Norway	lost	0-2			Ukraine	drew	0-0	
	Germany	drew	1-1		2004	Ukraine	drew	0-0	
1997	Ukraine	lost	0-1			Greece	lost	0-1	
	Armenia	drew	1-1			Norway	lost	1-4	
	Germany	drew	1-1			Serbia & Montenegro	drew	1-1	
	Albania	won	2-0		2005	Poland	lost	0-3	
						Wales	drew	2-2	

Willie Humphries

At school, Willie Humphries was a rugby scrum-half but also shone as a soccer player and joined Glentoran as an amateur while working as a clerical officer with the Belfast transport department.

His career began to take off when he joined Ards where his displays attracted the attention of a number of top English League clubs.

Leeds United beat Blackpool to his signature in September 1958 but he failed to settle at Elland Road and returned to Ireland to play for Ards in November 1959.

It was Coventry City manager Jimmy Hill who persuaded Humphries to have another attempt playing in the Football League and he made his debut for the Sky Blues against Hull City in April 1962. The following season he scored 10 goals in 51 first team games, his form winning him a recall to the Northern Ireland side, for whom he eventually won 14 caps. In 1963-64, Humphries had an outstanding season as Coventry won promotion to Division Two as Third Division Champions.

In March 1965 after scoring 24 goals in 126 games he left Highfield Road to join Swansea for £14,000. A regular member of the Irish League XI, appearing 12 times, he was unable to keep the Welsh club in the Second Division but did have three good seasons at the Vetch Field, scoring 22 goals in 143 games. On leaving Swansea, he returned to Ireland for his third and longest spell with Ards. During those years, he was voted 'Footballer of the Year' and led the side to success in the Irish Cup. On hanging up his boots, Willie Humphries managed Bangor from 1983 to 1985 before buying a newsagents business which he ran until he retired in 1991.

Personal File

Position: Outside-right
Born: William McCauley Humphries,
Belfast
8 June 1946
Clubs: Glentoran,
Ards,
Leeds United,
Ards,
Coventry City,
Swansea Town,
Ards

NI Caps: 14
NI Goals: 1

Games

Year	Opponent	Result	Score	G	Year	Opponent	Result	Score	G
1962	Wales	lost	0-4		1964	Scotland	won	2-1	
	Holland	lost	0-4			Spain	lost	0-1	
1963	Poland	won	2-0	1		England	lost	3-8	
	England	lost	1-3		1965	Scotland	lost	2-3	
	Scotland	lost	1-5			Holland	won	2-1	
	Wales	lost	1-4			Wales	lost	0-5	
	Spain	drew	1-1			Albania	won	4-1	

Allan Hunter

The winner of 53 full caps for Northern Ireland, centre-half Allan Hunter began his career with Coleraine for whom he played in the European Cup Winners' Cup competition before entering the Football League with Oldham Athletic in January 1967.

A virtual ever-present in the Latics' defence, he had made 83 League appearances for the Boundary Park club when in the summer of 1969 he joined their Lancashire neighbours Blackburn Rovers for a fee of £30,000.

He had a similar playing record with the Rovers and after appearing in 84 League games, left Ewood Park to join Ipswich Town in September 1971.

After making his debut against Leicester City alongside Derek Jefferson in the heart of the Ipswich defence, Hunter went on to play in all the remaining 25 games of that 1971-72 campaign. He formed a fine partnership with Kevin Beattie and missed very few matches over the next seven seasons. During his time at Portman Road, Hunter was voted the club's 'Player of the Year' in 1975-76, and was hailed as the best centre-half in the Football League. The highlight of his time with Ipswich Town was winning the FA Cup Final against Arsenal at Wembley in 1978. Hunter, who won 47 of his international caps whilst with the Suffolk club, left Ipswich in April 1982 after amassing 355 first team appearances to become player-manager at Colchester United.

The genial Irishman did not relish the managerial side of the game and resigned after only eight months in charge. Four years later he returned to Layer Road as coach but then following a spell out of the game, did commendable work teaching carpentry at the Belstead Special School. More recently he operated as a scout for his old boss Bobby Robson, at Newcastle United.

Fact: **Did you know that former Northern Ireland international Barry Hunter is Allan's nephew?**

Personal File

Position: Centre-half
Born: Allan Hunter,
Sion Mills
30 June 1946
Clubs: Coleraine,
Oldham Athletic,
Blackburn Rovers,
Ipswich Town,
Colchester United

NI Caps: 53
NI Goals: 1

Games

Year	Opponent	Result	Score	G	Year	Opponent	Result	Score	G
1970	USSR	lost	0-2		1975	Wales	won	1-0	
1971	Cyprus	won	3-0		1976	Sweden	lost	1-2	1
	Cyprus	won	5-0			Norway	won	3-0	
	England	lost	0-1			Yugoslavia	lost	0-1	
	Scotland	won	1-0			Israel	drew	1-1	
	Wales	won	1-0			Scotland	lost	0-3	
1972	USSR	lost	0-1			England	lost	0-4	
	USSR	drew	1-1			Wales	lost	0-1	
	Spain	drew	1-1		1977	Holland	drew	2-2	
	Scotland	lost	0-2			Belgium	lost	0-2	
	England	won	1-0			West			
	Wales	drew	0-0			Germany	lost	0-5	
1973	Bulgaria	lost	0-3			England	lost	1-2	
	Cyprus	lost	0-1			Scotland	lost	0-3	
	Portugal	drew	1-1			Wales	drew	1-1	
	Cyprus	won	3-0			Iceland	lost	0-1	
	England	lost	1-2		1978	Iceland	won	2-0	
	Scotland	won	2-1			Holland	lost	1-0	
	Wales	won	1-0			Belgium	won	3-0	
1974	Bulgaria	drew	0-0		1979	Republic			
	Scotland	won	1-0			of Ireland	drew	0-0	
	England	lost	0-1			Denmark	won	2-1	
	Wales	lost	0-1			Scotland	lost	0-1	
1975	Norway	lost	1-2			Wales	drew	1-1	
	Sweden	won	2-0			Denmark	lost	0-4	
	Yugoslavia	won	1-0		1980	England	lost	1-5	
	England	drew	0-0			Republic			
	Scotland	lost	0-3			of Ireland	won	1-0	

Burnley's Willie Irvine (r) climbs above West Ham United's Eddie Bovington (second r) to head for goal, watched by teammate Willie Morgan (l) and West Ham's Martin Peters (second l)

Willie Irvine

A prolific scorer throughout his entire Football League career, Willie Irvine started out with Burnley in 1960 where he spent a season finding his feet in the Lancashire League. His scoring exploits soon led to promotion to Central League level. He immediately served notice that he was a force to be reckoned with, scoring a hat-trick, having another effort disallowed and missing a penalty in a 6-1 win! Burnley's reserve team won the Central League Championship that season and again in 1962-63 when Irvine was his side's leading scorer.

It was inevitable that Irvine's form in front of goal would lead to a first team call-up but the Irish international selectors were quickest off the mark. After his first Under 23 appearance in February 1963, he was then chosen for the full Northern Ireland side to play against Wales in Belfast the following April. Although he didn't score and Wales won 4-1, Irvine must have felt in familiar surroundings playing alongside Burnley colleagues Jimmy McIlroy and Alex Elder with his brother Bobby of Stoke City in goal. He did eventually make Burnley's First Division side and on his debut at Arsenal, he scored the Clarets' first goal in a 3-2 win, following that up three days later with a hat-trick in a 3-1 defeat of Birmingham City at Turf Moor.

In three seasons from the summer of 1964, Irvine and his strike partner Andy Lochhead developed a marvellous partnership, hitting 118 League goals between them. That total included 29 from Irvine in 1965-66 (37 in all competitions) – a total that has only ever been exceeded by the prolific Bert Freeman and George Beel in the club's history.

A broken leg in an FA Cup tie at Everton in January 1967 signalled a downturn in Willie Irvine's Turf Moor career. Although he was back in first team action by the start of the following season, he took his total of goals for Burnley to 97 in 148 games when he was surprisingly allowed to join Preston North End.

After two seasons of struggle at Deepdale, he was in the side relegated in 1970 but not a regular in North End's Third Division Championship side of 1970-71, leaving for Brighton before the end of the season.

He scored on his Albion debut and quickly formed a useful strike force with Kit Napier. The following season Irvine and Napier top-scored with 16 goals each as Brighton finished runners-up to Aston Villa and were promoted to the Second Division. With the Seagulls immediately relegated, Irvine joined his last League club, Halifax Town.

After establishing a successful business in Burnley, he still lives and works in the town and watches the Clarets, his first love, as often as he can.

Personal File

Position: Centre-forward
Born: William John Irvine, Carrickfergus 18 June 1943
Clubs: Burnley, Preston North End, Brighton and Hove Albion, Halifax Town, Great Harwood

NI Caps: 23
NI Goals: 9

Games

Year	Opponent	Result	Score	G	Year	Opponent	Result	Score	G
1963	Wales	lost	1-4		1966	Mexico	won	4-1	
	Spain	drew	1-1	1	1967	England	lost	0-2	
1965	Switzerland	lost	1-2			Scotland	lost	1-2	
	Scotland	lost	2-3	1	1968	England	lost	0-2	
	Holland	won	2-1			Wales	lost	0-2	
	Wales	lost	0-5		1969	Israel	won	3-2	2
	Holland	drew	0-0			Turkey	won	4-1	
	Albania	won	4-1	1		England	lost	1-3	
1966	Scotland	won	3-2	1	1972	Scotland	lost	0-2	
	Scotland	lost	1-2	1		England	won	1-0	
	Albania	drew	1-1	1		Wales	drew	0-0	
	Wales	won	4-1	1					

(L-R) Northern Ireland's Tommy Jackson, Martin O'Neill and Roy Coyle in a rather desultory training session

Tommy Jackson

A tenacious and willing performer, Tommy Jackson was spotted by Everton playing for Glentoran against Benfica in the European Cup and was snapped up by the Merseysiders for a fee of just £10,000 in February 1968. He made his debut in the FA Cup semi-final but found himself in and out of the side before helping the Goodison club win the League Championship title in 1969-70.

Despite not being a regular in the Everton side, Jackson won the first of his 35 international caps for Northern Ireland when he played in a 3-2 win over Israel in Tel Aviv, creating goals for both Dougan and Irvine.

The midfielder was then traded to Nottingham Forest in exchange for Henry Newton and though he was a regular member of the City Ground club's side, he couldn't prevent their relegation from the top flight at the end of the 1971-72 season. He stayed with Forest until the summer of 1975 when he was given a free transfer and was immediately signed by Manchester United, who wanted him to captain their Central League side.

Due to unforeseen circumstances however, Jackson found himself in United's first team for the early games of the 1975-76 season – their first campaign back in the top flight – but then Gordon Hill arrived on the scene and Jackson lost his place as United went for an adventurous 4-2-4 system.

After three seasons at Old Trafford, Jackson was given a free transfer and returned to Ireland where after managing several clubs, he worked as a self-employed upholsterer for Bannon & Co in Belfast.

Personal File

Position: Midfielder
Born: Thomas Jackson,
Belfast
3 November 1946
Clubs: Glentoran,
Everton,
Nottingham Forest,
Manchester United

NI Caps: 35

Games

Year	Opponent	Result	Score	G	Year	Opponent	Result	Score	G
1969	Israel	won	3-2		1974	Wales	lost	0-1	
	England	lost	1-3		1975	Norway	lost	1-2	
	Scotland	drew	1-1			Sweden	won	2-0	
	Wales	drew	0-0			Yugoslavia	won	1-0	
1970	USSR	drew	0-0			England	drew	0-0	
	USSR	lost	0-2			Scotland	lost	0-3	
1971	Spain	lost	0-3			Wales	won	1-0	
1972	Scotland	lost	0-2		1976	Sweden	lost	1-2	
	England	won	1-0			Norway	won	3-0	
	Wales	drew	0-0			Yugoslavia	lost	0-1	
1973	Cyprus	won	3-0		1977	Holland	drew	2-2	
	England	lost	1-2			Belgium	lost	0-2	
	Scotland	won	2-1			West			
	Wales	won	1-0			Germany	lost	0-5	
1974	Bulgaria	drew	0-0			England	lost	1-2	
	Portugal	drew	1-1			Scotland	lost	0-3	
	Scotland	won	1-0			Wales	drew	1-1	
	England	lost	0-1			Iceland	lost	0-1	

Pat Jennings

At his peak, Pat Jennings was the best goalkeeper in the world and certainly a candidate for the best of all time.

Having played Gaelic football for North Down Schools, he turned to football with Newry United, Newry Town's junior club. After a season with the juniors and six months with Newry Town, he joined Watford in the summer of 1963. A year later he was on his way to White Hart Lane as Spurs' boss Bill Nicholson paid Watford £27,000.

In August 1967 Pat Jennings performed a coveted and extremely rare feat for a goalkeeper when he scored a goal with a long downfield punt in the 2:2 draw against Manchester United at Old Trafford in the FA Charity Shield.

In a 13-year spell at Tottenham, Jennings won an FA Cup winners' medal against Chelsea in 1967, two League Cup winners' medals against Aston Villa and Norwich City in 1971 and 1973 respectively and a UEFA Cup winners' medal by beating Wolves in 1972. He was also the PFA 'Player of the Year' in 1976. He went on to set a record number of appearances for Spurs, a figure bettered only by Steve Perryman. He was awarded the MBE for his services to the game in the 1976 Queen's Birthday Honours list. His achievements were also honoured by Spurs with a testimonial game against Arsenal in November 1976. He was tough and rarely injured but he did succumb to a serious ankle injury in 1976-77 – during his enforced absence, Spurs were relegated!

Even worse, manager Keith Burkinshaw allowed Jennings to join rivals Arsenal, then managed by his former Spurs boss and international colleague, Terry Neill. Jennings spent eight seasons at Highbury, making over 300 senior appearances, winning another FA Cup winners' medal in 1979 and a European Cup Winners' Cup medal in 1980.

Jennings' proudest moment came when the province reached the second round phase of the 1982 World Cup Finals in Spain. In the same group as the hosts Spain and Yugoslavia, the Irish were tipped for the earliest flight home. A draw against the Yugoslavs and a 1-0 win against Spain with Jennings in outstanding form booked their place.

"I have no regrets that I was not born in a more powerful football nation."

- *Pat Jennings*

Personal File

Position: Goalkeeper
Born: Patrick Anthony Jennings, Newry 12 June 1945
Clubs: Newry Town, Watford, Tottenham Hotspur, Arsenal

NI Caps: 119

Games

Year	Opponent	Result	Score	G	Year	Opponent	Result	Score	G
1964	Wales	won	3-2		1972	Spain	drew	1-1	
	Uruguay	won	3-0			Scotland	lost	0-2	
1965	England	lost	3-4			England	won	1-0	
	Switzerland	won	1-0			Wales	drew	0-0	
	Switzerland	lost	1-2		1973	Bulgaria	lost	0-3	
	Scotland	lost	2-3			Cyprus	lost	0-1	
1965	Holland	drew	0-0			Portugal	drew	1-1	
	Albania	won	4-1			England	lost	1-2	
1966	Scotland	won	3-2			Scotland	won	2-1	
	Scotland	lost	1-2			Wales	won	1-0	
	Albania	drew	1-1		1974	Portugal	drew	1-1	
	Wales	won	4-1			Scotland	won	1-0	
	West Germany	lost	0-2			England	lost	0-1	
1967	England	lost	0-2			Wales	lost	0-1	
	Scotland	lost	1-2		1975	Norway	lost	1-2	
1968	Scotland	won	1-0			Sweden	won	2-0	
	England	lost	0-2			Yugoslavia	won	1-0	
	Wales	lost	0-2			England	drew	0-0	
1969	Israel	won	3-2			Scotland	lost	0-3	
	Turkey	won	4-1			Wales	won	1-0	
	Turkey	won	3-0		1976	Sweden	lost	1-2	
	England	lost	1-3			Norway	won	3-0	
	Scotland	drew	1-1			Yugoslavia	lost	0-1	
	Wales	drew	0-0			Israel	drew	1-1	
1970	USSR	drew	0-0			Scotland	lost	0-3	
	USSR	lost	0-2			England	lost	0-4	
	Scotland	lost	0-1			Wales	lost	0-1	
	England	lost	1-3		1977	Holland	drew	2-2	
1971	Cyprus	won	3-0			Belgium	lost	0-2	
	Cyprus	won	5-0			West Germany	lost	0-5	
	England	lost	1-0			England	lost	1-2	
	Scotland	won	1-0			Scotland	lost	0-3	
	Wales	won	1-0			Wales	drew	1-1	
1972	USSR	drew	1-1			Iceland	lost	0-1	

Pat Jennings

In May 1985, Jennings was granted a second testimonial, this time against Spurs. On the verge of retiring, he returned to White Hart Lane as goalkeeping cover for Ray Clemence and also to keep fit for Northern Ireland ahead of the 1986 World Cup Finals.

He won another nine caps in his second spell with Spurs, giving him a world record total of 119. The conclusion of the World Cup saw Jennings officially retire, though later that year he did captain the Rest of the World XI against the Americas in a FIFA/UNICEF charity match. Since then, the popular keeper has shared his time between coaching the goalkeepers at White Hart Lane and making personal appearances.

"Pat had enormous hands like shovels and he could grab the ball out of the air as easily as an elephant grabs buns."

-Ron Burgess (Welsh international) who brought him to Watford

Games Continued

Year	Opponent	Result	Score	G	Year	Opponent	Result	Score	G
1978	Iceland	won	2-0			Spain	won	1 0	
	Holland	lost	0-1			France	lost	1-4	
	Belgium	won	3-0		1983	Albania	won	1-0	
1979	Republic					Scotland	drew	0-0	
	of Ireland	drew	0-0			England	drew	0-0	
	Denmark	won	2-1			Wales	lost	0-1	
	Bulgaria	won	2-0		1984	Austria	won	3-1	
	England	lost	0-4			Turkey	lost	0-1	
	Bulgaria	won	2-0			West			
	England	lost	0-2			Germany	won	1-0	
	Scotland	lost	0-1			Scotland	won	2-0	
	Wales	drew	1-1			Wales	drew	1-1	
	Denmark	lost	0-4			Finland	lost	1-1	
1980	England	lost	1-5		1985	Romania	won	3-2	
	Republic					Finland	won	2-1	
	of Ireland	won	1-0			England	lost	0-1	
	Israel	drew	0-0			Spain	drew	0-0	
1981	Scotland	drew	1-1			Turkey	won	2-0	
	Portugal	won	1-0		1986	Turkey	drew	0-0	
	Scotland	lost	0-2			Romania	won	1-0	
	Sweden	lost	0-1			England	drew	0-0	
1982	Scotland	drew	0-0			France	drew	0-0	
	Israel	won	1-0			Denmark	drew	1-1	
	England	lost	0-4			Morocco	won	2-1	
	Wales	lost	0-3			Algeria	drew	1-1	
	Yugoslavia	drew	0-0			Spain	lost	1-2	
	Honduras	drew	1-1			Brazil	lost	0-3	

Damien Johnson

A Northern Ireland youth international, he began his career with Blackburn Rovers but actually made his Football League debut for Nottingham Forest after being loaned out to the City Ground club in January 1998 to gain experience.

In his short spell with Forest he demonstrated that he was going to be a star of the future and on his return to Ewood Park he won Northern Ireland Under 21 honours. During the 1998-99 close season, he proved that he was equipped to challenge for a role wide on the Rovers' right, and must have been disappointed that he had to wait until the UEFA Cup tie in Lyon for his baptism. Over the course of that 1998-99 season, the youngster gave several displays where he employed quick feet and strong running and despite his size, he got up well to head the ball. The goal he scored against Arsenal was a great example of his intelligent positioning at the far post. Not surprisingly, he won full international honours when he played in the 1-0 defeat of the Republic of Ireland as well as winning five more caps at Under 21 level.

A player of great industry and a fearless tackler, he made only occasional appearances during the following season, though he remained an important member of the Northern Ireland side. Following the appointment of Graeme Souness, Johnson was switched to a central midfield role and this looked like being a success until he was sidelined by a back problem. After regaining full fitness, he returned to the Blackburn side and netted a superb goal in the Worthington Cup tie against Manchester City

In March 2002 he was allowed to join Birmingham City and impressed by scoring on his home debut against Grimsby Town. He then made a quick return to the Premiership via the play-offs. In the first half of the 2002-03 season, Johnson was easily City's most consistent player and scored the club's 'Goal of the Season' against Leeds United. However, a hamstring injury knocked him off his stride and he struggled to regain his best form. Last season he was back to his best, maintaining a reliable level of consistency, even when asked to help out at right-back on several occasions.

Personal File

Position:	Midfielder
Born:	Damien Micheal Johnston, Lisburn 18 November 1978
Clubs:	Blackburn Rovers Nottingham Forest (loan), Birmingham City
NI Caps:	36

Games

Year	Opponent	Result	Score	G	Year	Opponent	Result	Score	G
1999	Republic of Ireland	won	1-0		2003	Ukraine	drew	0-0	
2000	France	lost	0-1			Finland	lost	0-1	
	Luxembourg	won	3-1			Armenia	lost	0-1	
	Malta	won	3-0			Greece	lost	0-2	
	Hungary	lost	0-1			Italy	lost	0-2	
2001	Yugoslavia	lost	1-2			Spain	drew	0-0	
	Malta	won	1-0		2004	Ukraine	drew	0-0	
	Iceland	lost	0-1			Armenia	lost	0-1	
	Norway	lost	0-4			Norway	lost	1-4	
	Bulgaria	lost	3-4			Barbados	drew	1-1	
	Bulgaria	lost	0-1			St Kitts & Nevis	won	2-0	
	Czech Republic	lost	1-3			Trinidad and Tobago	won	3-0	
2002	Malta	won	1-0		2005	Switzerland	drew	0-0	
	Poland	lost	1-4			Poland	lost	0-3	
	Liechtenstein	drew	0-0			Wales	drew	2-2	
	Spain	lost	0-5			Azerbaijan	drew	0-0	
2003	Cyprus	drew	0-0			Austria	drew	3-3	
	Spain	lost	0-3			England	lost	0-4	

Dick Keith

A one-time tinsmith, Dick Keith arrived on Tyneside as one of the most promising youngsters to come out of Ulster, joining Newcastle United from Irish League side Linfield for £9,000 in September 1956.

He was immediately handed a Football League debut as a replacement for the injured Bobby Cowell at right-back for the match against Manchester United and thereafter became a Magpies' regular for the next seven seasons.

Keith made the first of his 23 appearances for Northern Ireland against England at Wembley in November 1957, replacing Willie Cunningham in a remarkable 3-2 win.

Partnering his Newcastle team-mate Alf McMichael at full-back they soon became an accomplished duo for both club and country. They appeared together in Northern Ireland's positive World Cup campaign of 1958 and played as a full-back pairing in 13 of Dick Keith's 23 games.

Dick Keith had a cool, assured manner on the field and attempted to play football from defence whenever possible. His polished style served the Magpies well, being captain of the club as his period of first team football at St James Park came to an end after relegation in 1960-61.

Moving to Dean Court in February 1964 after appearing in 223 League and Cup games for United, Dick Keith continued his career with Bournemouth before later playing non-League football for Weymouth.

He was killed when sadly only 33 years of age following an accident in a builder's yard whilst dismantling an automatic garage door. Dick Keith's skull was fractured and he died soon afterwards.

Fact: **Dick Keith played for Northern Ireland with his Newcastle United team mate, Alf McMichael. Both players joined Newcastle United after playing for Linfield.**

Personal File

Position: Right-back
Born: Richard Matthewson Keith,
Belfast
15 May 1933
Died: 28 February 1967
Clubs: Linfield,
Newcastle United,
Bournemouth,
Weymouth

NI Caps: 23

Games

Year	Opponent	Result	Score	G	Year	Opponent	Result	Score	G
1958	England	won	3-2		1960	Scotland	lost	0-4	
	Italy	drew	2-2			England	lost	1-2	
	Wales	drew	1-1		1961	England	lost	2-5	
	Czechoslovakia	won	1-0			West			
	Argentina	lost	1-3			Germany	lost	3-4	
	West					Scotland	lost	2-5	
	Germany	drew	2-2			Wales	lost	1-5	
	Czechoslovakia	won	2-1			Italy	lost	2-3	
	France	lost	0-4			Greece	lost	1-2	
1959	England	drew	3-3			West			
	Spain	lost	2-6			Germany	lost	1-2	
	Scotland	drew	2-2		1962	Wales	lost	0-4	
	Wales	won	4-1			Holland	lost	0-4	

Peter Kennedy (right)

Peter Kennedy

Peter Kennedy began his career as a speedy left-winger with Portadown before a £100,000 transfer took him to Notts County in the summer of 1996. He settled down quickly, his early displays showing him to be comfortable on the ball and a provider of excellent crosses. Then things started to go wrong and he was on the verge of leaving the game after a depressing spell in County's reserves.

Then he was signed by Watford manager Graham Taylor and repaid his faith in him by scoring his first-ever hat-trick in a 3-0 win at Southend United. Despite cracking a bone in his leg, he had done enough to secure selection for the PFA Second Division team and still finished the season as the Hornets' leading scorer, with 13 goals and a Second Division Championship medal. The club's only ever-present in their first season back in Division One, Kennedy's form was such that he won the first of 20 full caps for Northern Ireland.

Following Watford's promotion to the Premiership – he had the distinction of scoring the club's first goal in the top flight – his season was disrupted by a mysterious back injury and a cartilage operation. There followed an Achilles tendon operation: having scored 22 goals in 134 games he was placed on the 'open to offers' list in the summer of 2001.

Kennedy became Paul Jewell's first signing when the Wigan boss paid £300,000 for his services. Though he made a somewhat slow start, he eventually began to provide a more balanced look in the centre of the park. Having helped the Latics win the Second Division Championship in 2002-03, he was then loaned out to Derby County and though he continued to be a regular in the Northern Ireland side, he was released by the Latics.

On leaving the JJB stadium Kennedy joined Peterborough United. In a season during which he was blighted by injuries, he was unable to prevent the "Posh's" relegation to the league's basement.

Personal File

Position: Full-back/Midfielder
Born: Peter Henry James Kennedy,
Lurgan
10 September 1973
Clubs: Portadown,
Notts County,
Watford,
Wigan Athletic,
Derby County (loan)
Peterborough United

NI Caps: 20

Games

Year	Opponent	Result	Score	G	Year	Opponent	Result	Score	G
1999	Moldova	drew	2-2			Iceland	won	3-0	
	Germany	lost	0-3			Malta	won	1-0	
2000	France	lost	0-1			Poland	lost	1-4	
	Turkey	lost	0-3		2003	Cyprus	drew	0-0	
	Germany	lost	0-4			Finland	lost	0-1	
	Finland	lost	1-4			Italy	lost	0-2	
2001	Norway	lost	0-4			Spain	drew	0-0	
	Bulgaria	lost	3-4		2004	Ukraine	drew	0-0	
	Czech Republic	lost	1-3			Greece	lost	0-1	
2002	Denmark	drew	1-1			Norway	lost	1-4	

Neil Lennon

Briefly on the books of Manchester City, midfielder Neil Lennon made his name with Crewe Alexandra where he became an important member of the Railwaymen's side. Easily recognised by his red hair, he was capped by Northern Ireland at several levels while at Gresty Road. His consistency also saw him selected by fellow professionals both in 1994 and 1995 to the teams that won the PFA Divisional Awards.

Ambitious for a higher grade of football, he joined First Division Leicester City for a fee of £750,000 in February 1996 and gave an outstanding performance at Wembley as the Foxes reached the Premiership via the play-offs. Lennon was also elected to the PFA award-winning Second Division team for his performances before he joined Leicester for a third year running. Though the following season saw him fined by the FA after an alleged gesture following a match against Newcastle, his impressive non-stop displays against Middlesbrough in the Coca Cola Cup Final both at Wembley and in the replay at Hillsborough were a major factor in City lifting the trophy for the first time since the competition began.

Lennon continued to develop as a key member of the midfield for both club and country and by 1998-99 had fully inherited the role of chief playmaker. The following season he helped Leicester to another League Cup win as they beat Tranmere Rovers in the final, running Matt Elliott close for the 'Man-of-the-Match' award.

In 2000-01 Lennon played under the mounting speculation about an impending transfer to Celtic. He eventually linked up with his former mentor, Martin O'Neill in December 2000 where he collected an array of medals as the Bhoys walked off with the Scottish League Cup, FA Cup and Premiership title.

A regular for Northern Ireland, he was treated disgracefully by some sections of his own supporters during a subsequent World Cup tie in Belfast because of his Catholic background and his new club allegiance, but showed great character to put those incidents behind him as the sporting world rallied to his support. Lennon continued to win silverware with the Parkhead club but sadly after making 40 appearances for Northern Ireland decided to retire somewhat prematurely from international football.

Personal File

Position: Midfielder
Born: Neil Francis Lennon, Lurgan 25 June 1971
Clubs: Manchester City, Crewe Alexandra, Leicester City, Glasgow Celtic

NI Caps: 40
NI Goals: 2

Games

Year	Opponent	Result	Score	G	Year	Opponent	Result	Score	G
1994	Mexico	lost	0-3		1999	Turkey	lost	0-3	
1995	Chile	lost	1-2			Finland	won	1-0	
1996	Portugal	drew	1-1			Moldova	drew	2-2	1
	Liechtenstein	won	4-0			Germany	lost	0-3	
	Austria	won	5-3			Moldova	drew	0-0	
	Norway	lost	0-2			Republic			
1997	Ukraine	lost	0-1			of Ireland	won	1-0	
	Armenia	drew	1-1	1	2000	France	lost	0-1	
	Germany	drew	1-1			Turkey	lost	0-3	
	Albania	won	2-0			Germany	lost	0-4	
	Belgium	won	3-0			Malta	won	3-0	
	Portugal	drew	0-0			Finland	lost	1-4	
	Ukraine	lost	1-2			Hungary	lost	0-1	
	Armenia	drew	0-0		2001	Denmark	drew	1-1	
	Thailand	drew	0-0			Iceland	lost	0-1	
1998	Germany	lost	1-3			Norway	lost	0-4	
	Albania	lost	0-1			Czech			
	Portugal	lost	0-1			Republic	lost	0-1	
	Slovakia	won	1-0			Bulgaria	lost	3-4	
	Switzerland	won	1-0			Bulgaria	lost	0-1	
	Spain	lost	1-4		2002	Poland	lost	1-4	

Steve Lomas

A competitive and hard-tackling midfielder, Steve Lomas was spotted by a Manchester City scout playing for Coleraine at the age of 15. Having worked his way up through the ranks, he made his Football League debut for the then Maine Road club in a 1-0 win at Sheffield United in November 1993.

His meteoric rise was capped with a full international debut for Northern Ireland in a 2-0 win over Romania at Windsor Park in March 1994.

A valued member of the City squad, he continued to show his consistency, playing under all five managers who had been in charge of the club, but surprisingly in March 1997 after playing in 137 games he was transferred to West Ham United for £1.6 million.

Appointed as the Hammers' captain, he led the club into Europe via fifth place in the Premiership and skippered the national side in the games against Moldova, Germany and Canada.

He continued to impress for both West Ham and Northern Ireland until midway through the 1999-2000 season when he broke a toe playing for his country against Malta.

A good ball winner and accurate passer of the ball, he also possesses a long throw that often causes problems for opposition defences. Following a cruciate ligament injury, Lomas was out of the game for almost a year, but on his return he soon began to demonstrate the battling qualities and leadership that had been sorely missed. Unable to prevent the Hammers from losing their Premiership status, he then missed virtually all of the 2003-04 campaign due to an ongoing ankle injury.

"He's a natural leader. Harry Redknapp spotted this and made him skipper – it's easy to see why. The other players respond to him."

- Lawrie McMenemy

Personal File

Position: Midfielder
Born: Stephen Martin Lomas,
Hanover, Germany
18 January 1974
Clubs: Manchester City,
West Ham United

NI Caps: 45
NI Goals: 3

Games

Year	Opponent	Result	Score	G	Year	Opponent	Result	Score	G
1994	Romania	won	2-0		1998	Albania	lost	0-1	
	Liechtenstein	won	4-1	1		Portugal	lost	0-1	
	Colombia	lost	0-2			Slovakia	won	1-0	1
	Mexico	lost	0-3			Switzerland	won	1-0	
1995	Portugal	lost	1-2		1999	Moldova	drew	2-2	
	Austria	won	2-1			Germany	lost	0-3	
1996	Portugal	drew	1-1			Moldova	drew	0-0	
	Liechtenstein	won	4-0			Canada	drew	1-1	
	Austria	won	5-3		2000	France	lost	0-1	
	Norway	lost	0-2			Turkey	lost	0-3	
	Sweden	lost	1-2			Germany	lost	0-4	
	Germany	drew	1-1			Luxembourg	won	3-1	
1997	Ukraine	lost	0-1			Malta	won	3-0	
	Armenia	drew	1-1		2001	Malta	won	1-0	
	Germany	drew	1-1			Denmark	drew	1-1	
	Albania	won	2-0			Iceland	lost	0-1	
	Italy	lost	0-2		2002	Poland	lost	1-4	1
	Belgium	won	3-0			Liechtenstein	drew	0-0	
	Portugal	drew	0-0		2003	Spain	lost	0-3	
	Ukraine	lost	1-2			Ukraine	drew	0-0	
	Armenia	drew	0-0			Finland	lost	0-1	
	Thailand	drew	0-0			Armenia	lost	0-1	
						Greece	lost	0-2	

November 1954: The players of Manchester City Football Club, a side with a good chance of winning the league Championship. From the back row and from left to right: Laurie Barnet (trainer), Bill McAdams, Dave Ewing, Ken Barnes, Bert Trautmann, Roy Little, Ken Branagan, Fred Tilson, (assistant trainer), Les McDowall (manager), Jim McClelland (coach), Fionan Gagan, Don Revie, Roy Paul (captain), Johnny Hart, and Roy Clarke.

Bill McAdams

Bill McAdams was a centre-forward who worked as an apprentice heating engineer and played for Banbridge Town and Glenavon before turning down Burnley after trials. His performances for the Irish League club Distillery prompted Manchester City to sign him in December 1953 and he scored on his debut the following month in a 2-1 home win over Sunderland. In only his second game for the Blues he netted a hat-trick in a 5-2 FA Cup defeat of Bradford City.

Despite this impressive start, Bill McAdams found his first few years at Maine Road hampered by injuries, notably a slipped disc and he failed to make the starting line-ups for both the 1955 and 1956 FA Cup Finals. It was 1957-58 before he became a regular in the City side, scoring 19 goals in 28 games including a hat-trick in a 4-1 home win over West Bromwich Albion. His best season in terms of goals scored was 1959-60 when his total of 21 in 31 games included trebles in the games against Wolverhampton Wanderers, Preston North End and Newcastle United. He had scored 65 goals in 134 League and Cup games when in September 1960 he was transferred to Bolton Wanderers. In his first season with the then Burnden Park club, he scored 18 goals in 27 games including a hat-trick against Aston Villa. Whilst with Bolton, his form for Northern Ireland was most impressive, and after scoring both Ireland's goals in a 5-2 home defeat at the hands of England, he then netted a hat-trick in a World Cup qualifying game against West Germany – a match the Irish lost 4-3!

In December 1961 his former Manchester City team-mate Don Revie signed him for Leeds United to boost a struggling attack. Although he gained his 15th and final international cap with the Yorkshire club, he was soon on the move, joining Brentford in the summer of 1962. He won a Fourth Division Championship medal with the Bees before later playing for Queen's Park Rangers and Barrow, where he continued to score goals.

Personal File

Position: Centre-forward
Born: William John McAdams, Belfast 20 January 1934
Died: 13 October 2002
Clubs: Glenavon, Distillery, Manchester City, Bolton Wanderers, Leeds United, Brentford, Queen's Park Rangers, Barrow

NI Caps: 15
NI Goals: 7

Games

Year	Opponent	Result	Score	G	Year	Opponent	Result	Score	G
1954	Wales	won	2-1		1961	Wales	lost	1-5	
1955	Scotland	drew	2-2	1		Italy	lost	2-3	1
1957	England	drew	1-1			Greece	lost	1-2	
1958	Scotland	drew	1-1			West Germany	lost	1-2	
	Italy	drew	2-2		1962	Greece	won	2-0	
1961	England	lost	2-5	2		England	drew	1-1	
	West Germany	lost	3-4	3		Holland	lost	0-4	
	Scotland	lost	2-5						

Jon McCarthy

Having been unable to make much of an impression with his first club Hartlepool United, Jon McCarthy drifted into non-League football with Shepshed Charterhouse before joining York City in March 1990.

At his most dangerous when operating wide on the right-wing, his electrifying pace and sheer persistence caused problems for most defences. McCarthy was voted the Minstermen's 'Clubman of the Year' on two occasions and had made 233 appearances before Port Vale paid £450,000 for his services in the summer of 1995.

He scored the winning goal against Everton in the FA Cup during a spell of being on the mark five times in eight games and earned his first international honours at Northern Ireland 'B' level before stepping up to the full squad against Sweden. It is hardly surprising that he won the supporters' 'Player of the Year' award. He continued to impress for the Valiants, his play going a long way in helping the club into one of their highest-ever finishing positions in 1996-97.

During the early part of the following season, McCarthy joined Birmingham City in a £1.85 million deal and though he initially struggled at St Andrew's, he finally won over the crowd. However, a broken leg in the game against Tranmere Rovers during the course of the 1999-2000 season saw him out of action until April. Then, just four games into his comeback, he suffered a second fracture in the same place while playing against Manchester City. The following season saw him play in the Worthington Cup Final against Liverpool but he broke his right leg for a third time within 18 months – this just after he'd fought his way back into the Northern Ireland squad.

On recovering from his third broken leg, he went on loan to Sheffield Wednesday before brief spells with former clubs Port Vale and York City and finally Carlisle United, whom he helped avoid relegation to the Conference. McCarthy later played non-League football for Hucknall Town.

Personal File

Position: Midfielder
Born: Jonathan David McCarthy, Middlesbrough, 18 August 1970
Clubs: Hartlepool United, Shepshed Charterhouse, York City, Port Vale, Birmingham City, Sheffield Wednesday (loan), Port Vale, York City, Carlisle United, Hucknall Town

NI Caps: 18

Games

Year	Opponent	Result	Score	G	Year	Opponent	Result	Score	G
1996	Sweden	lost	1-2		1999	Canada	drew	1-1	
1997	Italy	lost	0-2			Republic			
	Armenia	drew	0-0			of Ireland	won	1-0	
	Thailand	drew	0-0		2000	France	lost	0-1	
1998	Portugal	lost	0-1			Turkey	lost	0-3	
	Slovakia	won	1-0			Germany	lost	0-4	
	Spain	lost	1-4			Finland	lost	1-4	
1999	Finland	won	1-0		2001	Norway	lost	0-4	
	Moldova	drew	2-2			Bulgaria	lost	3-4	
	Germany	lost	0-3						

Left: Jon McCarthy (left)

George McCartney

Sunderland defender George McCartney made his first team bow during the 2000-01 season in the Worthington Cup tie against Luton Town and went on to appear in a handful more games over the campaign. Also that season he appeared for Northern Ireland at Under 21 level before sitting on the bench for the end of season World Cup qualifiers against Bulgaria and the Czech Republic.

Primarily a left-back who can also operate in central defence, he won his first full cap for Northern Ireland in September 2001 and even managed a goal in a 3-0 win over Iceland.

He signed a new long-term contract and then enjoyed a run in the side towards the end of the season, impressing supporters with his calm assured play, which belied his relative inexperience.

The 2002-03 season saw him understudy to Michael Gray but when manager Howard Wilkinson moved Gray into midfield, McCartney took his place and impressed with his confident use of the ball and all-round defending. The following season saw McCartney firmly establish himself at left-back for Sunderland, finishing the campaign as club captain.

An excellent attacker down the flank, he formed a superb partnership with Julio Arca which produced many a goal for the Wearsiders. He led Sunderland to the FA Cup and play-off semi-finals and although the Black Cats fell short on both fronts, the experience was invaluable for the youngster.

With the club missing out on promotion, it was a relief to Sunderland fans when McCartney signed a new contract that will keep the Northern Ireland defender at the Stadium of Light for the foreseeable future. Last season, McCartney was outstanding as the Black Cats won promotion to the Premiership as winners of the Championship.

Personal File

Position: Left-back/Central Defender
Born: George McCartney,
Belfast
29 April 1981
Clubs: Sunderland

NI Caps: 19
NI Goals: 1

Games

Year	Opponent	Result	Score	G	Year	Opponent	Result	Score	G
2002	Iceland	won	3-0	1	2003	Italy	lost	0-2	
	Malta	won	1-0			Spain	drew	0-0	
	Poland	lost	1-4		2004	Ukraine	drew	0-0	
	Liechtenstein	drew	0-0			Armenia	lost	0-1	
	Spain	lost	0-5			Greece	lost	0-1	
2003	Cyprus	drew	0-0			Norway	lost	1-4	
	Spain	lost	0-3		2005	Wales	drew	2-2	
	Ukraine	drew	0-0			Austria	drew	3-3	
	Finland	lost	0-1			Canada	lost	0-1	
	Greece	lost	0-2						

John McClelland

Multi-capped Northern Ireland international defender John McClelland began his career with Portadown before trying his luck in the Football League with Cardiff City. Coming off the bench on his debut against Bristol Rovers, he scored a late equaliser in a 2-2 draw. Even though he played in a handful of games towards the end of that 1974-75 season, League football had come too early for the young McClelland and he joined Bangor City in the summer of 1975.

Mansfield Town gave him a second chance at League level and it was while he was at Field Mill that his career took off in a big way, when Scottish giants Glasgow Rangers paid £90,000 to take him to Ibrox.

With Rangers he won a Scottish Cup winners' medal in 1983-84 before First Division Watford paid £225,000 for his services.

McClelland played in Northern Ireland's 1982 and 1986 World Cup final teams and represented the Football League against the Rest of the World at Wembley in August 1987. In the summer of 1989 he joined Leeds United but struggled with injury during his time at Elland Road and was loaned to former club Watford in January 1990. Despite these injuries, he managed his final appearance for Northern Ireland, playing in the 3-2 home defeat by Norway in March 1990.

After a loan spell with Notts County, McClelland joined St Johnstone as player-coach, later being elevated to player-manager. After losing his job with Saints, he turned out briefly for Carrick Rangers before having spells with Arbroath, Wycombe Wanderers and Yeovil Town. McClelland then had a brief spell as assistant-manager to Chris Kamara at Bradford City before linking up with Darlington as player-coach. Having made just one appearance for the Quakers, he then tragically broke his leg at Hartlepool. Having decided finally to hang up his boots, he was assistant-manager at Leeds United for a spell and has remained at Elland Road as the Yorkshire club's Tours and PR manager.

**"Mine eyes have seen
The glory of Espana '82,
When little Northern Ireland
Showed the world what we can do."**

- Northern Ireland Supporters Song

Personal File

Position: Central defender
Born: John McClelland, Belfast 7 December 1955
Clubs: Portadown, Cardiff City, Bangor City, Mansfield Town, Glasgow Rangers, Watford, Leeds United, Watford (loan), Notts County (loan), St Johnstone, Carrick Rangers, Arbroath, Wycombe Wanderers, Yeovil Town, Darlington

NI Caps: 53
NI Goals: 1

Games

Year	Opponent	Result	Score	G	Year	Opponent	Result	Score	G
1980	Scotland	won	1-0		1984	Scotland	won	2-0	
	Australia	won	2-1			England	lost	0-1	
	Australia	drew	1-1			Wales	drew	1-1	
	Australia	won	2-1			Finland	lost	0-1	
1981	Sweden	won	3-0		1985	Romania	won	3-2	
	Scotland	drew	1-1			Israel	won	3-0	
	Scotland	lost	0-2			Finland	won	2-1	
	Sweden	lost	0-1			England	lost	0-1	
1982	Scotland	drew	1-1			Spain	drew	0-0	
	Wales	lost	0-3			Turkey	won	2-0	
	Yugoslavia	drew	0-0		1986	Turkey	drew	0-0	
	Honduras	drew	1-1			France	drew	0-0	
	Spain	won	1-0		1987	England	lost	0-3	
	Austria	drew	2-2			Turkey	drew	0-0	
	France	lost	1-4			Israel	drew	1-1	
1983	Austria	lost	0-2			England	lost	0-2	
	West Germany	won	1-0			Yugoslavia	lost	1-2	
	Albania	drew	0-0		1988	Turkey	won	1-0	
	Turkey	won	2-1	1		Greece	lost	2-3	
	Albania	won	1-0			France	drew	0-0	
	Scotland	drew	0-0			Malta	won	2-0	
	England	drew	0-0		1989	Republic of Ireland	drew	0-0	
	Wales	lost	0-1			Hungary	lost	0-1	
1984	Austria	won	3-1			Spain	lost	0-4	
	Turkey	lost	0-1			Spain	lost	0-2	
	West Germany	won	1-0			Malta	won	2-0	
					1990	Norway	lost	2-3	

David McCreery

David McCreery developed through the junior ranks at Old Trafford during Tommy Docherty's reign as manager of Manchester United. He turned professional in October 1974 and made his Football League debut almost immediately when he came on as a substitute for Willie Morgan at Portsmouth. In fact, David McCreery was United's own 'super-sub' as he came off the bench in nearly half the 87 League games in which he appeared for the club. He also wore the No.12 shirt in the 1976 and 1977 FA Cup Finals, replacing Gordon Hill in both games.

Docherty left United for Derby County but when the former Reds' boss began a second spell as Queen's Park Rangers manager, he took McCreery to Loftus Road for £200,000 in August 1979. In the summer months he played in the NASL for Tulsa Roughnecks but in October 1982, McCreery joined Newcastle United, teaming up with former Liverpool stars Keegan and McDermott.

The vastly under-rated midfielder, whose game was full of fire and determination, helped the Magpies to win promotion to Division One at the end of the 1983-84 season.

McCreery had won the first of his 67 full caps for Northern Ireland in 1976 when he came off the bench against Scotland at Hampden Park. He played in all five of his country's matches in the 1982 World Cup Finals in Spain and was also a member of the Northern Ireland side four years later.

McCreery, who had appeared in 270 games for the Magpies, left St James Park in the summer of 1989 and had a couple of months in Sweden with Sundsvaal before joining Heart of Midlothian in September. He later returned to the Football League as player-manager of Hartlepool United but after criticism that he didn't play himself enough, he left to have a brief spell with Coleraine before taking up a similar post with Carlisle United. He then returned to take charge of Hartlepool for a second time, later scouting for Barnet and acting as consultant to Blyth Spartans. After leaving the game, he ran a hospitality company as well as being a European consultant for MLS, the new American soccer organisation.

**"Green is the colour.
Football is the game.
We're all together,
And winning is our aim."**

- Northern Ireland Supporters' Song

Personal File

Position: Midfielder
Born: David McCreery,
Belfast
16 September 1957
Clubs: Manchester United,
Queen's Park Rangers,
Tulsa Roughnecks (USA),
Newcastle United,
Heart of Midlothian,
Sundsvaal (Sweden),
Hartlepool United,
Coleraine, Carlisle United,
Hartlepool United
NI Caps: 67

Games

Year	Opponent	Result	Score	G	Year	Opponent	Result	Score	G
1976	Scotland	lost	0-3		1981	Portugal	won	1-0	
	England	lost	0-4			Scotland	lost	0-2	
	Wales	lost	0-1		1982	Scotland	drew	0-0	
1977	Holland	drew	2-2			Israel	won	1-0	
	Belgium	lost	0-2			England	lost	0-4	
	West Germany	lost	0-5			France	lost	0-4	
	England	lost	1-2			Yugoslavia	drew	0-0	
	Scotland	lost	0-3			Honduras	drew	1-1	
	Wales	drew	1-1			Spain	won	1-0	
	Iceland	lost	0-1			Austria	drew	2-2	
1978	Iceland	won	2-0			France	lost	1-4	
	Holland	lost	0-1		1983	Austria	lost	0-2	
	Belgium	won	3-0		1984	Turkey	lost	0-1	
	Scotland	drew	1-1		1985	Romania	won	3-2	
	England	lost	0-1			Spain	drew	0-0	
	Wales	lost	0-1		1986	Turkey	drew	0-0	
1979	Republic of Ireland	drew	0-0			Romania	won	1-0	
	Denmark	won	2-1			England	drew	0-0	
	Bulgaria	won	2-0			France	drew	0-0	
	England	lost	0-4			Denmark	drew	1-1	
	Bulgaria	won	2-0			Algeria	drew	1-1	
	Wales	drew	1-1			Spain	lost	1-2	
	Denmark	lost	0-4			Brazil	lost	0-3	
1980	England	lost	1-5		1987	Turkey	drew	0-0	
	Republic of Ireland	won	1-0			England	lost	0-2	
	Scotland	won	1-0			Yugoslavia	lost	1-2	
	England	drew	1-1		1988	Yugoslavia	lost	0-3	
	Wales	won	1-0		1989	Spain	lost	0-4	
	Australia	won	2-1			Malta	won	2-0	
	Australia	drew	1-1			Chile	lost	0-1	
1981	Sweden	won	3-0		1990	Hungary	lost	1-2	
	Portugal	lost	0-1			Republic of Ireland	lost	0-3	
	Scotland	drew	1-1			Norway	lost	2-3	
						Uruguay	won	1-0	

(L-R) PFA Chairman Jimmy Hill turns around in his seat to talk to Arsenal's Mel Charles, Jimmy Magill, Billy McCullough and David Herd, at a meeting called by the PFA to discuss the Football League's latest proposals regarding the wages and contracts dispute

Billy McCullough

Full-back Billy McCullough was a footballing buccaneer who rejoiced in the nickname 'Flint' after a character in the TV series 'Wagon Train'. The tag was justified not only by a shared surname but also by the sharp-edged tackles which he dispensed freely in his role of Arsenal's left-back throughout the first half of the sixties.

McCullough arrived at Highbury as a £5,000 recruit from Portadown in September 1958 – one of manager George Swindin's first signings. Three months after putting pen to paper, McCullough made his League debut for Arsenal as a replacement for out-of-form Dennis Evans against Luton Town. He eclipsed his countryman Billy Bingham, one of the most dangerous wingers in Britain, to play a stirring part in a 1-0 victory. He continued to make steady progress and when injury ended Evans' career in 1959-60, McCullough became a first team regular.

Billy McCullough's trademark was aggression, both in his vigorous approach to opposing wingers and his penchant for adventurous forays along his touchline.

His 10 appearances for Northern Ireland were played mostly at left-half due to the competition from the excellent Alex Elder.

Back at Highbury, McCullough eventually lost his place in the Arsenal side to the up and coming Peter Storey. Transfer listed in the summer of 1966, he moved on to Millwall before following a spell at Bedford Town, he became player-manager of Cork Celtic and later Derry City.

On hanging up his boots he became an electrical engineer but Billy McCullough will be remembered as one of the most consistent full-backs Arsenal has ever had, playing in nearly 300 first team games.

Personal File

Position: Left-back
Born: William James McCullough, Larne 27 July 1935
Clubs: Portadown, Arsenal, Millwall, Bedford Town, Cork Celtic, Derry City

NI Caps: 10

Games

Year	Opponent	Result	Score	G
1961	Italy	lost	2-3	
1963	Spain	drew	1-1	
1964	Scotland	won	2-1	
	Spain	lost	0-1	
	England	lost	3-8	
	Wales	won	3-2	
	Uruguay	won	3-0	
1965	England	lost	3-4	
	Switzerland	won	1-0	
1967	England	lost	0-2	

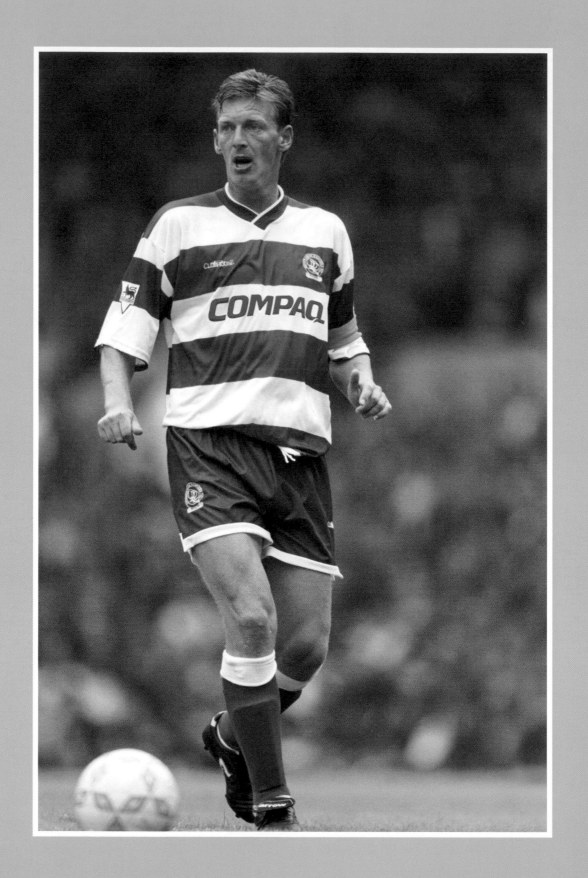

Alan McDonald

Though he turned professional with Queen's Park Rangers in the summer of 1980, Alan McDonald actually made his Football League debut whilst on loan to Charlton Athletic in April 1983.

He played his first League game for Rangers the following season in a 4-0 win at Wolverhampton Wanderers and scored his first goal for the club two games later in a resounding 8-1 League Cup win over Crewe Alexandra. Over the next few seasons, Alan McDonald established himself as one of the best central defenders in the First Division.

In October 1985 he won the first of 52 international caps, when he played for Northern Ireland in a 1-0 win over Romania in Bucharest and a month later, was one of the stars of a brave performance against England at Wembley – a goalless draw sealing Northern Ireland's place in the 1986 World Cup Finals. That season he was an integral member of the Rangers side that reached the League Cup Final against Oxford United, but a winners' medal eluded him as Rangers lost 3-0. McDonald was one of Rangers' most consistent players throughout the early nineties, missing very few games for the club. Rock solid and reliable, he gave every striker he came up against a hard time.

Captain of Queen's Park Rangers, Alan McDonald always led by example and spent 17 seasons at Loftus Road, during which time he scored 17 goals in 478 League and Cup games before being released in the summer of 1997.

McDonald joined Swindon Town, making an immediate impact as he helped to tighten up a Robins' rearguard, which had leaked too many goals the previous season. On his return to Loftus Road with the Swindon side, he became a stand-in goalkeeper following the first-half dismissal of Fraser Digby. He would simply not be beaten as Town's 10-men recorded a vital away win!

Personal File

Position: Central Defender
Born: Alan McDonald,
Belfast
12 October 1963
Clubs: Queen's Park Rangers,
Charlton Athletic (loan),
Swindon Town

NI Caps: 52
NI Goals: 3

Games

Year	Opponent	Result	Score	G	Year	Opponent	Result	Score	G
1986	Romania	won	1-0		1991	Austria	drew	0-0	
	England	drew	0-0			Faroe Islands	drew	1-1	
	France	drew	0-0		1992	Faroe Islands	won	5-0	1
	Denmark	drew	1-1	1		Scotland	lost	0-1	
	Morocco	won	2-1			Lithuania	drew	2-2	
	Algeria	drew	1-1			Germany	drew	1-1	
	Spain	lost	1-2		1993	Albania	won	3-0	
	Brazil	lost	0-3			Spain	drew	0-0	
1987	England	lost	0-3			Denmark	lost	0-1	
	Turkey	drew	0-0			Albania	won	2-1	1
	Israel	drew	1-1			Republic of Ireland	lost	0-3	
	England	lost	0-2			Spain	lost	1-3	
	Yugoslavia	lost	1-2			Lithuania	won	1-0	
1988	Yugoslavia	lost	0-3			Latvia	won	2-1	
	Turkey	won	1-0		1994	Denmark	lost	0-1	
	Poland	drew	1-1			Republic of Ireland	drew	1-1	
	France	drew	0-0		1995	Portugal	lost	1-2	
	Malta	won	3-0			Austria	won	2-1	
1989	Republic of Ireland	drew	0-0			Republic of Ireland	drew	1-1	
	Hungary	lost	0-1			Latvia	won	1-0	
	Spain	lost	0-4			Canada	lost	0-2	
	Chile	lost	0-1			Chile	lost	1-2	
1990	Hungary	lost	1-2			Latvia	lost	1-2	
	Republic of Ireland	lost	0-3		1996	Austria	won	5-3	
	Uruguay	won	1-0			Norway	lost	0-2	
1991	Yugoslavia	lost	0-2						
	Denmark	drew	1-1						

Willie McFaul

After initially being rejected by Newcastle United, Willie McFaul took up a joinery apprenticeship and played semi-pro for Coleraine before joining Linfield. Here he won Irish League and Cup medals and played in European football.

During September 1966, Newcastle United played Linfield in a friendly – the Magpies putting seven goals past McFaul – but he still made a number of outstanding saves and was signed by the Tyneside club for £7,000. During his first two seasons at St James Park, his appearances were spasmodic but after playing in the opening game of the 1968-69 season at West Ham, he never looked back. The blond haired keeper was quick and acrobatic and what he lacked in inches, he made up for with instinct and reflex agility.

In his first full season, he was instrumental in the Magpies winning the UEFA Cup, making a series of fabulous saves over the two legs.

McFaul was a consistent performer over the next five years, ranked in the top half-dozen keepers in the country along with Banks, Clemence, Bonetti and Pat Jennings, his rival at international level.

McFaul was unlucky to have such an accomplished contemporary as Jennings and subsequently never won the haul of caps worthy of his talent. A second choice to the Spurs keeper for Northern Ireland, he only appeared six times for his country, although he was on the substitute's bench on over 40 occasions.

McFaul also played his part in United's run to the 1974 FA Cup Final at Wembley – his saves in the latter stages of the competition making him a hero. The appointment of Gordon Lee as manager marked the end of McFaul's dominance as Newcastle's keeper. He stayed at St James Park as assistant-coach to the juniors, then reserves and had a spell as caretaker boss when Richard Dinnis was sacked. When Jack Charlton resigned as manager, McFaul applied for the job and got it but after three years in charge, he parted company with the club.

He then managed Coleraine, the Londonderry club having been bottom of the Irish League and in dire straits when McFaul took over, before becoming assistant-coach to Northern Ireland manager Bryan Hamilton.

Personal File

Position: Goalkeeper
Born: William Stewart McFaul,
Coleraine
1 October 1943
Clubs: Coleraine,
Linfield,
Newcastle United

NI Caps: 6

Games

Year	Opponent	Result	Score	G
1967	England	lost	0-2	
1970	Wales	lost	0-1	
1971	Spain	lost	0-3	
1972	USSR	lost	0-1	
1973	Cyprus	won	3-0	
1974	Bulgaria	drew	0-0	

"It is debatable whether there's a better goalkeeper in the country."

- Bill Shankly on Willie McFaul

Chris McGrath

The term 'enigma' is often over-used when discussing gifted footballers who fail to do justice to their talent. In the case of Chris McGrath, it is especially apt.

The dark, softly spoken Ulsterman had exquisite skill that might have graced either Tottenham flank for a decade, and he made a stirring start to his White Hart Lane career before inexorably fading into obscurity. The promising young striker who proved particularly effective in European matches, scored several important goals during the 1973-74 UEFA Cup run and appeared in both legs of the final with Feyenoord.

Although he had to be content with a runners-up medal as Spurs lost the first major final in their history, consolation came in the form of international honours, with his first appearance for Northern Ireland in May 1974 against Scotland. Unfortunately the talent he displayed that first season did not develop as expected and under Terry Neill, who as manager of Northern Ireland gave McGrath his international chance, he was rarely able to get a first team game. He was not helped by a general uncertainty as to his most effective position, sometimes playing on the wing, sometimes as a central striker and even in a more withdrawn midfield role.

Following a loan spell with Millwall, McGrath, still only 21, joined Manchester United for £35,000, leaving the feeling that he had simply underachieved.

Although he was at Old Trafford for five years, McGrath played only 12 full League games for the Reds and in fact, made 16 appearances at international level, more than for his club! He spent the summers of 1981 and 1982 with Tulsa Roughnecks and when released by United, joined the South China club of Hong Kong. He was last heard of working at an armaments factory in Enfield.

Personal File

Position: Winger
Born: Roland Christopher McGrath, Belfast
29 November 1954
Clubs: Tottenham Hotspur, Millwall (loan), Manchester United

NI Caps: 21
NI Goals: 4

Games

Year	Opponent	Result	Score	G	Year	Opponent	Result	Score	G
1974	Scotland	won	1-0			Wales	drew	1-1	
	England	lost	0-1			Iceland	lost	0-1	
	Wales	lost	0-1		1978	Iceland	won	2-0	1
1975	Norway	lost	1-2			Holland	lost	0-1	
1976	Israel	drew	1-1			Belgium	won	3-0	1
1977	Holland	drew	2-2	1		Scotland	drew	1-1	
	Belgium	lost	0-2			England	lost	0-1	
	West Germany	lost	0-5			Wales	lost	0-1	
	England	lost	1-2	1	1979	Bulgaria	won	2-0	
	Scotland	lost	0-3			England	lost	0-4	
						England	lost	0-2	

**"Oh I was only little
When my father said to me,
C'mon we'll go to Windsor to
Cheer the boys in emerald green."**

- Northern Ireland Supporters' Song

Jimmy McIlroy

Of all the players who wore the claret and blue of Burnley Football Club since the Second World War, to the vast majority of Clarets' fans, the greatest of them all was the magical Irishman Jimmy McIlroy.

In his formative years in a village on the outskirts of Belfast, the young McIlroy never had any doubts that he wanted to be a footballer when he grew up. He was influenced and encouraged by his father Harry, a part-time player with Distillery and his uncle Willie McIlroy, who was a professional with Portadown.

He practiced constantly with a tennis ball and though he was a slightly built youngster, at the age of 10 he represented the school team, playing with and against 14 year olds, who were of course, much bigger than himself. He left school at 15 to do manual work to build himself up and earn some money to pay back his parents for their earlier sacrifices. He began playing for the Craigavad Club near Bangor, and the scouts from Glentoran were soon monitoring his performances. After signing for that club, he soon became a regular and came under constant scrutiny from the English talent scouts.

In March 1950 Burnley manager Frank Hill paid Glentoran £8,000 and Jimmy was on his way to Turf Moor. In October of that year, four days before his 19th birthday, Jimmy McIlroy made his First Division debut for Burnley, embarking on a truly memorable Football League career.

Within a year, in October 1951 and still a teenager, he won his first international cap against Scotland in Belfast. Although the Irish were beaten 3-0, McIlroy's performance ensured that he would be virtually a permanent member of his country's line-up for well into the next decade.

In August 1955, Jimmy McIlroy was acknowledged as one of the finest football talents in these islands when he was chosen for a Great Britain representative side to play the Rest of Europe in a match at Windsor Park to commemorate the 75th anniversary of the formation of the Irish FA.

In the Championship-winning season of 1959-60 and the two campaigns that followed, McIlroy was at his best and in 1962 he almost led the Clarets to a League and Cup double. An inexplicable loss of form by the whole team over the closing weeks of the season deprived Burnley of immortality. As it was, McIlroy was just edged into second place in the 'Footballer of the Year' poll by his captain Jimmy Adamson.

Then in February 1963, the unbelievable happened, McIlroy was transferred to Second Division Stoke City for just £25,000. Joining players such as Jackie Mudie, Dennis Viollet and the immortal Stanley Matthews at the Victoria Ground, he helped the Potters win the Second Division Championship and in 1964 helped them reach the League Cup Final.

Personal File

Position: Inside-forward
Born: James McIlroy, Lambeg nr Befast, 25 October 1931
Clubs: Glentoran, Burnley, Stoke City, Oldham Athletic

NI Caps: 55
NI Goals: 10

Games

Year	Opponent	Result	Score	G	Year	Opponent	Result	Score	G
1952	Scotland	lost	0-2		1958	Czechoslovakia	won	2-1	
	England	lost	0-2			France	lost	0-4	
	Wales	lost	0-3		1959	England	drew	3-3	
1953	England	drew	2-2			Spain	lost	2-6	1
	Scotland	drew	1-1			Scotland	drew	2-2	2
	Wales	lost	2-3			Wales	won	4-1	1
1954	England	lost	1-3		1960	Scotland	lost	0-4	
	Scotland	lost	1-3			England	lost	1-2	
	Wales	won	2-1			Wales	lost	2-3	
1955	England	lost	0-2		1961	England	lost	2-5	
	Scotland	drew	2-2			West Germany	lost	3-4	
	Wales	lost	2-3			Wales	lost	1-5	
1956	England	lost	0-3			Greece	lost	1-2	1
	Scotland	won	2-1			West Germany	lost	1-2	1
	Wales	drew	1-1		1962	Scotland	lost	1-6	
1957	England	drew	1-1	1		Greece	won	2-0	
	Scotland	lost	0-1			England	drew	1-1	1
	Portugal	drew	1-1			Holland	lost	0-4	
	Wales	drew	0-0		1963	Poland	won	2-0	
	Italy	lost	0-1			England	lost	1-3	
	Portugal	won	3-0	1		Scotland	lost	1-5	
1958	Scotland	drew	1-1			Poland	won	2-0	
	England	won	3-2	1		Wales	lost	1-4	
	Italy	drew	2-2		1966	Scotland	won	3-2	
	Italy	lost	1-3			Scotland	lost	1-2	
	Wales	drew	1-1			Albania	drew	1-1	
	Czechoslovakia	won	1-0						
	Argentina	lost	1-3						
	West Germany	drew	2-2						

Jimmy McIlroy

In January 1966 he was recruited by Oldham Athletic, struggling in Division Three as their player-manager. In August 1967 he returned to Stoke as their chief coach before in August 1970 spending just 16 days as manager of Bolton Wanderers!

McIlroy spent many years as a respected journalist and though now retired, Jimmy Mac will forever be a sporting hero in Burnley, the town he made his home as a teenager five decades ago.

"One of the greatest inside forwards in Britain today, he can manipulate the ball beautifully and split open a defence with accurate, devastating passes."

- Malcolm Brodie

Left: Chelsea goalkeeper Mathews dives across the goalmouth to save a penalty shot taken by Burnley inside-right Jimmy McIlroy(right) during the First Division match at Stamford Bridge, London.

Sammy McIlroy

As with so many Belfast schoolboys, Manchester United was the only team Sammy McIlroy set his sights on, and he followed in the footsteps of George Best, crossing the Irish Sea to Manchester as a 15-year-old.

Signing with the distinction of being the last Busby babe, McIlroy announced his arrival in the Reds' first team in bold print in 1971 with a sizzling debut in which he scored one goal and got two 'assists' in United's derby fixture at Maine Road which finished in a 3-3 draw. Yet the fairytale soon turned sour and a motorcycle accident kept him sidelined for over half the 1972-73 season.

Once restored to full fitness, McIlroy claimed a regular place in the United side under Tommy Docherty that was destined for relegation.
McIlroy, who'd won his first international cap against Spain in February 1972 before his accident, soon became as important a part of the Northern Ireland side as he was United's.

He won 88 caps and was an integral part of the most glorious chapter in Northern Ireland's soccer history – which in part explains why he was awarded the MBE – as they went on to World Cup glory in Spain in 1982 and Mexico in 1986.

A midfielder full of energy and attacking purpose whose inspiration was important as United clinched the Second Division Championship, played in the 1976 FA Cup Final and won a winners' medal the following year. In 1979, Arsenal with Liam Brady giving a 'man of the match' performance, were cruising to a 2-0 victory with just five minutes to go. The Arsenal manager, former Northern Ireland international Terry Neill, decided to take the luxury of replacing midfielder David Price with the youngster Steve Walford. Then Gordon McQueen scrambled a goal for United and almost immediately, Sammy McIlroy made a jinking run through the crowded defence before unleashing a bending shot past his Northern Irish colleague Pat Jennings. The Arsenal players looked totally baffled and dejected. Somehow though, Liam Brady found a last drop of energy to set up a movement, which led to Alan Sunderland sensationally scoring a last-gasp winner. McIlroy captured the mood of the United players; 'It was like picking eight draws and then finding the pools coupon still in your pocket.'

Though McIlroy was a permanent fixture in the Northern Ireland side, new manager Ron Atkinson didn't see him as part of Manchester United's future plans and in February 1982 after scoring 69 goals in 408 games, he joined Stoke City for £350,000.

A free transfer later saw him quit Stoke for the other half of Manchester but he played just a dozen games in blue. He next tried his luck in Sweden with Orgryte before joining Bury and then another spell abroad in Austria with VFB Molding was followed by a period with Preston North End.

Personal File

Position: Midfielder
Born: Samuel Baxter McIlroy, Belfast 2 August 1954
Clubs: Manchester United, Stoke City, Manchester City, Orgryte (Sweden), Bury, VFB Modling (Austria), Preston North End

NI Caps: 88
NI Goals: 5

Games

Year	Opponent	Result	Score	G	Year	Opponent	Result	Score	G
1972	Spain	drew	1-1		1979	England	lost	0-2	
	Scotland	lost	0-2			Scotland	lost	0-1	
1974	Scotland	won	1-0			Wales	drew	1-1	
	England	lost	0-1			Denmark	lost	0-4	
	Wales	lost	0-1		1980	England	lost	1-5	
1975	Norway	lost	1-2			Republic of Ireland	won	1-0	
	Sweden	won	2-0			Israel	drew	0-0	
	Yugoslavia	won	1-0			Scotland	won	1-0	
	England	drew	0-0			England	drew	1-1	
	Scotland	lost	0-3			Wales	won	1-0	
	Wales	won	1-0		1981	Sweden	won	3-0	1
1976	Sweden	lost	1-2			Portugal	lost	0-1	
	Norway	won	3-0	1		Scotland	drew	1-1	
	Yugoslavia	lost	0-1			Portugal	won	1-0	
	Scotland	lost	0-3			Scotland	lost	0-2	
	England	lost	0-4			Sweden	lost	0-1	
	Wales	lost	0-1		1982	Scotland	drew	0-0	
1977	Holland	drew	2-2			Israel	won	1-0	
	Belgium	lost	0-2			England	lost	0-4	
	England	lost	1-2			France	lost	0-4	
	Scotland	lost	0-3			Scotland	drew	1-1	1
	Wales	drew	1-1			Wales	lost	0-3	
	Iceland	lost	0-1			Yugoslavia	drew	0-0	
1978	Iceland	won	2-0	1		Honduras	drew	1-1	
	Holland	lost	0-1			Spain	won	1-0	
	Belgium	won	3-0			Austria	drew	2-2	
	Scotland	drew	1-1			France	lost	1-4	
	England	lost	0-1		1983	Austria	lost	0-2	
	Wales	lost	0-1			West Germany	won	1-0	
1979	Republic of Ireland	drew	0-0			Albania	drew	0-0	
	Denmark	won	2-1			Turkey	won	2-1	
	Bulgaria	won	2-0			Albania	won	1-0	
	England	lost	0-4			Scotland	drew	0-0	
	Bulgaria	won	2-0						

Sammy McIlroy

After hanging up his boots, McIlroy became manager of then non-League Macclesfield, whom he led to two Conference titles and victory in the 1996 FA Trophy. After winning promotion to the Football League, McIlroy took the Silkmen into Division Two in the club's first season in the competition. McIlroy parted company with Macclesfield in 2000 to take over the reins of the national side. The popular McIlroy resigned after the last European Championship qualifier against Greece in Athens to join Stockport County, but has since parted company with the Edgeley Park club.

"It was like picking eight draws and then finding the pools coupon still in your pocket."

- Sammy McIlroy on the 1976 FA Cup Final.

Games Continued

Year	Opponent	Result	Score	G	Year	Opponent	Result	Score	G
	England	drew	0-0		1986	Turkey	drew	0-0	
	Wales	lost	0-1			Romania	won	1-0	
1984	Austria	won	3-1			England	drew	0-0	
	Turkey	lost	0-1			France	drew	0-0	
	Scotland	won	2-0	1		Denmark	drew	1-1	
	England	lost	0-1			Morocco	won	2-1	
	Wales	drew	1-1			Algeria	drew	1-1	
	Finland	lost	0-1			Spain	lost	1-2	
1985	Finland	won	2-1			Brazil	lost	0-3	
	England	lost	0-1		1987	England	lost	0-3	
	Turkey	won	2-0						

Northern Ireland's manager Sammy McIlroy celebrates with his players.

Alf McMichael

One of the most prominent of Newcastle United's many fine full-backs over the years, Alf McMichael was captain of both club and country in a spell of 14 seasons at St James Park.

Only a handful of players have appeared more for the Magpies and no-one has been capped as often as McMichael.

At left-back, the Irishman from Belfast played throughout the fifties for United. In an era with so much glory, he was rarely given headlines, content to stay in the background as others took the spotlight. He signed for Cliftonville when just 15 but in 1945 he was picked up by Linfield and his game developed quickly after that, winning an Irish Cup medal in 1948 and League representative honours a year later. Though he was soon to cross the Irish Sea, he created something of a unique achievement when he actually managed to get the Linfield v Cliftonville fixture in 1949 brought forward by 15 minutes so he could dash to catch a train bound for Dublin with his new bride!

McMichael eventually joined Newcastle United for a fee of £23,000 in September 1949 and within 24 hours of putting pen to paper, he made his debut in a 4-2 defeat of Manchester City. McMichael was first honoured at full international level by Northern Ireland in October 1949 but it proved an awful outing for the full-back as Scotland won 8-2 at Windsor Park. He kept his place for the next game – a 9-2 defeat by England – and though he was then dropped, he soon returned to the international stage to become a regular fixture in the Irish line-up.

In 1951 the Ulsterman was unlucky to miss United's FA Cup Final Wembley success when he slipped in training and broke a wrist. Though he was back at Wembley a year later to receive a winners' medal, he again missed out in 1955 with ligament trouble.

McMichael captained Northern Ireland until Danny Blanchflower took over and was a proud member of their 1958 World Cup giant-killing side. He was also honoured by being picked for the Rest of the UK team to play Wales and was recognised as being one of the top defenders in football during the fifties. All told he played on 40 occasions for his country, by far the most capped individual with the club. With well over 400 games behind him and netting a solitary goal against Cardiff City in 1955, Alf McMichael joined South Shields as player-manager in 1963. Within a year he had netted a testimonial at St James Park. He turned South Shields into one of the game's most feared FA Cup minnows before later returning to Ireland to manage Bangor. On ending his involvement with the game, he worked in the Harland and Wolff shipyard.

Personal File

Position: Full-back
Born: Alfred McMichael,
Belfast
1 October 1927
Clubs: Linfield,
Newcastle United,
South Shields

NI Caps: 40

Games

Year	Opponent	Result	Score	G	Year	Opponent	Result	Score	G
1950	Scotland	lost	2-8		1957	Wales	drew	0-0	
	England	lost	2-9			Italy	lost	0-1	
1951	England	lost	1-4			Portugal	won	3-0	
	Scotland	lost	1-6		1958	Scotland	drew	1-1	
	France	drew	2-2			England	won	3-2	
1952	Scotland	lost	0-2			Italy	drew	2-2	
	England	lost	0-2			Italy	lost	1-3	
	Wales	lost	0-3			Wales	drew	1-1	
1953	England	drew	2-2			Czechoslovakia	won	1-0	
	Scotland	drew	1-1			Argentina	lost	1-3	
	France	lost	1-3			West Germany	drew	2-2	
	Wales	lost	2-3			Czechoslovakia	won	2-1	
1954	Scotland	lost	1-3			France	lost	0-4	
	England	lost	1-3		1959	Spain	lost	2-6	
	Wales	won	2-1			Scotland	drew	2-2	
1955	England	lost	0-2			Wales	won	4-1	
	Wales	lost	2-3		1960	Scotland	lost	0-4	
1956	Wales	drew	1-1			England	lost	1-2	
1957	England	drew	1-1			Wales	lost	2-3	
	Scotland	lost	0-1						
	Portugal	drew	1-1						

Eric McMordie

But for a bout of homesickness, Eric McMordie could have been a member of the great Manchester United side of the late 1960s. Instead he became an integral part of a very impressive Middlesbrough side who were never quite good enough to climb out of the old Second Division. Consequently, McMordie – whose Christian name was actually Alexander – spent his entire career outside the top flight of the Football League when his talents would have fitted easily at the highest level.

Spotted by Manchester United as a youngster in Belfast, 15-year-old McMordie had a short trial at Old Trafford with fellow Irish youngster George Best. Both returned to Ireland feeling homesick but, while Best was persuaded to return for a second spell, McMordie stayed in Ireland. The rest, as they say, is history. However, the young McMordie did well enough for local amateur side Dundela to earn a recommendation to Middlesbrough manager Raich Carter from the club's Irish-based scout Matt Willis and joined Boro as a professional in September 1964.

It was not until September of the following year that he made his first team debut at inside-forward against Plymouth Argyle, but he became an immediate hit by scoring on his home debut in a 4-0 defeat of Rotherham United. However, the season ended in relegation to the Third Division for the first time in Middlesbrough's history and McMordie initially struggled to establish himself in Stan Anderson's rejuvenated team.

However, he became an important member of the team in a midfield role over the next six seasons and won the first of 21 caps for Northern Ireland against Israel in 1968, going on to score three goals in his first five appearances.

Although initially part of Jack Charlton's successful side of 1973-74, he made way for Bobby Murdoch on the Scot's arrival from Celtic and it quickly became clear that he had no future at Ayresome Park. A loan spell with Sheffield Wednesday, which brought him six goals in nine games, surprisingly failed to end in a permanent deal. McMordie had not started a first team game for Middlesbrough for almost 18 months when he signed for York City in the summer of 1975, having scored 26 goals in 277 League and Cup games for the Teeside club.

Although still in his 20s, Eric McMordie's career was in decline and he later moved on to Hartlepool United after just 42 league games at Bootham Crescent. He made a further 46 appearances for Hartlepool before ending his playing days at the early age of just 31.

Since his retirement, McMordie has continued to live and work on Teeside, where he runs a chain of green-grocers.

Personal File

Position: Midfielder
Born: Alexander McMordie,
Belfast
12 April 1946
Clubs: Dundela,
Middlesbrough,
Sheffield Wednesday,
York City,
Hartlepool United

NI Caps: 21
NI Goals: 3

Games

Year	Opponent	Result	Score	G	Year	Opponent	Result	Score	G
1969	Israel	won	3-2		1971	Cyprus	won	3-0	
	Turkey	won	4-1	1		Cyprus	won	5-0	
	Turkey	won	3-0			England	lost	0-1	
	England	lost	1-3	1		Scotland	won	1-0	
	Scotland	drew	1-1	1		Wales	won	1-0	
	Wales	drew	0-0		1972	USSR	drew	1-1	
1970	USSR	drew	0-0			Spain	drew	1-1	
	Scotland	lost	0 1			Scotland	lost	0-2	
	England	lost	1-3			England	won	1-0	
	Wales	lost	0-1			Wales	drew	0-0	
					1973	Bulgaria	lost	0-3	

"**Whether it be on the pitch or in training, he always had time for a laugh or a joke. He was also a great midfield player who could get forward or back.**"

- David Armstrong on Eric McMordie

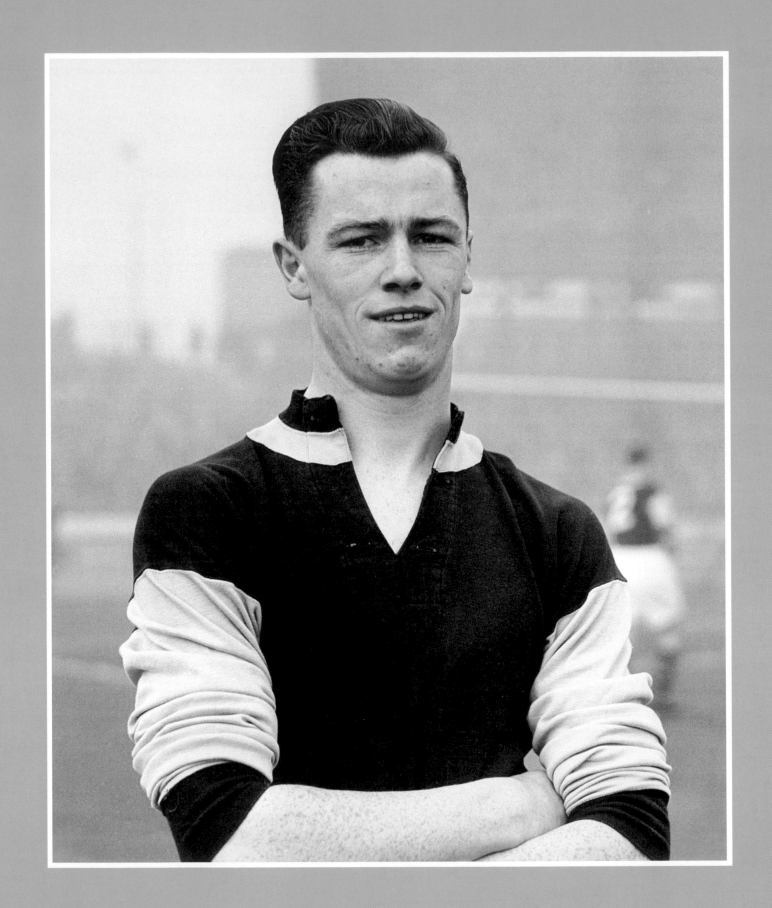

Peter McParland

One of Aston Villa's greatest post-war goalscoring wingers, Peter McParland joined the Midlands outfit from League of Ireland club Dundalk for £3,880 in the summer of 1952. He made an immediate impact with Villa, his form leading to him winning the first of 34 full international caps for Northern Ireland when in March 1954 he scored both his country's goals in a 2-1 defeat of Wales at Wrexham's Racecourse Ground.

McParland was also the scorer of both Villa's goals when they beat Manchester United 2-1 to win the 1957 FA Cup Final. During the course of this game, it was the Northern Ireland international who collided with United keeper Ray Wood, forcing him to be carried from the field.

In 1958, McParland represented Northern Ireland in the World Cup Finals in Sweden and scored both his side's goals in a 2-2 draw against West Germany and in the 2-1 play-off win over Czechoslovakia.

Back on the domestic front, he won a Second Division Championship medal in 1959-60 and represented the Football League against the Italian League. In the two-legged League Cup Final of 1961, he netted the winner against Rotherham United. He topped the club's scoring charts in 1956-57 but his best season in terms of goals scored was 1959-60 when he netted 25 League and Cup goals in 46 appearances.

He left Aston Villa in January 1962 after scoring 120 goals in 340 games – a phenomenal record for an out-and-out winger, to play for Villa's neighbours, Wolverhampton Wanderers. A year later he joined Plymouth Argyle, then played for Worcester City before in 1970-71 managing Glentoran. In 1972 he had a spell as manager of Bournemouth but afterwards spent much of his time coaching abroad, particularly in Cyprus, Kuwait and Hong Kong from his base on the south coast.

"Peter McParland scored both goals against Germany, the first was against the run of play but they hit back and scored twice before we levelled again."

- Harry Gregg

Personal File

Position: Outside-left
Born: Peter James McParland,
      Newry
      25 April 1934
Clubs: Dundalk,
       Aston Villa,
       Wolverhampton Wanderers,
       Plymouth Argyle,
       Worcester City

NI Caps: 34
NI Goals: 10

Games

Year	Opponent	Result	Score	G	Year	Opponent	Result	Score	G
1954	Wales	won	2-1	2	1958	France	lost	0-4	
1955	England	lost	0-2		1959	England	drew	3-3	
	Scotland	drew	2-2			Spain	lost	2-6	
1956	Scotland	won	2-1			Scotland	drew	2-2	
	England	lost	0-3			Wales	won	4-1	2
1957	England	drew	1-1		1960	Scotland	lost	0-4	
	Scotland	lost	0-1			England	lost	1-2	
	Portugal	drew	1-1			Wales	lost	2-3	
	Wales	drew	0-0		1961	England	lost	2-5	
1958	Scotland	drew	1-1			West Germany	lost	3-4	
	England	won	3-2			Scotland	lost	2-5	
	Italy	drew	2-2			Wales	lost	1-5	
	Italy	lost	1-3	1		Italy	lost	2-3	
	Wales	drew	1-1			Greece	lost	1-2	
	Czechoslovakia	won	1-0			West Germany	lost	1-2	
	Argentina	lost	1-3	1	1962	Holland	lost	0-4	
	West Germany	drew	2-2	2					
	Czechoslovakia	won	2-1	2					

Eddie Magill

Full-back Eddie Magill joined Arsenal from Irish League side Portadown in the summer of 1959 and after some impressive displays for the Gunners' reserve side, made a traumatic Football League debut against Sheffield Wednesday in December of that year, a match the Owls won 5-1.

Settling into the Arsenal side alongside another former Portadown player, Billy McCullough, there was a tendency among supporters of opposing teams to think of them as peas from the same pod; yet Magill and McCullough could hardly have offered a wider contrast. While Billy McCullough's approach was based on fire and forcefulness, Eddie Magill was not noted for the ferocity of his tackles. He preferred to jockey his opponents away from the danger area, watching for an opportunity to clear the ball out of harm's way – relying on stealth rather than strength.

Despite some heavy defeats during his early days at Highbury, Eddie Magill held on to his place for a 19-match run in his first season at the club, but then lost out to both Dave Bacuzzi and Len Wills.

In 1961-62 he shared the full-back duties with Bacuzzi and won the first of 26 full international caps for Northern Ireland when he played against Scotland at Windsor Park in a match the visitors won 6-1.

He later became a regular in the Arsenal defence, eventually losing his place after 116 league appearances when England international Don Howe was signed from West Bromwich Albion in April 1964.

With little option but to seek a future elsewhere, Magill made a £6,000 switch to Brighton and Hove Albion, spending three seasons at the Goldstone Ground before taking up coaching and management posts in Denmark.

Personal File

Position: Full-back
Born: Edward James Magill,
Lurgan
17 May 1939
Clubs: Portadown,
Arsenal,
Brighton and Hove Albion

NI Caps: 26

Games

Year	Opponent	Result	Score	G	Year	Opponent	Result	Score	G
1962	Scotland	lost	1-6		1965	England	lost	3-4	
	Greece	won	2-0			Switzerland	won	1-0	
	England	drew	1-1			Switzerland	lost	1-2	
1963	Poland	won	2-0			Scotland	lost	2-3	
	England	lost	1-3			Holland	drew	0-0	
	Scotland	lost	1-5			Albania	won	4-1	
	Poland	won	2-0		1966	Scotland	won	3-2	
	Wales	lost	1-4			Scotland	lost	1-2	
	Spain	drew	1-1			Albania	drew	1-1	
1964	Scotland	won	2-1			Wales	won	4-1	
	Spain	lost	0-1			West				
	England	lost	3-8			Germany	lost	0-2	
	Wales	won	3-2			Mexico	won	4-1	
	Uruguay	won	3-0						

Sammy Morgan

A tall striker with aerial ability, Sammy Morgan played his early football for Gorleston before joining Port Vale, initially on trial in January 1970. Despite scoring on his first appearance as a substitute in a 1-1 draw at Newport County in March of that year, he had to wait until the opening game of the following season before making his full debut for the club, scoring Vale's second goal in a 2-0 win at Swansea.

In 1971-72 he scored seven goals in 36 games and after helping to make many others for his colleagues, was voted the club's 'Player of the Year'. His form that season led to him winning the first of 18 full caps for Northern Ireland against Spain at Hull's Boothferry Park, where he netted his country's goal in a 1-1 draw.

The following season, Morgan was Vale's joint-top scorer but at the end of this 1972-73 campaign, having scored 27 goals in 126 League and Cup games, he was sold to Aston Villa for £22,000 plus eventually an extra £5,000 through a goalscoring clause.

His stay at Villa Park was brief and he left just before the start of the 1974-75 season to continue his career with Brighton and Hove Albion. After later ending his Football League career with Cambridge United, he went to play in Holland, initially with Sparta Rotterdam and then FC Groningen.

His career then came full circle as he rejoined Gorleston to become their team manager. He subsequently became the secretary and chairman of Great Yarmouth Schools FA, a schoolboy coach in the United States and finally a schoolboy coach to Norwich City.

"It is all about people – not facilities."

- Sammy Morgan

Personal File

Position: Forward
Born: Samuel John Morgan,
Belfast
3 December 1946
Clubs: Gorleston, Port Vale,
Aston Villa,
Brighton and Hove Albion,
Cambridge United,
Sparta Rotterdam,
FC Groningen

NI Caps: 18
NI Goals: 3

Games

Year	Opponent	Result	Score	G	Year	Opponent	Result	Score	G
1972	Spain	drew	1-1	1	1974	Scotland	won	1-0	
1973	Bulgaria	lost	0-3			England	lost	0-1	
	Portugal	drew	1-1		1975	Sweden	won	2-0	
	Cyprus	won	3-0	1	1976	Sweden	lost	1-2	
	England	lost	1-2			Norway	won	3-0	1
	Scotland	won	2-1			Yugoslavia	lost	0-1	
	Wales	won	1-0			Scotland	lost	0-3	
1974	Bulgaria	drew	0-0			Wales	lost	0-1	
	Portugal	drew	1-1		1979	Denmark	won	2-1	

Jim Magilton

Midfielder Jim Magilton joined Liverpool as an apprentice in May 1986 but as he was unable to break into the Reds' first team, he joined Oxford United for £100,000 in October 1990.

Impressive displays for the Manor Ground club, where he scored 39 goals in 167 games, led to a number of top flight clubs showing an interest in securing his services.

In February 1994, Southampton manager Alan Ball paid £600,000 for the Northern Ireland international – who'd scored from the penalty spot in a 3-1 defeat of Poland on his debut – and he made his first appearance for Saints in the 4-2 home win over Liverpool when Matt Le Tissier netted a hat-trick.

Jim Magilton was a commanding presence in the centre of the Southampton midfield, and a neat and indefatigable 'fetcher and carrier' between penalty areas. However he didn't seem to fit into new manager Dave Jones' plans and he made a surprise move to Hillsborough soon after the start of the 1997-98 season. The fact that the fee was £1.6 million showed just how highly Owls manager David Pleat rated him.

However, when Pleat was replaced by Ron Atkinson, Magilton's days with the Yorkshire club were numbered. On losing his place, he also found that his position in the Northern Ireland side was not assured.

After a loan spell with Ipswich Town, the move became permanent and in 1999-2000 he netted his first-ever professional hat-trick in the play-off semi-final win against Bolton Wanderers – he also had a second penalty attempt brilliantly saved by the Wanderers' keeper. To cap a fine season he was also recalled to the Northern Ireland team by new manager Sammy McIlroy, occasionally captaining the side. One of the main inspirations of Ipswich's successful return to the top flight, Magilton was then hampered by a series of niggling injuries and couldn't halt the club's slide back into the First Division. Appointed captain by new manager Joe Royle, Jim Magilton remains an important member of the East Anglian club and in the 2004-05 season led them to the play-offs where they lost to West Ham United over two legs.

Personal File

Position: Midfielder
Born: James Magilton,
      Belfast
      6 May 1969
Clubs: Liverpool,
       Oxford United,
       Southampton,
       Sheffield Wednesday,
       Ipswich Town

NI Caps: 52
NI Goals: 5

Games

Year	Opponent	Result	Score	G	Year	Opponent	Result	Score	G
1991	Poland	won	3-1	1		of Ireland	drew	1-1	
	Yugoslavia	lost	1-4			Canada	lost	0-2	
	Faroe Islands	drew	1-1			Chile	lost	1-2	
1992	Faroe Islands	won	5-0			Latvia	lost	1-2	
	Austria	won	2-1		1996	Portugal	drew	1-1	
	Denmark	lost	1-2			Norway	lost	0-2	
	Scotland	lost	0-1			Germany	drew	1-1	
	Lithuania	drew	2-2		1997	Ukraine	lost	0-1	
	Germany	drew	1-1			Armenia	drew	1-1	
1993	Albania	won	3-0	1		Belgium	won	3-0	1
	Denmark	lost	0-1			Portugal	drew	0-0	
	Albania	won	2-1	1	1998	Germany	lost	1-3	
	Republic of Ireland	lost	0-3			Portugal	lost	0-1	
	Lithuania	won	1-0			Spain	lost	1-4	
	Latvia	won	2-1	1	2000	Luxembourg	won	3-1	
1994	Latvia	won	2-0		2001	Yugoslavia	lost	1-2	
	Denmark	lost	0-1			Malta	won	1-0	
	Republic of Ireland	drew	1-1			Denmark	drew	1-1	
	Romania	won	2-0			Iceland	lost	0-1	
	Liechtenstein	won	4-1			Norway	lost	0-4	
	Colombia	lost	0-2			Czech Republic	lost	0-1	
	Mexico	lost	0-3			Bulgaria	lost	3-4	
1995	Portugal	lost	1-2		2002	Denmark	drew	1-1	
	Austria	won	2-1			Iceland	won	3-0	
	Republic of Ireland	lost	0-4			Malta	won	1-0	
	Republic					Poland	lost	1-4	
						Liechtenstein	drew	0-0	

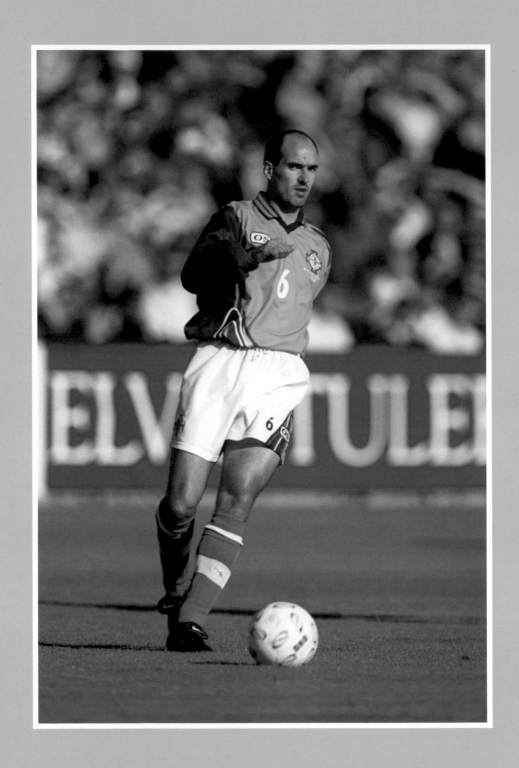

Steve Morrow

Steve Morrow was first spotted by Arsenal playing for his local side Bangor and after joining the North London club as an apprentice, turned professional in May 1988.

Although still to play a League game for the Gunners, his ability was recognised at full international level when he came off the bench for Northern Ireland against Uruguay in Belfast in May 1990. He continued to play for his country though still a reserve at Highbury and in January 1991 he went on loan to Reading, where he made his Football League debut against Exeter City. With his path to the Arsenal first team blocked by Nigel Winterburn, Morrow had three loan periods in 1991-92 with Watford, Reading again and Barnet.

He returned to Arsenal at the end of that season and made his League debut as a substitute against Norwich City at Carrow Road.

Morrow had been a member of the Arsenal FA Youth Cup winning team in 1987-88 and had suffered more than his fair share of injuries, which included a hernia and a groin strain. After originally winning a regular place at the expense of the injured Nigel Winterburn, he was moved into midfield, usually with a specific marking job in hand. Rarely has someone gone from the sublime to the ridiculous quite as quickly as the Ulsterman.

Having scored his first goal for the club in the League Cup Final against Sheffield Wednesday, he sustained a broken arm in the post-match celebrations and instead of collecting his medal, he left the field on a stretcher, requiring an oxygen mask! This injury kept him out of the FA Cup Final against the same opposition later in the season, though he did appear for the Gunners in two European Cup Winners' Cup Finals against Parma and Real Zaragosa.

Made captain of the Northern Ireland side, he was still never more than a squad player at Highbury and he eventually left to join Queen's Park Rangers for £1 million on transfer deadline day in March 1997. Despite playing under a number of different managers during his time at Loftus Road, he was never able to gain regular selection. He also ruptured ligaments in his shoulder and this required a number of operations before he went on loan to Peterborough United, prior to deciding to retire.

Personal File

Position: Midfielder/Defender
Born: Stephen Joseph Morrow,
Bangor
2 July 1970
Clubs: Arsenal,
Reading (loan),
Watford (loan),
Reading (loan),
Barnet (loan),
Queen's Park Rangers,
Petersborough United (loan)

NI Caps: 39
NI Goals: 1

Games

Year	Opponent	Result	Score	G	Year	Opponent	Result	Score	G
1990	Uruguay	won	1-0		1996	Portugal	drew	1-1	
1991	Austria	drew	0-0			Sweden	lost	1-2	
	Poland	won	3-1		1997	Ukraine	lost	0-1	
	Yugoslavia	lost	1-4			Germany	drew	1-1	
1992	Faroe Islands	won	5-0			Albania	won	2-0	
	Scotland	lost	0-1			Italy	lost	0-2	
	Germany	drew	1-1			Belgium	won	3-0	
1993	Spain	drew	0-0			Portugal	drew	0-0	
	Albania	won	2-1			Ukraine	lost	1-2	
	Republic of Ireland	lost	0-3			Armenia	drew	0-0	
1994	Romania	won	2-0	1	1998	Germany	lost	1-3	
	Colombia	lost	0-2			Portugal	lost	0-1	
	Mexico	lost	0-3			Slovakia	won	1-0	
1995	Portugal	lost	1-2			Switzerland	won	1-0	
	Republic of Ireland	lost	0-4			Spain	lost	1-4	
	Republic of Ireland	drew	1-1		1999	Turkey	lost	0-3	
	Latvia	lost	1-2			Finland	won	1-0	
						Moldova	drew	2-2	
						Germany	lost	0-3	
						Moldova	drew	0-0	
					2000	Germany	lost	0-4	
						Finland	lost	1-4	

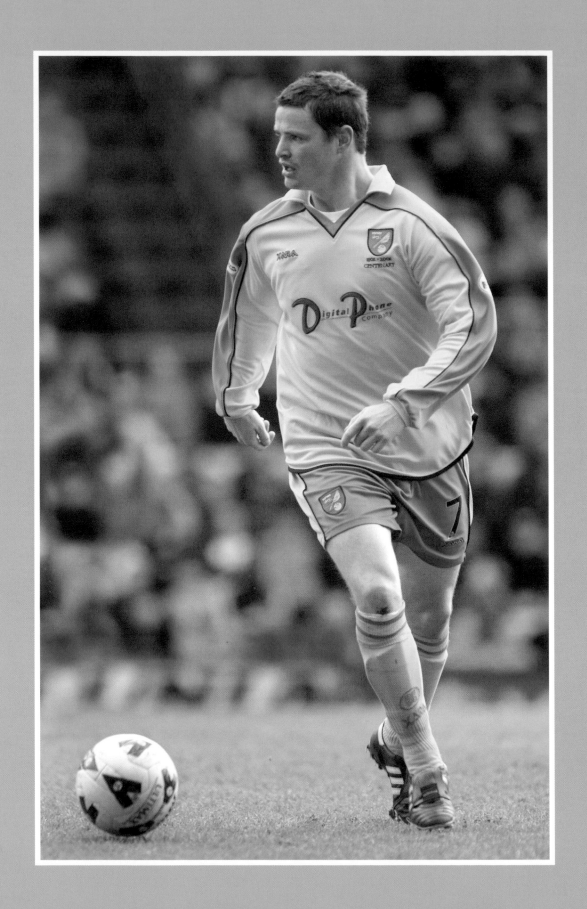

Phil Mulryne

A member of Manchester United's FA Youth Cup winning side of 1994-95, he made a promising start to his senior career at Old Trafford with an excellent performance against Ipswich in the Coca Cola Cup in October 1997.

Already a full international, having scored on his Northern Ireland debut when he came off the bench to score in a 3-0 win over Belgium, Phil Mulryne looked to have a bright future. Yet after just a handful of first team appearances for United, he was allowed to join Norwich City in transfer deadline week in March 1999 for a knockdown price of £500,000.

A highly talented midfielder whose senior opportunities at Old Trafford had been severely limited by the likes of Roy Keane, David Beckham, Paul Scholes and Nicky Butt, he scored on his full debut for the Canaries against Grimsby Town.

A player who likes to dictate the pattern of play and is always available to receive a pass, Phil Mulryne is also something of a dead-ball specialist. Sadly, at the start of the 1999-2000 campaign, he had the misfortune to suffer a double compound fracture of his right leg, which resulted in over seven months on the sidelines. Another injury-interrupted campaign in 2000-01 prevented him from making the impact at club level he so badly desired, though he did towards the end of the season return to the full Northern Ireland set-up.

In 2001-02 he completed his first season of regular first team football and became an integral part of Nigel Worthington's side. Steering clear of injuries, he proved there are few better playmakers outside the top flight than the Northern Ireland international. At one time it looked as if he would be leaving Carrow Road on a 'Bosman' free transfer but he decided his footballing future lay in East Anglia by signing a new three-year deal. Having helped the Canaries into the Premiership, Phil Mulryne remains a vital cog for both club and country and though they lost their top flight status after one season, he will be hoping to be part of a Norwich side that bounces straight back.

Personal File

Position: Midfielder
Born: Phillip Patrick Mulryne, Belfast
1 January 1978
Clubs: Manchester United, Norwich City

NI Caps: 26
NI Goals: 3

Games

Year	Opponent	Result	Score	G	Year	Opponent	Result	Score	G
1997	Belgium	won	3-0	1	2002	Poland	lost	1-4	
	Armenia	drew	0-0			Liechtenstein	drew	0-0	
	Thailand	drew	0-0		2003	Spain	lost	0-3	
1998	Albania	lost	0-1			Ukraine	drew	0-0	
	Spain	lost	1-4		2004	Ukraine	drew	0-0	
1999	Turkey	lost	0-3			Armenia	lost	0-1	
	Finland	won	1-0			Estonia	won	1-0	
	Canada	drew	1-1			Serbia &			
2001	Yugoslavia	lost	1-2			Montenegro	drew	1-1	
	Denmark	drew	1-1			Barbados	drew	1-1	
	Bulgaria	lost	0-1			St Kitts &			
	Czech					Nevis	won	2-0	
	Republic	lost	1-3	1		Trinidad &			
2002	Denmark	drew	1-1	1		Tobago	won	3-0	
	Iceland	won	3-0		2005	Canada	lost	0-1	

Colin Murdock

One of a trio of Manchester United players to join Preston North End during the summer of 1997, Colin Murdock developed over the following season into a more than useful left-sided defender. Benefiting from regular first team football, his partnership with Michael Jackson at the heart of the North End defence blossomed. Particularly strong in the air, he was called into the Northern Ireland 'B' squad during the early part of the 1998-99 season and was unlucky not to win full international honours.

He eventually made his full international debut for Northern Ireland in February 2000 when he came off the bench against Luxembourg and then won further caps against Malta and Hungary.

During the course of that 1999-2000 season when North End won the Second Division Championship, Murdock's dominance in the air and timely tackles were seen to good effect. At the end of the campaign, David Moyes gave him a new contract – just reward for his contribution to the club's success.

In the higher grade of football, Murdock displayed his growing skill and confidence but after receiving his marching orders in the game at Nottingham Forest, he took a while to win back his place. Maturing into a solid and most reliable team member, he continued to represent Northern Ireland, adding several more caps over the course of the season.

A threat at set pieces, he scored his first goal for 18 months and the club's opening goal of the 2001-02 campaign against Walsall before following this with another in the next game! Missing a number of matches due to injury and suspension, he was again a regular for Northern Ireland.

In 2002-03 Murdock had to share the central defensive duties with Marlon Broomes who arrived at Deepdale from Burnley – this was after the club dispensed with playing three centre-halves and reverted to two. Murdock was made captain in the absence of Chris Lucketti for the game at Ipswich but in January 2003 he was injured in the match against Nottingham Forest and was forced to sit out the rest of the season.

Colin Murdock had appeared in 212 League and Cup games for North End but after refusing to sign a new contract, he was placed on the transfer list and later joined Hibernian, where in his first season at Easter Road he scored a number of vital goals from set pieces.

After one season at Easter Road Murdock returned to the Football League with Crewe Alexandra for whom his outstanding displays at the heart of the Railwaymen's defence was paramount in keeping their place in the championship.

He scored his first international goal in a 3-3 draw with Austria during the 2004-05 season.

Personal File

Position: Central defender
Born: Colin James Murdock,
Ballymena
2 July 1975
Clubs: Manchester United,
Preston North End,
Hibernian,
Crewe Alexandra

NI Caps: 27
NI Goals: 1

Games

Year	Opponent	Result	Score	G	Year	Opponent	Result	Score	G
2000	Luxembourg	won	3-1		2003	Cyprus	drew	0-0	
	Malta	won	3-0			Spain	lost	0-3	
	Hungary	lost	0-1			Ukraine	drew	0-0	
2001	Yugoslavia	lost	1-2		2004	Greece	lost	0-1	
	Malta	won	1-0			Barbados	drew	1-1	
	Denmark	drew	1-1			St Kitts			
	Iceland	lost	0-1			& Nevis	won	2-0	
	Norway	lost	0-4			Trinidad &			
	Czech					Tobago	won	3-0	
	Republic	lost	0-1		2005	Switzerland	drew	0-0	
	Bulgaria	lost	3-4			Wales	drew	2-2	
	Bulgaria	lost	0-1			Azerbaijan	drew	0-0	
	Czech					Austria	drew	3-3	1
	Republic	lost	1-3			Canada	lost	0-1	
2002	Denmark	drew	1-1			England	lost	0-4	
	Malta	won	1-0						

Terry Neill

From the moment he walked into Highbury as a 17-year-old recruit from Irish League Bangor City in December 1959, there was no doubting Terry Neill's dedication. There followed two and a half years of steady but unspectacular progress, in and out of the League side until his career gathered momentum with the appointment of Billy Wright.

At the age of 18, Neill won the first of his 59 caps against Italy and in 1961-62 at the age of 19, he became Arsenal's youngest-ever captain.

Over the next three seasons, although a regular in the Northern Ireland side, he could not claim a regular place in the Gunner's League side. In 1964-65 he recaptured his form and for the next three seasons he missed very few games, including playing against Leeds United in the 1968 League Cup Final. Around this time, Terry Neill was appointed captain of Northern Ireland as well as becoming the PFA secretary. In 1968-69 a series of injuries, including contracting jaundice, forced him to miss half a season including the League Cup Final against Swindon Town.

One of the most memorable moments of Terry Neill's career came in his 50th international appearance – he scored the winning goal at Wembley in a rare Irish victory over England. Neill, who went on to become at the time, the most capped Arsenal player, later broke Danny Blanchflower's record of Irish caps, though this in turn was to be broken by Pat Jennings.

A thoughtful and articulate captain of his country, he was clearly prime management material, and it came as no surprise when he left Highbury to become player-manager at Hull City.

At 29, he was the youngest boss in the League, going on to assume the same dual role for Northern Ireland.

His management career was eventually to lead him to Tottenham in 1974 and then to Highbury in 1976 to succeed Bertie Mee. His masterstroke was to bring back coach Don Howe from Leeds. Their partnership guided the Gunners to their three successive FA Cup Finals in 1978, '79 and '80 plus their near miss in the Cup Winners' Cup in 1980 when they lost to Valencia on penalties.

Even this favourite son of Highbury could not escape the usual fate of managers when things begin to go wrong and after eight seasons in charge, he was sacked at the end of 1983. It was the first real setback in a 25-year career in football for the serious-minded self-confident Ulsterman.

Personal File

Position: Centre-half
Born: William John Terence Neill,
          Belfast
          8 May 1942
Clubs: Bangor City,
          Arsenal,
          Hull City

NI Caps: 59
NI Goals: 2

Games

Year	Opponent	Result	Score	G	Year	Opponent	Result	Score	G
1961	Italy	lost	2-3		1967	Scotland	lost	1-2	
	Greece	lost	1-2			Wales	drew	0-0	
	West				1968	Scotland	won	1-0	
	Germany	lost	1-2			England	lost	0-2	
1962	Scotland	lost	1-6		1969	Israel	won	3-2	
	Greece	won	2-0			Turkey	won	4-1	
	England	drew	1-1			Turkey	won	3-0	
	Wales	lost	0-4			England	lost	1-3	
1963	England	lost	1-3			Scotland	drow	1 1	
	Poland	won	2-0			Wales	drew	0-0	
	Wales	lost	1-4		1970	USSR	drew	0-0	
	Spain	drew	1-1			USSR	lost	0-2	
1964	Scotland	won	2-1			Scotland	lost	0-1	
	Spain	lost	0-1			England	lost	1-3	
	England	lost	3-8			Wales	lost	0-1	
	Wales	won	3-2		1971	Spain	lost	0-3	
	Uruguay	won	3-0			Cyprus	won	3-0	
1965	England	lost	3-4		1972	USSR	lost	0-1	
	Switzerland	won	1-0			USSR	drew	1-1	
	Scotland	lost	2-3			Spain	drew	1-1	
	Holland	won	2-1	1		Scotland	lost	0-2	
	Wales	lost	0-5			England	won	1-0	1
	Holland	drew	0-0			Wales	drew	0-0	
	Albania	won	4-1		1973	Bulgaria	lost	0-3	
1966	Scotland	won	3-2			Cyprus	lost	0-1	
	Scotland	lost	1-2			Portugal	drew	1-1	
	Albania	drew	1-1			Cyprus	won	3-0	
	Wales	won	4-1			England	lost	1-2	
	West					Scotland	won	2-1	
	Germany	lost	0-2			Wales	won	1-0	
	Mexico	won	4-1						

Sammy Nelson

When Sammy Nelson joined Arsenal, he was a left-winger but was soon converted to a left-back, the position in which he was to win 51 full international caps for Northern Ireland – scoring his only goal in a 1-1 draw against Wales in June 1977.

Nelson played his first League game for the Gunners against Ipswich Town in October 1969, a season in which he also made his international debut against Wales at Swansea's then Vetch Field ground.

Quick and agile, Sammy Nelson boasted a fine touch with his left foot, though his right was considerably less precise. He was capable of adding fire power to the Gunners' attack – a scorcher in the 7-0 League Cup defeat of Leeds United at Highbury later that year still lingers with Arsenal fans of that generation. During the 'double' winning season of 1970-71, Nelson was Bob McNab's understudy. The following season after an injury to the England defender, Nelson won a regular place. McNab was released shortly afterwards and Nelson missed very few games in the seasons that followed. He played in all three FA Cup Finals between 1978 and 1980 picking up a winners medal in 1979, and made a European Cup Winners' Cup Final appearance against Valencia in 1980.

Sammy Nelson was effective in the air and a redoubtable tackler, unfailingly brave if a little inclined to make the occasional wild challenge. This aggression in the heat of the battle concealed a disarmingly gentle and humorous nature. Various antics – he once bared his behind to the crowd in a moment of levity – endeared him to the public, while his Arsenal team-mates will never forget the night a fire alarm sounded at their hotel and he emerged wearing only his underpants and clutching his wallet!

Following the arrival of Kenny Sansom at Highbury in June 1980, Sammy Nelson found himself with no future at the North London club and after a testimonial match against Celtic, he was transferred to Brighton and Hove Albion in September 1981 for £10,000. He was a member of the Seagulls' squad that reached the FA Cup Final in 1983 but shortly afterwards he hung up his boots to remain at the Goldstone Ground as the south coast club's coach.

Personal File

Position: Left-back
Born: Samuel Nelson,
Belfast
1 April 1949
Clubs: Arsenal
Brighton and Hove Albion

NI Caps: 51
NI Goals: 1

Games

Year	Opponent	Result	Score	G	Year	Opponent	Result	Score	G
1970	England	lost	1-3		1977	Wales	drew	1-1	1
	Wales	lost	0-1			Iceland	lost	0-1	
1971	Spain	lost	0-3		1978	Iceland	won	2-0	
	Cyprus	won	3-0			Holland	lost	0-1	
	England	lost	0-1			Belgium	won	3-0	
	Scotland	won	1-0		1979	Republic			
	Wales	won	1-0			of Ireland	drew	0-0	
1972	USSR	lost	0-1			Denmark	won	2-1	
	USSR	drew	1-1			Bulgaria	won	2-0	
	Spain	drew	1-1			England	lost	0-4	
	Scotland	lost	0-2			Bulgaria	won	2-0	
	England	won	1-0			England	lost	0-2	
	Wales	drew	0-0			Scotland	lost	0-1	
1973	Bulgaria	lost	0-3			Wales	drew	1-1	
	Cyprus	lost	0-1			Denmark	lost	0-4	
	Portugal	drew	1-1		1980	England	lost	1-5	
1974	Scotland	won	1-0			Republic			
	England	lost	0-1			of Ireland	won	1-0	
1975	Sweden	won	2-0			Israel	drew	0-0	
	Yugoslavia	won	1-0		1981	Scotland	drew	1-1	
1976	Sweden	lost	1-2			Portugal	won	1-0	
	Norway	won	3-0			Scotland	lost	0-2	
	Israel	drew	1-1			Sweden	lost	0-1	
	England	lost	0-4		1982	England	lost	0-4	
1977	Belgium	lost	0-2			Scotland	drew	1-1	
	West					Spain	won	1-0	
	Germany	lost	0-5			Austria	drew	2-2	

Chris Nicholl

Chris Nicholl played his first Football League game for Halifax Town after joining the Shaymen from non-League Witton Albion in the summer of 1968, having previously been on the books of Burnley. At Halifax he came under the tutelage of Alan Ball senior, who instantly recognised the youngster's potential to be one of the country's top central defenders.

His next move was to Luton Town where he was an important member of the Hatters' defence when they won promotion from the Third Division.

Later at Aston Villa, Nicholl, by now having fulfilled that potential, made history by becoming the only player to score two goals for each side in the same match, from open play!

He won two League Cup tankards with Villa, scoring one of the goals that defeated Everton in the third meeting between the two clubs in the 1977 final. Southampton manager Lawrie McMenemy paid £80,000 to take Nicholl to The Dell. It was a shrewd piece of business as the Northern Ireland international, who scored on his debut against Sweden made an immediate impact.

Nicholl had won instant promotion with every club he had joined and sure enough, he maintained that record with the Saints, who regained their place in the First Division in 1978. He appeared for the south coast club in the League Cup Final of 1979 and in Europe during the early eighties.

He later played for Grimsby Town but it was no surprise when, after McMenemy left Southampton rudderless in the summer of 1985, the directors replaced him with Chris Nicholl. Managerially he was more cautious than McMenemy and though that might not have suited the fans, he did keep the Saints afloat in Division One. He was sacked in June 1991 and remained out of the game for three years until taking over at Walsall.

Lawrie McMenemy invited him into his Northern Ireland international set-up in 1998 and during 2001-02 he had another brief spell at the Bescot Stadium working under Ray Graydon. Still living in Walsall, he is now working as a football statistician for the Press Association.

Games

Year	Opponent	Result	Score	G	Year	Opponent	Result	Score	G
1975	Sweden	won	2-0	1	1980	England	drew	1-1	
	Yugoslavia	won	1-0			Wales	won	1-0	
	England	drew	0-0			Australia	won	2-1	1
	Scotland	lost	0-3			Australia	drew	1-1	
	Wales	won	1-0			Australia	won	2-1	
1976	Sweden	lost	1-2		1981	Sweden	won	3-0	
	Norway	won	3-0			Portugal	lost	0-1	
	Yugoslavia	lost	0-1			Scotland	drew	1-1	
	Scotland	lost	0-3			Portugal	won	1-0	
	England	lost	0-4			Scotland	lost	0-2	
	Wales	lost	0-1			Sweden	lost	0-1	
1977	Wales	drew	1-1		1982	Scotland	drew	0-0	
1978	Belgium	won	3-0			Israel	won	1-0	
	Scotland	drew	1-1			England	lost	0-4	
	England	lost	0-1			France	lost	0-4	
	Wales	lost	0-1			Wales	lost	0-3	
1979	Republic of Ireland	drew	0-0			Yugoslavia	drew	0-0	
	Bulgaria	won	2-0			Honduras	drew	1-1	
	England	lost	0-4			Spain	won	1-0	
	Bulgaria	won	2-0	1		Austria	drew	2-2	
	England	lost	0-2			France	lost	1-4	
	Wales	drew	1-1		1983	Scotland	drew	0-0	
1980	Republic of Ireland	won	1-0			England	drew	0-0	
	Israel	drew	0-0			Wales	lost	0-1	
	Scotland	won	1-0		1984	Austria	won	3-1	
						Turkey	lost	0-1	

Jimmy Nicholl

Perhaps the only Canadian-born player to ever turn out for Manchester United, Jimmy Nicholl, though born across the Atlantic, moved back to England with his family while still a teenager. Perhaps even more unusual, he went on to win 73 caps for Northern Ireland.

Jimmy Nicholl made his United debut during the 1974-75 season, coming off the bench to replace Martin Buchan in a 1-0 win at Southampton.

A fine defender, he was one of a new breed of young footballers developed by the club in the mid 1970s. The following season he took over the right-back position from Alex Forsyth and by the start of the 1976-77 campaign, Nicholl had laid claim to Forsyth's jersey and was to be a permanent fixture in the Red Devils side over the next five seasons.

He won an FA Cup winners' medal in the 1977 final against Liverpool but was on the losing side two years later against Arsenal. His United career came to an abrupt end in 1981 with the signing of John Gidman, and he was loaned out to Sunderland before returning to Canada to play for Toronto Blizzards. Nicholl, who had appeared in 247 games for United, returned to Roker Park to play for Sunderland in September 1982. He then had a brief spell with Glasgow Rangers in 1983-84 before signing for West Bromwich Albion. He had made 56 League appearances for the Baggies when he returned to Rangers at the start of the 1986-87 season for a fee of £50,000.

Jimmy Nicholl has an impressive record with Northern Ireland, with caps at youth and Under 21 levels as well as his appearances at full international level. One of Northern Ireland's stars in the 1982 World Cup Finals, Nicholl also went with his country to the 1986 finals in Mexico.

On hanging up his boots, he had two spells managing Raith Rovers either side of a period in charge of Millwall, before becoming assistant-coach at Dunfermline Athletic. Unlucky not to succeed Sammy McIlroy as Northern Ireland manager, Nicholl is currently assistant-manager at Aberdeen.

"The first thing that struck me about Jimmy was his enthusiasm."

- Jim Magilton on Nicholl

Personal File

Position: Right-back
Born: James Michael Nicholl,
Canada
28 December 1954
Clubs: Manchester United,
Sunderland,
Toronto Blizzards (Canada),
Glasgow Rangers,
West Bromwich Albion

NI Caps: 73
NI Goals: 1

Games

Year	Opponent	Result	Score	G	Year	Opponent	Result	Score	G
1976	Israel	drew	1-1		1981	Scotland	lost	0-2	
	Wales	lost	0-1			Sweden	lost	0-1	
1977	Holland	drew	2-2		1982	Scotland	drew	0-0	
	Belgium	lost	0-2			Israel	won	1-0	
	England	lost	1-2			England	lost	0-4	
	Scotland	lost	0-3			France	lost	0-4	
	Wales	drew	1-1			Wales	lost	0-3	
	Iceland	lost	0-1			Yugoslavia	drew	0-0	
1978	Iceland	won	2-0			Honduras	drew	1-1	
	Holland	lost	0-1			Spain	won	1-0	
	Belgium	won	3-0			Austria	drew	2-2	
	Scotland	drew	1-1			France	lost	1-4	
	England	lost	0-1		1983	Austria	lost	0-2	
	Wales	lost	0-1			West			
1979	Republic					Germany	won	1-0	
	of Ireland	drew	0-0			Albania	drew	0-0	
	Denmark	won	2-1			Turkey	won	2-1	
	Bulgaria	won	2-0			Albania	won	1-0	
	England	lost	0-4			Scotland	drew	0-0	
	Bulgaria	won	2-0			England	drew	0-0	
	England	lost	0-2			Wales	lost	0-1	
	Scotland	lost	0-1		1984	Turkey	lost	0-1	
	Wales	drew	1-1			West			
	Denmark	lost	0-4			Germany	won	1-0	
1980	England	lost	1-5			Scotland	won	2-0	
	Republic					England	lost	0-1	
	of Ireland	won	1-0			Finland	lost	0-1	
	Israel	drew	0-0		1985	Romania	won	3-2	
	Scotland	won	1-0			Finland	won	2-1	
	England	drew	1-1			England	lost	0-1	
	Wales	won	1-0			Spain	drew	0-0	
	Australia	won	2-1			Turkey	won	2-0	
	Australia	drew	1-1		1986	Turkey	drew	0-0	
	Australia	won	2-1			Romania	won	1-0	
1981	Sweden	won	3-0	1		England	drew	0-0	
	Portugal	lost	0-1			France	drew	0-0	
	Scotland	drew	1-1			Algeria	drew	1-1	
	Portugal	won	1-0			Spain	lost	1-2	
						Brazil	lost	0-3	

Jimmy Nicholson

Jimmy Nicholson was already an Irish schoolboy international when he signed amateur forms for Northern Ireland in May 1958, yet he was once chosen for an England youth side!

However, he went on to gain Northern Ireland Under 23 caps and was in their 'B' team at the age of 16.

Nicholson turned professional for United in February 1960, making his League debut for the Red Devils against Everton at Goodison Park the following August. Three months later he became the youngest player in the 20th century to appear in a full international when, at 17 years and 8 months old, he played for Northern Ireland against Scotland at Hampden Park.

At a time when Manchester United were enjoying much success, his career took a nose-dive and at one stage, he was dropped to the Old Trafford club's third team.

In December 1964 with 68 League and Cup games behind him, Nicholson teamed up with Tom Johnson at Huddersfield Town. The former Busby babe initially signed on trial, his eventual £7,500 transfer having to be considered as one of Town's all-time bargains, despite the fact that he scored an own goal on his debut!

After starring in attack and defence, Nicholson developed into a skilful, industrious midfielder with an eye for goal. Under chief coach Ian Greaves, Nicholson regained his appetite for the game and within a matter of weeks was back in the Northern Ireland side. He went on to become Huddersfield Town's most capped international, with 31 appearances for Northern Ireland between March 1965 and October 1971. On his last appearance for his country, Nicholson scored his side's goal in a 1-1 draw with the USSR at Windsor Park.

In 1969-70 he skippered the Huddersfield side back to Division One as one of seven ever-presents but in December 1973, Nicholson, who had scored 28 goals in 310 League and Cup games, was transferred to Bury. He helped them gain promotion from Division Four in his first season at Gigg Lane.

At the end of the 1975-76 season, Nicholson left the Shakers to play non-League football, first for Mossley and then Stalybridge Celtic. Nicholson is now manager of a Sales Sports Centre.

Personal File

Position: Midfielder
Born: James Joseph Nicholson,
Belfast
27 February 1943
Clubs: Manchester United,
Huddersfield Town,
Bury,
Mossley,
Stalybridge Celtic

NI Caps: 41
NI Goals: 6

Games

Year	Opponent	Result	Score	G	Year	Opponent	Result	Score	G
1961	Scotland	lost	2-5		1968	Scotland	won	1-0	
	Wales	lost	1-5			England	lost	0-2	
1962	Greece	won	2-0			Wales	lost	0-2	
	England	drew	1-1		1969	Turkey	won	4-1	
	Wales	lost	0-4			Turkey	won	3-0	1
	Holland	lost	0-4			England	lost	1-3	
1963	Poland	won	2-0			Scotland	drew	1-1	
	England	lost	1-3			Wales	drew	0-0	
	Scotland	lost	1-5		1970	USSR	drew	0-0	
	Poland	won	2-0			USSR	lost	0-2	
1965	Holland	won	2-1			Scotland	lost	0-1	
	Wales	lost	0-5			England	lost	1-3	
	Holland	drew	0-0			Wales	lost	0-1	
	Albania	won	4-1		1971	Cyprus	won	3-0	1
1966	Scotland	won	3-2			Cyprus	won	5-0	1
	Scotland	lost	1-2			England	lost	0-1	
	Albania	drew	1-1			Scotland	won	1-0	
	Wales	won	4-1			Wales	won	1-0	
	Mexico	won	4-1	1	1972	USSR	lost	0-1	
1967	Scotland	lost	1-2	1		USSR	drew	1-1	1
	Wales	drew	0-0						

John O'Neill (right)

John O'Neill

Having played his early football with Derry Boys Club, John O'Neill was still a Loughborough undergraduate, playing for Leicester City on a non-contract basis while completing his Economics studies, when Jock Wallace gave him his debut against Burnley on the opening day of the 1978-79 season.

The gamble soon paid off as O'Neill quickly developed into a cool, polished central defender.

Already capped by Northern Ireland at Under 21 level prior to his League bow, he soon began adding full international caps on a regular basis, as his fine reading of the game brought him the added responsibility of the Leicester captaincy. Though he was occasionally criticised for an apparently over-casual on-field approach, O'Neill saved the Foxes many a goal with his intelligent interventions. Experience gained in two World Cup campaigns for his country stood City's defence in good stead during the up and down struggles of the early 1980s.

In 1986, John O'Neill surpassed Gordon Banks' record as the most capped Leicester City player but a year later having appeared in 345 League and Cup games for the Foxes, he was allowed to move to Queen's Park Rangers for £150,000.

O'Neill made just a handful of appearances as the Loftus Road club enjoyed a brief flurry of Division One success and after just five months with the club, moved on to Norwich City. After only 34 minutes of his Canaries' debut he suffered a crippling knee injury, and some months later he had to concede that his career had come to a sadly premature end. Norwich very honourably held a testimonial match on his behalf in May 1989.

In February 1990 he was appointed manager of League of Ireland side Finn Harps but two years later, he concentrated on a wine and spirits business in Derry.

In October 1994 he hit the headlines again with a High Court action for negligence against John Fashanu and Wimbledon FC which terminated with an out-of-court settlement of £70,000 in John O'Neill's favour.

Personal File

Position: Central defender
Born: John Patrick O'Neill, Derry
11 March 1958
Clubs: Derry BC, Leicester City, Queen's Park Rangers Norwich City

NI Caps: 39
NI Goals: 2

Games

Year	Opponent	Result	Score	G	Year	Opponent	Result	Score	G
1980	Israel	drew	0-0		1983	Albania	drew	0-0	
	Scotland	won	1-0			Turkey	won	2-1	
	England	drew	1-1			Albania	won	1-0	
	Wales	won	1-0			Scotland	drew	0-0	
	Australia	won	2-1	1	1984	Scotland	won	2-0	
	Australia	drew	1-1		1985	Israel	won	3-0	
	Australia	won	2-1			Finland	won	2-1	1
1981	Portugal	lost	0-1			England	lost	0-1	
	Scotland	drew	1-1			Spain	drew	0-0	
	Portugal	won	1-0			Turkey	won	2-0	
	Scotland	lost	0-2		1986	Turkey	drew	0-0	
	Sweden	lost	0-1			Romania	won	1-0	
1982	Scotland	drew	0-0			England	drew	0-0	
	Israel	won	1-0			France	drew	0-0	
	England	lost	0-4			Denmark	drew	1-1	
	France	lost	0-4			Morocco	won	2-1	
	Scotland	drew	1-1			Algeria	drew	1-1	
	France	lost	1-4			Spain	lost	1-2	
1983	Austria	lost	0-2			Brazil	lost	0-3	
	West Germany	won	1-0						

Martin O'Neill

Having just won an Irish Cup winners' medal with Distillery in a 3-0 win over Derry City, Martin O'Neill signed for Nottingham Forest in October 1971. Making his Football League debut as a substitute for the injured John Robertson, O'Neill scored Forest's second goal in a 4-1 win over West Bromwich Albion at the City Ground, a month after putting pen to paper. He then faded from the Forest first team and was languishing in the club's reserves side and on the transfer list – but the appointment of Brian Clough as manager seemed to transform O'Neill into a tenacious midfield player and it wasn't long before he was back playing first team football.

An automatic choice for Northern Ireland throughout his career, winning 64 caps, Martin O'Neill won a League Championship medal in 1977-78, two League Cup winners' medals in 1977-78 and 1978-79 and a European Cup winners' medal in 1979-80 as the Reds beat Hamburg SV – having been left out of the Forest side to face Malmö the previous season!

O'Neill had scored 62 goals in 371 League and Cup games for Forest, including a spectacular hat-trick in a 6-0 win over Chelsea in March 1979, when he was allowed to leave the City Ground and join Norwich City.

He helped the Canaries avoid relegation in 1981-82 before joining Manchester City. After less than a year at Maine Road, O'Neill rejoined Norwich for a second spell, eventually helping them win promotion to the First Division.

In 1983 he returned to the City of Nottingham – but this time to County, where unfortunately injury ended his playing career.

He then moved into non-League management, first with Grantham Town and then Shepshed Charterhouse before business commitments forced him to quit. Wycombe Wanderers lured him back in February 1990 and he led them into the Football League in 1993. Despite resisting offers from larger clubs, Martin O'Neill finally returned to one of his former clubs, Norwich City, as manager in June 1995 but left six months later to take over at Leicester City. He lost his first nine matches in charge as Leicester slipped out of the First Division play-off race. But seven wins from their last 10 matches was enough to earn Leicester a place in the play-offs. In the play-off final at Wembley they met Crystal Palace who had been relegated with them from the Premiership the season before. An extra-time winner saw the Foxes win 2-1 and win a place in the top flight.

Personal File

Position: Midfielder
Born: Martin Hugh Michael O'Neill, Kilrea
1 March 1952
Clubs: Distillery,
Nottingham Forrest,
Norwich City,
Manchester City,
Notts County

NI Caps: 64
NI Goals: 8

Games

Year	Opponent	Result	Score	G	Year	Opponent	Result	Score	G
1972	USSR	drew	1-1		1980	Australia	drew	1-1	1
	Spain	drew	1-1			Australia	won	2-1	
	Wales	drew	0-0		1981	Sweden	won	3-0	
1973	Portugal	drew	1-1	1		Portugal	lost	0-1	
	Cyprus	won	3-0			Portugal	won	1-0	
	England	lost	1-2			Scotland	lost	0-2	
	Scotland	won	2-1	1		Sweden	lost	0-1	
	Wales	won	1-0		1982	Scotland	drew	0-0	
1974	Bulgaria	drew	0-0			England	lost	0-4	
	Portugal	drew	1-1			France	lost	0-4	
	England	lost	0-1			Scotland	drew	1-1	
	Wales	lost	0-1			Yugoslavia	drew	0-0	
1975	Sweden	won	2-0	1		Honduras	drew	1-1	
	Yugoslavia	won	1-0			Spain	won	1-0	
	England	drew	0-0			Austria	drew	2-2	
	Scotland	lost	0-3			France	lost	1-4	
1976	Yugoslavia	lost	0-1		1983	Austria	lost	0-2	
1977	England	lost	1-2			West			
	Scotland	lost	0-3			Germany	won	1-0	
1978	Iceland	won	2-0			Albania	drew	0-0	
	Holland	lost	0-1			Turkey	won	2-1	1
	Scotland	drew	1-1	1		Albania	won	1-0	
	England	lost	0-1			Scotland	drew	0-0	
	Wales	lost	0-1			England	drew	0-0	
1979	Republic of Ireland	drew	0-0		1984	Austria	won	3-1	1
	Denmark	won	2-1			Turkey	lost	0-1	
	Bulgaria	won	2-0			West			
	England	lost	0-4			Germany	won	1-0	
	Bulgaria	won	2-0			England	lost	0-1	
	Denmark	lost	0-4			Wales	drew	1-1	
1980	Republic of Ireland	won	1-0			Finland	lost	0-1	
	Israel	drew	0-0		1985	Romania	won	3-2	1
	Australia	won	2-1			Finland	won	2-1	

Martin O'Neill

O'Neill kept the Foxes in the top half of the Premiership for the next four seasons before in the summer of 2000 leaving to manage Celtic.

In his first season at Parkhead, O'Neill, who said it took him two and a half seasons to agree to join the Glasgow giants, led the Bhoys to the Scottish Premier title and to Scottish Cup and League Cup success. Since then, O'Neill has led Celtic to the UEFA Cup Final in 2003 and to more domestic silverware in all competitions, most recently the Scottish Cup in May 2005. But despite this success he decided to resign from Parkhead to look after Geraldine, his wife who has been suffering from ill-health for some time.

"I've never planned anything in my life. I'm Irish – I don't plan!"

- Martin O'Neill on himself

Michael O'Neill

Michael O'Neill was playing for Coleraine when he joined Newcastle United as an 18-year-old in October 1987. The transfer created a record £100,000 fee for a Northern Ireland club.

Though he was very much a raw talent, he made a big impact on the First Division scene. His intricate style and ball skills knitted with those of Paul Gascoigne and in his first season he netted 13 goals in 21 games to be voted United's 'Player of the Season'.

But then he was struck by illness and injury, losing form dramatically. After being in and out of the side during the following campaign, he was transferred to Dundee United for £350,000.

O'Neill later had trials with both Everton and Middlesbrough before moving to Hibernian. He rediscovered much of the talent that had delighted the Tyneside crowd during his time at Easter Road, and this prompted a £300,000 transfer to Coventry City in the summer of 1996.

O'Neill, who won 31 caps for Northern Ireland came very close to netting a hat-trick at international level, for after scoring two of Northern Ireland's goals in a 5-3 defeat of Austria, he placed a shot against the post.

O'Neill failed to settle at Highfield Road and after an extended loan to Aberdeen in January1998, he was loaned to Reading until the end of the campaign. Playing either on the left-hand side or centre of midfield, O'Neill became the new Wigan manager Ray Mathias' first signing when he arrived at Springfield Park in September 1998. Still a quality performer, he went on to score the winner in the Autowindscreen Shield area final second leg at Wrexham as the Latics went on to win the trophy at Wembley.

He was enjoying an excellent 1999-2000 season until injuries forced him to miss the final third of the campaign including the play-offs.

The hardworking midfielder was made available for transfer in the close season and joined St Johnstone where he became a great favourite with the McDiarmid Park crowd.

Personal File

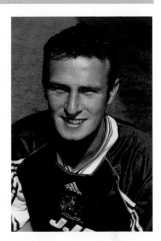

Position: Forward/Midfielder
Born: Michael Andrew Martin O'Neill,
Portadown
5 July 1969
Clubs: Coleraine,
Newcastle United,
Dundee United,
Hibernian,
Coventry City, Aberdeen (loan),
Reading (loan),
Wigan Athletic,
St Johnstone

NI Caps: 31
NI Goals: 4

Games

Year	Opponent	Result	Score	G	Year	Opponent	Result	Score	G
1988	Greece	lost	2-3		1993	Albania	won	3-0	
	Poland	drew	1-1			Albania	won	2-1	
	France	drew	0-0			Republic			
	Malta	won	3-0			of Ireland	lost	0-3	
1989	Republic					Spain	lost	1-3	
	of Ireland	drew	0-0			Lithuania	won	1-0	
	Hungary	lost	0-1			Latvia	won	2-1	
	Spain	lost	0-4		1994	Liechtenstein	won	4-1	
	Spain	lost	0-2		1995	Austria	won	2-1	
	Malta	won	2-0	1		Republic			
	Chile	lost	0-1			of Ireland	lost	0-4	
1990	Hungary	lost	1-2		1996	Liechtenstein	won	4-0	1
	Republic					Austria	won	5-3	2
	of Ireland	lost	0-3			Norway	lost	0-2	
1991	Poland	won	3-1			Sweden	lost	1-2	
1992	Faroe Islands	won	5-0		1997	Ukraine	lost	0-1	
	Scotland	lost	0-1			Armenia	drew	1-1	
	Germany	drew	1-1						

Darren Patterson

Able to play at right-back or in central defence, Darren Patterson began his career with West Bromwich Albion but in April 1989 after being unable to force his way into the club's League side, he left the Hawthorns to join Wigan Athletic on a free transfer.

He had to wait until the fifth game of the 1989-90 season before making his Football League debut, coming on as a substitute to replace Steve Senior in a 1-0 defeat at Leyton Orient. Though he appeared in 29 games in that campaign, more than half of those appearances were in the role of substitute. It was a similar story the following season but in 1991-92, this versatile player established himself as a first team regular.

O'Neill's form was so impressive that at the end of the season, Crystal Palace paid £225,000 for his services. He spent two seasons in the Eagles' reserve side before being given his chance in their League side. Shortly afterwards, despite making the first of 17 full international appearances for Northern Ireland, he was sold to Luton Town for £100,000.

However, his debut for the Hatters was delayed due to a tendon injury. The strong-tackling defender was later hampered by injuries, and had a brief loan spell at Preston North End before leaving Kenilworth Road to try his luck north of the border with Scottish Premier League side Dundee United.

He spent two seasons at Tannadice but during much of his time there, he was plagued by injuries. He then had a brief spell with York City before joining Oxford United. He spent virtually all the 2001-02 season recovering from an Achilles injury, and after making 20 appearances for the Manor Ground club, he was forced to retire.

Patterson stayed with the 'U's' after being appointed the club's Youth Teams coach and in November 2004 replaced Graham Rix as the club's manager. However, shortly afterwards he left the Manor Ground to be replaced by the Argentinian Ramon Diaz, who in turn parted company with the club towards the end of the 2004-05 season.

Personal File

Position: Defender
Born: Darren James Patterson, Belfast
15 October 1969
Clubs: West Bromwich Albion, Wigan Athletic, Crystal Palace, Luton Town, Preston North End (loan), Dundee United, York City, Oxford United

NI Caps: 17
NI Goals: 1

Games

Year	Opponent	Result	Score	G	Year	Opponent	Result	Score	G
1994	Colombia	lost	0-2		1996	Norway	lost	0-2	
	Mexico	lost	0-3			Sweden	lost	1-2	
1995	Republic of Ireland	lost	0-4		1998	Switzerland	won	1-0	1
	Republic of Ireland	drew	1-1			Spain	lost	1-4	
	Latvia	won	1-0		1999	Finland	won	1-0	
	Canada	lost	0-2			Moldova	drew	2-2	
	Chile	lost	1-2			Germany	lost	0-3	
	Latvia	lost	1-2			Moldova	drew	0-0	
						Republic of Ireland	won	1-0	

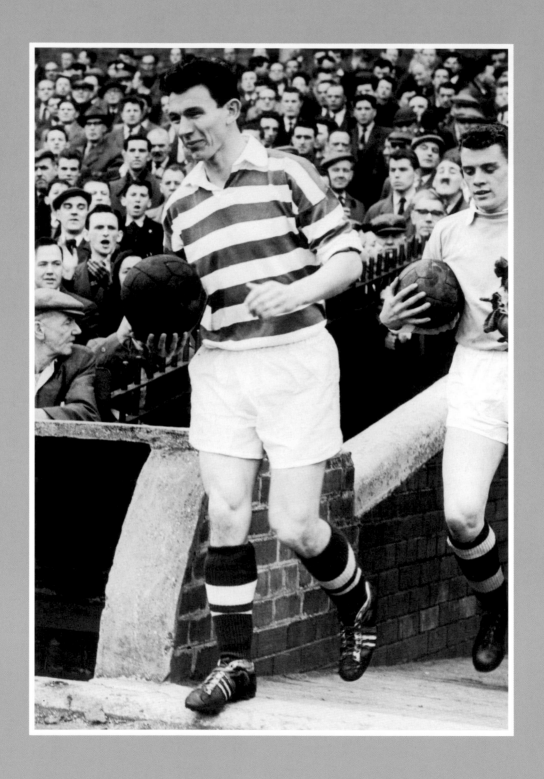

Bertie Peacock

Having started his career with Coleraine, Bertie Peacock joined Glentoran, for whom he scored the only goal of the 1949 Irish Cup Final against Barney Cannon's Derry City. Shortly afterwards he joined Celtic and made his debut at inside-left in a Scottish League Cup tie against Aberdeen.

After netting the only goal of the game against East Fife on the opening day of the 1950-51 season, Bertie Peacock became an established member of the Celtic side. He was Charlie Tully's left-wing partner in the youngest-ever Celtic team to win the Scottish Cup when Motherwell were beaten at Hampden Park in April 1951.

Northern Ireland picked him and Tully for the game against Scotland at Windsor Park in October 1951 but the visitors won 2-0. A year later, Peacock dropped back to left-half and it wasn't long before the great Celtic half-back line of Evans, Stein and Peacock began to feature regularly for the Bhoys.

After helping Celtic win the double in 1953-54 he was a member of the first-ever Celtic team to win the League Cup in 1956. He was then appointed Celtic's captain and in October 1957 helped the club retain the League Cup by beating Rangers 7-1 at Hampden.

Peacock was part of the wonderful Irish performance in the World Cup of 1958 when his energy so impressed the Swedish journalists, they nicknamed him 'The Little Black Ant' because his jet black hair seemed to be all over the park against Czechoslovakia (twice), Argentina and West Germany. In the play-off game against the Czechs, Peacock was badly injured but still managed to 'score' a disallowed goal in extra-time.

After missing the Cup Final against Hibs in 1961, he was fit for the replay but was told he could play for Northern Ireland in Rome if he wanted. Celtic lost the Cup while the discarded skipper played the three games of his life against Italy, Greece and West Germany and all away from home.

Peacock, who scored 50 goals in 453 games was an all-time Celtic great and not a bad manager either, taking charge of the national team from 1962 to 1967 and later taking his beloved Coleraine to their first-ever Irish League Championship in 1974.

Personal File

Position: Left-Half
Born: Robert Peacock,
Coleraine
29 September 1928
Died: 22 July 2004
Clubs: Coleraine, Glentoran,
Glasgow Celtic,
Coleraine,
Morton (loan),
Hamilton Steelers (Canada)

NI Caps: 31
NI Goals: 2

Games

Year	Opponent	Result	Score	G	Year	Opponent	Result	Score	G
1952	Scotland	lost	0-2		1958	West Germany	drew	2-2	
1953	France	lost	1-3			Czechoslovakia	won	2-1	
1954	Wales	won	2-1		1959	England	drew	3-3	1
1955	England	lost	0-2			Scotland	drew	2-2	
	Scotland	drew	2-2			Wales	won	4-1	1
1956	Scotland	won	2-1		1960	Scotland	lost	0-4	
	England	lost	0-3			England	lost	1-2	
1957	Wales	drew	0-0		1961	England	lost	2-5	
	Italy	lost	0-1			West Germany	lost	3-4	
	Portugal	won	3-0			Scotland	lost	2-5	
1958	Scotland	drew	1-1			Italy	lost	2-3	
	England	won	3-2			Greece	lost	1-2	
	Italy	drew	2-2			West Germany	lost	1-2	
	Italy	lost	1-3		1962	Scotland	lost	1-6	
	Wales	drew	1-1						
	Czechoslovakia	won	1-0						
	Argentina	lost	1-3						

Jim Platt

A Middlesbrough career that was to span more than a decade and see probably the best ever Boro side, began when manager Stan Anderson paid £7,000 for the 18-year-old Jim Platt. The young keeper had impressed playing for Ballymena and before joining the Teeside club, had interested Liverpool. Platt had a three-week trial at Anfield but the signing of Ray Clemence thwarted the move and Liverpool's loss proved to be Middlesbrough's gain.

After a homesick season on the sidelines, Platt replaced Willie Whigham as the club's first choice keeper and ended that 1971-72 season, his first in the side, as the club's 'Player of the Year'.

The following season, Platt was ever-present and he played a crucial role as Boro stormed to the Second Division title in 1973-74, conceding just 28 goals in 40 games including an impressive 23 clean sheets. Following the arrival of Jim Stewart, Platt's appearances were restricted and he spent loan spells with both Hartlepool United and Cardiff City. But he soon bounced back and it wasn't until midway through the 1982-83 season that he once again lost his place.

His sterling performances for Middlesbrough brought him recognition for Northern Ireland. He earned 23 caps and it was only the presence of the great Pat Jennings that restricted his appearances. Platt made his debut for Northern Ireland in 1976 as a substitute against Israel and went on to feature in his country's strongest period and played one game in the 1982 World Cup Finals.

Having played in 481 first team games, Platt left Ayresome Park and returned to Northern Ireland and Ballymena where he was player-manager. After working with several clubs and running his own printing and wholesaling business, he returned to the north-east as assistant to former Boro team-mate David Hodgson at Darlington. When Hodgson left, Platt took over the reins but was dismissed early in the 1996-97 season, though he later managed non-League Gateshead.

Personal File

Position: Goalkeeper
Born: James Archibald Platt,
Ballymena
26 January 1952
Clubs: Ballymena,
Middlesbrough,
Hartlepool United (loan),
Cardiff City (loan),
Ballymena

NI Caps: 23

Games

Year	Opponent	Result	Score	G	Year	Opponent	Result	Score	G
1976	Israel	drew	1-1		1982	France	lost	1-4	
1978	Scotland	drew	1-1			Scotland	drew	1-1	
	England	lost	0-1			Wales	lost	0-3	
	Wales	lost	0-1			Austria	drew	2-2	
1980	Scotland	won	1-0		1983	Austria	lost	0-2	
	England	lost	1-5			West			
	Wales	won	1-0			Germany	won	1-0	
	Australia	won	2-1			Albania	won	1-0	
	Australia	drew	1-1			Turkey	won	2-1	
	Australia	won	2 1		1984	England	lost	0-1	
1981	Sweden	lost	0-1			Wales	drew	1-1	
	Portugal	won	1-0		1986	Morocco	won	2-1	

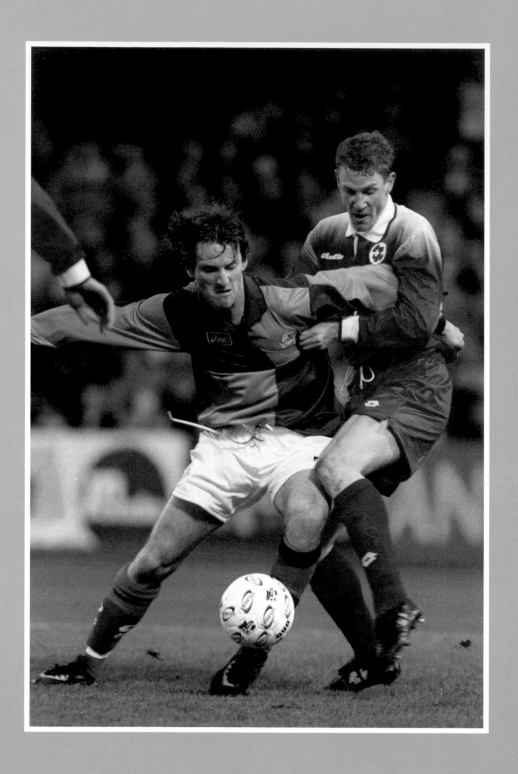

James Quinn

James Quinn began his Football League career with Birmingham City but after just four appearances for the Blues, he left St Andrew's and joined Blackpool in a £25,000 deal.

After making his Seasiders' debut as a substitute for Bryan Griffiths in a 3-2 defeat at Cambridge United on the opening day of the 1993-94 season and scoring Blackpool's second goal, he found himself just starting one game in that campaign!

Following a loan spell with Stockport County, Quinn continued to improve. Using his pace to unsettle defenders, he found more steadiness in front of goal, scoring 10 times in 42 games. In the opening game of the 1995-96 season, Quinn scored one of the campaign's quickest goals as he netted just seconds into the 1-1 draw at Bristol City.

His 14 goals led to him being called up for Northern Ireland's full squad, having scored for the 'B' side against the Norwegian Olympic XI.

Over the next season or so, the young Blackpool striker continued to be the subject of transfer speculation and though a bad injury forced him to miss a number of games, within weeks of returning to first team action, he had joined West Bromwich Albion for £500,000 in February 1998.

Quinn, who had scored 47 goals in 182 games for the Seasiders, was an important member of the Baggies' squad in his early days at the Hawthorns but following the appointment of Gary Megson as Albion manager, he found himself in and out of the side. Preferring to occupy a withdrawn midfield role, he found it difficult to play up front alongside Lee Hughes. However, he still managed to add to his collection of international caps for Northern Ireland whilst battling away in the reserves and on loan at Notts County and Bristol Rovers. Quinn who has now made 36 appearances for his country, later left Albion to continue his career in Dutch football with Willem II.

"I am happy to play the role of a foil for David Healy. As long as the team does well I am happy."

- James Quinn on the Northern Ireland Football team

Personal File

Position: Striker
Born: Stephen James Quinn, Coventry 15 December 1974
Clubs: Birmingham City, Blackpool, Stockport County (loan), West Bromwich Albion, Notts County (loan), Bristol Rovers (loan), Willem II (Holland)

NI Caps: 36
NI Goals: 4

Games

Year	Opponent	Result	Score	G	Year	Opponent	Result	Score	G
1996	Sweden	lost	1-2		2000	Luxembourg	won	3-1	1
1997	Albania	won	2-0			Malta	won	3-0	1
	Italy	lost	0-2		2001	Yugoslavia	lost	1-2	
	Belgium	won	3-0	1		Bulgaria	lost	0-1	
	Portugal	drew	0-0			Czech Republic	lost	1-3	
	Ukraine	lost	1-2		2002	Malta	won	1-0	
	Armenia	drew	0-0		2003	Cyprus	drew	0-0	
	Thailand	drew	0-0			Finland	lost	0-1	
1998	Germany	lost	1-3			Armenia	lost	0-1	
	Albania	lost	0-1			Greece	lost	0-2	
	Slovakia	won	1-0		2004	Serbia & Montenegro	drew	1-1	1
	Switzerland	won	1-0			Barbados	drew	1-1	
1999	Turkey	lost	0-3			Trinidad & Tobago	won	3-0	
	Finland	won	1-0		2005	Poland	lost	0-3	
	Republic of Ireland	won	1-0			Wales	drew	2-2	
2000	France	lost	0-1			Azerbaijan	drew	0-0	
	Turkey	lost	0-3			Austria	drew	3-3	
	Germany	lost	0-4						
	Finland	lost	1-4						

Jimmy Quinn

Jimmy Quinn was playing non-League football for Oswestry Town when Swindon Town signed him in December 1981. In his first two seasons at the County Ground, Quinn made just a handful of appearances and it was midway through the 1983-84 season before he established himself as a first team regular with the Robins.

Surprisingly he was allowed to leave Swindon in the close season and joined Blackburn Rovers for £32,000. It was while on Rovers' books that Quinn made the first of his 46 international appearances, scoring for Northern Ireland in a 3-0 defeat of Israel. He netted 17 goals in 71 League games for the Ewood Park club before returning to Swindon for a second spell in December 1986.

Playing alongside Dave Bamber he began to develop a predatory knack for goalscoring and after scoring nine goals in 22 games, helped the club win promotion to the Second Division in his second season back at the County Ground. In 1987-88 Quinn was the club's top scorer with 21 goals in 42 games as they finished in mid-table in Division Two.

In June 1988 Leicester City signed Quinn for a tribunal-set fee of £210,000. He was at Filbert Street for only six months, with more than half his 31 League outings for the Foxes being as a substitute. His next stop was Bradford City before he joined West Ham United in December 1989. That season he scored 13 goals in 20 games but in the club's promotion-winning season of 1990-91 he made only 16 starts due to the fierce competition from Frank McAvennie and the newly signed Iain Dowie. After scoring 22 goals in 57 games for the Hammers he joined Bournemouth, before moving on to Reading in the summer of 1992.

He led Reading's Second Division Championship effort from the front and was the League's top scorer with 35 goals. When Mark McGhee left, Quinn became Reading's player-manager. He led the club to the play-off final against Bolton, which they lost 4-3.

In July 1997 Quinn moved to Peterborough United as Barry Fry's right-hand man and took his total of goals for his eight clubs to 211 in 571 games before replacing Steve McMahon as Swindon manager. Later losing out to Colin Todd, he took over the reins at non-League Weymouth.

Personal File

Position: Forward
Born: James Martin Quinn,
Belfast
18 November 1959
Clubs: Oswestry Town,
Swindon Town,
Blackburn Rovers,
Swindon Town,
Leicester City, Bradford City,
West Ham United,
Bournemouth, Reading,
Peterborough United

NI Caps: 46
NI Goals: 12

Games

Year	Opponent	Result	Score	G	Year	Opponent	Result	Score	G
1985	Israel	won	3-0	1	1990	Hungary	lost	1-2	
	Finland	won	2-1			Norway	lost	2-3	1
	England	lost	0-1		1991	Yugoslavia	lost	1-4	
	Spain	drew	0-0		1992	Lithuania	drew	2-2	
	Turkey	won	2-0		1993	Spain	drew	0-0	
1986	Turkey	drew	0-0			Denmark	lost	0-1	
	Romania	won	1-0	1		Albania	won	2-1	
	England	drew	0-0			Republic of			
	France	drew	0-0			Ireland	lost	0-3	
	Denmark	drew	1-1			Latvia	won	2-1	
	Morocco	won	2-1	1	1994	Latvia	won	2-0	1
1987	England	lost	0-3			Denmark	lost	0-1	
	Turkey	drew	0-0			Republic of			
1988	Yugoslavia	lost	0-3			Ireland	drew	1-1	1
	Turkey	won	1-0	1		Romania	won	2-0	
	Greece	lost	2-3			Liechtenstein	won	4-1	2
	Poland	drew	1-1			Colombia	lost	0-2	
	France	drew	0-0			Mexico	lost	0-3	
	Malta	won	3-0	1	1995	Portugal	lost	1-2	1
1989	Republic of					Austria	won	2-1	
	Ireland	drew	0-0			Latvia	won	1-0	
	Hungary	lost	0-1		1996	Liechtenstein	won	4-0	1
	Spain	lost	0-4			Austria	won	5-3	
	Spain	lost	0-2						
	Malta	won	2-0						
	Chile	lost	0-1						

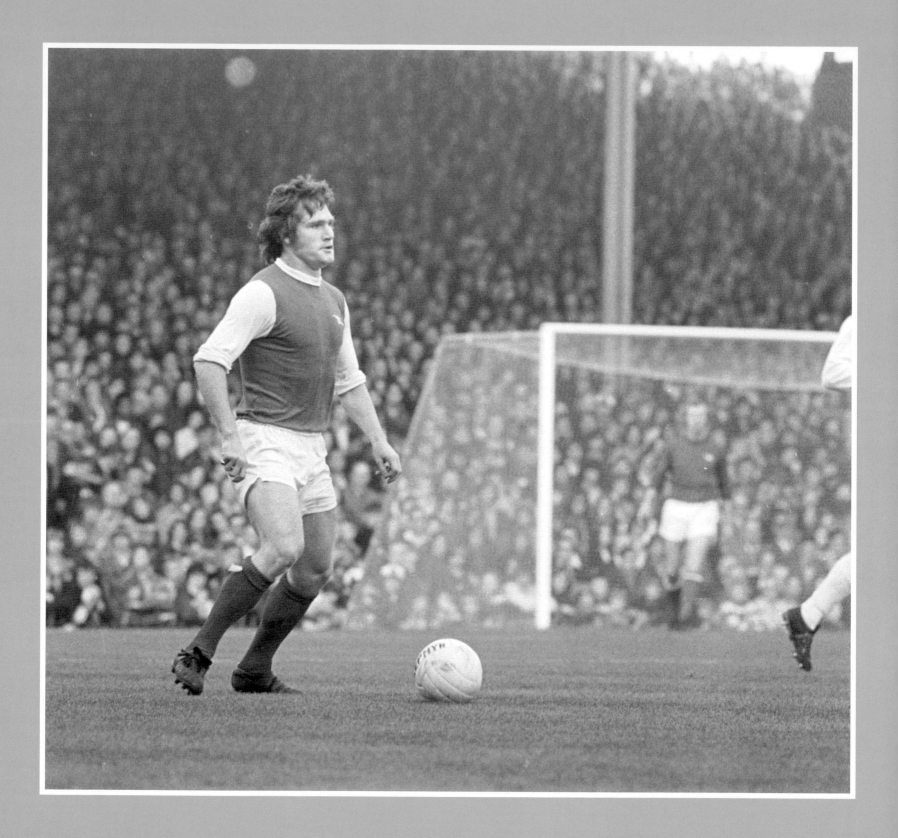

Pat Rice

Everyone remembers Charlie George as the Arsenal fan that grew up to play for the team. But this was also the case with Pat Rice – having moved to London with his family when he was 10. Whereas George never fulfilled his enormous potential, Rice, a determined, quick and agile full-back, exceeded even his own expectations in a fabulous playing career at Highbury, spanning 18 years from 1964 to 1982.

One of the most loyal players the club has ever had, Rice played in no fewer than five Wembley FA Cup Finals – a record he shares with Joe Hulme, Frank Stapleton and Johnny Giles. He also won 49 caps for Northern Ireland and played in 527 League and Cup games for the Gunners – a total only bettered by George Armstrong and David O'Leary.

Despite this, Pat's career had a very unimpressive start. He appeared in just a handful of first team matches in his first five years at Highbury. However, when Peter Storey switched from right-back to midfield, Pat Rice was drafted into the right-back position for the beginning of the 1970-71 season.

In his first full season, he helped Arsenal to the incredible League and FA Cup double and over the next 10 seasons, Pat Rice was undoubtedly Arsenal's most consistent player. Appearing in every league match during 1971-72, 1975-76 and 1976-77 Rice became one of the few Arsenal players to be an ever-present in three different seasons.

Rice was made Arsenal captain in 1977 and skippered them to three consecutive FA Cup Finals between 1978 and 1980 and the European Cup Winners' Cup Final of 1980. By this time he was also leading his country and won the last of his caps against England in October 1979.

The following month, Rice was transferred to Watford, helping the Hornets gain promotion to the First Division in 1981-82 and then finish next season as runners-up to Liverpool.

In 1984 Rice returned to Highbury as youth team coach and over the next ten years he helped the Gunners to two FA Youth Cup Final wins, and discovered the likes of Andy Cole, Kevin Campbell, Paul Merson, David Rocastle and Michael Thomas to name but a few.

Now the club's assistant-manager, having helped the Gunners to the double in 1997-98 and the Premier League title in seasons 2001-02 and 2003-04, Pat Rice will forever be remembered for his dedication to the club he loves and supports.

Personal File

Position: Right-back
Born: Patrick James Rice,
Belfast
17 March 1949
Clubs: Arsenal,
Watford

NI Caps: 49

Games

Year	Opponent	Result	Score	G	Year	Opponent	Result	Score	G
1969	Israel	won	3-2		1976	Norway	won	3-0	
1970	USSR	lost	0-2			Yugoslavia	lost	0-1	
1971	England	lost	0-1			Israel	drew	1-1	
	Scotland	won	1-0			Scotland	lost	0-3	
	Wales	won	1-0			England	lost	0-4	
1972	USSR	drew	1-1			Wales	lost	0-1	
	Spain	drew	1-1		1977	Holland	drew	2-2	
	England	won	1-0			Belgium	lost	0-2	
	Scotland	lost	0-2			West			
	Wales	drew	0-0			Germany	lost	0-5	
1973	Bulgaria	lost	0-3			England	lost	1-2	
	Cyprus	lost	0-1			Scotland	lost	0-3	
	England	lost	1-2			Iceland	lost	0-1	
	Scotland	won	2-1		1978	Iceland	won	2-0	
	Wales	won	1-0			Holland	lost	0-1	
1974	Bulgaria	drew	0-0			Belgium	won	2-0	
	Portugal	drew	1-1		1979	Republic			
	Scotland	won	1-0			of Ireland	drew	0-0	
	England	lost	0-1			Denmark	won	2-1	
	Wales	lost	0-1			England	lost	0-4	
1975	Norway	lost	1-2			England	lost	0-2	
	Yugoslavia	won	1-0			Scotland	lost	0-1	
	England	drew	0-0			Wales	drew	1-1	
	Scotland	lost	0-3			Denmark	lost	0-4	
	Wales	won	1-0		1980	England	drew	1-1	
1976	Sweden	lost	1-2						

Derek Spence

Blond striker Derek Spence began his career with Crusaders before joining Oldham Athletic in September 1970. Unable to win a regular place at Boundary Park, he moved to Bury and in 1973-74, helped the Shakers win promotion to the Third Division. He had scored 44 goals in 140 League games when Blackpool manager Allan Brown brought him to Bloomfield Road in October 1976.

He made his Seasiders' debut in a 1-0 win over Brian Clough's Nottingham Forest, complementing the skills of Mickey Walsh and Bob Hatton. Sadly a serious injury forced him to miss the entire 1977-78 season when the club were relegated to the Third Division for the first time in their history. In 1978-79, Spence was back to his best and was the club's leading scorer with 17 goals including a hat-trick in a 3-1 home win over Carlisle United. Midway through the following season, Spence, who had scored 24 goals in 98 games left Bloomfield Road to play for Olympiakos of Greece.

He later returned to Football League action with Fourth Division Southend United. The fact that Spence was still playing international football for Northern Ireland while playing in the League's basement, marked him out as something special. His 21 goals in the Shrimps' Championship-winning season of 1980-81 including a hat-trick against York, was rounded off with a typical Spence goal. A deep diagonal cross, met after a surging run, shrugging off the full-back on the way and a one-on-one which was unfair in its equality as the ball was smashed past the keeper, un-muddied by the pointlessness of diving.

Derek Spence later saw out his career with another spell at Bury, prior to playing in Hong Kong and coaching youngsters.

Personal File

Position: Forward
Born: Derek William Spence, Belfast 18 January 1952
Clubs: Crusaders, Oldham Athletic, Bury, Blackpool, Olympiakos (Greece), Southend United, Bury, Sea Bee (Hong Kong)

NI Caps: 29
NI Goals: 3

Games

Year	Opponent	Result	Score	G	Year	Opponent	Result	Score	G
1975	Yugoslavia	won	1-0		1979	Republic of Ireland	drew	0-0	
	England	drew	0-0			Denmark	won	2-1	1
	Scotland	lost	0-3			England	lost	0-4	
	Wales	won	1-0			Bulgaria	won	2-0	
1976	Sweden	lost	1-2			England	lost	0-2	
	Israel	drew	1-1			Scotland	lost	0-1	
	Scotland	lost	0-3			Wales	drew	1-1	1
	England	lost	0-4			Denmark	lost	0-4	
	Wales	lost	0-1		1980	Republic of Ireland	won	1-0	
1977	Holland	drew	2-2	1		Israel	drew	0-0	
	West Germany	lost	0-5			Australia	won	2-1	
	England	lost	1-2		1981	Scotland	drew	1-1	
	Scotland	lost	0-3			Sweden	lost	0-1	
	Wales	drew	1-1		1982	France	lost	0-4	
	Iceland	lost	0-1						

Ian Stewart

A winger with great control and a clever, but direct style, Ian Stewart was a triallist with Everton as a schoolboy but it was Queen's Park Rangers who took him on as a professional in May 1980. Developing through the youth scheme, he made his debut for the Loftus Road club as a substitute for Tommy Langley in a 2-1 defeat at Blackburn Rovers during October 1980.

After a handful of appearances the following season, Stewart won a regular place in the Rangers side and in 1982-83 helped them win the Second Division Championship, although an injury at Derby midway through the campaign restricted his appearances. On his return to full fitness he had a brief loan spell with Millwall, but in 1983-84 he was back in the No.8 shirt as Rangers finished fifth in the top flight. Never a prolific scorer, he did net in consecutive wins over Stoke City and Arsenal, but they proved to be his only league goals in his stay at Loftus Road.

He also scored two goals in his 31 appearances for Northern Ireland, each time his strike proving to be the only goal of the game as West Germany were beaten by a stunning volley in November 1982 and Albania the following April.

In August 1985, Stewart joined Newcastle United, with manager Willie McFaul paying £100,000 for the player's services. Early impressions of Ian Stewart's talent were most favourable. He could provide a dangerous cross and was able on occasions to hit a powerful shot, but by the time of his last outing for the Magpies during the 1986-87 season, he had been labelled with the 'inconsistent' tag.

Taking part in the 1986 World Cup Finals, Ian Stewart never fulfilled his potential, and after leaving St James Park his career declined. After brief appearances for Portsmouth and Brentford, he ended his first-class days with Aldershot though he rarely showed the skill that had taken him almost to the top.

Personal File

Position: Left-winger
Born: Ian Edwin Stewart,
Belfast
10 September 1961
Clubs: Queen's Park Rangers,
Millwall (loan),
Newcastle United,
Portsmouth,
Brentford (loan),
Aldershot

NI Caps: 31
NI Goals: 2

Games

Year	Opponent	Result	Score	G	Year	Opponent	Result	Score	G
1982	France	lost	0-4		1985	Romania	won	3-2	
1983	Austria	lost	0-2			Israel	won	3-0	
	West					Finland	won	2-1	
	Germany	won	1-0	1		England	lost	0-1	
	Albania	drew	0-0			Spain	drew	0-0	
	Turkey	won	2-1			Turkey	won	2-0	
	Albania	won	1-0	1	1986	Romania	won	1-0	
	Scotland	drew	0-0			England	drew	0-0	
	England	drew	0-0			Denmark	drew	1-1	
	Wales	lost	0-1			Morocco	won	2-1	
1984	Austria	won	3-1			Algeria	drew	1-1	
	Turkey	lost	0-1			Spain	lost	1-2	
	West					Brazil	lost	0-3	
	Germany	won	1-0		1987	England	lost	0-3	
	Scotland	won	2-0			Israel	drew	1-1	
	England	lost	0-1						
	Wales	drew	1-1						
	Finland	lost	0-1						

Gerry Taggart

He began with his local side Hillsborough Boys before spending a season with Glenavon. Manchester City signed him as a trainee and during 1988-89 he was a member of their youth side that reached the final of the FA Youth Cup. After making his first team debut in a 1-0 win at Portsmouth in February 1989, he gave some impressive displays in helping City to runners-up spot in the Second Division.

City's former manager Mel Machin paid £75,000 to take him to Barnsley and after scoring on his debut helped the Yorkshire club avoid the drop from the Second Division.

In March 1990 he won the first of his 51 full international caps to add to youth and Under 23 honours when he played against Norway at Windsor Park.

Taggart went on to play in 247 games for Barnsley before signing for Bolton Wanderers in the summer of 1995. He suffered with injuries and loss of form in his first season at Bolton, but bounced back with some sterling performances the following term. While at Burnden Park he earned a recall into the Northern Ireland squad and celebrated by scoring in a World Cup qualifying 1-1 draw against Germany in Nuremburg.

Taggart earned his little piece of Burnden history by scoring in the Wanderers' final game against Charlton Athletic, taking great delight in letting his team-mates know that it was down to his new red boots! Selected as a member of the PFA award-winning First Division side, he again suffered with injuries and after appearing in 81 games, joined Leicester City on a free transfer under the Bosman ruling.

In 1999-2000, he was voted the Foxes' 'Player of the Year' and as well as winning a Worthington Cup winners' medal, earned a recall to the national side when he captained Northern Ireland against Hungary. He also captained the national side when gaining his 50th cap but Norway spoiled the occasion by winning 4-0. A serious knee injury then restricted his appearances for Leicester but he played his part in helping the club reach the Premiership prior to a move to Stoke City in 2003.

"You have to go into every match with self-belief."

-Gerry Taggart

Personal File

Position: Central defender
Born: Gerald Paul Taggart,
Belfast
18 October 1970
Clubs: Manchester City,
Barnsley,
Bolton Wanderers,
Leicester City,
Stoke City

NI Caps: 51
NI Goals: 7

Games

Year	Opponent	Result	Score	G	Year	Opponent	Result	Score	G
1990	Norway	lost	2-3			Colombia	lost	0-2	
	Uruguay	won	1-0			Mexico	lost	0-3	
1991	Yugoslavia	lost	0-2		1995	Portugal	lost	1-2	
	Denmark	drew	1-1			Austria	won	2-1	
	Austria	drew	0-0			Republic			
	Poland	won	3-1	2		of Ireland	lost	0-4	
	Faroe Islands	drew	1-1			Republic			
1992	Faroe Islands	won	5-0			of Ireland	drew	1-1	
	Austria	won	2-1			Canada	lost	0-2	
	Denmark	lost	1-2	1		Chile	lost	1-2	
	Scotland	lost	0-1			Latvia	lost	1-2	
	Lithuania	drew	2-2	1	1997	Germany	drew	1-1	1
	Germany	drew	1-1			Albania	won	2-0	
1993	Albania	won	3-0			Italy	lost	0-2	
	Spain	drew	0-0			Belgium	won	3-0	
	Denmark	lost	0-1			Portugal	drew	0-0	
	Albania	won	2-1			Ukraine	lost	1-2	
	Republic					Armenia	drew	0-0	
	of Ireland	lost	0-3		1998	Germany	lost	1-3	
	Spain	lost	1-3			Portugal	lost	0-1	
	Lithuania	won	1-0			Spain	lost	1-4	1
	Latvia	won	2-1	1	2000	Hungary	lost	0-1	
1994	Latvia	won	2-0		2001	Malta	won	1-0	
	Denmark	lost	0-1			Denmark	drew	1-1	
	Republic					Iceland	lost	0-1	
	of Ireland	drew	1-1			Norway	lost	0-4	
	Romania	won	2-0		2003	Spain	lost	0-3	
	Liechtenstein	won	4-1						

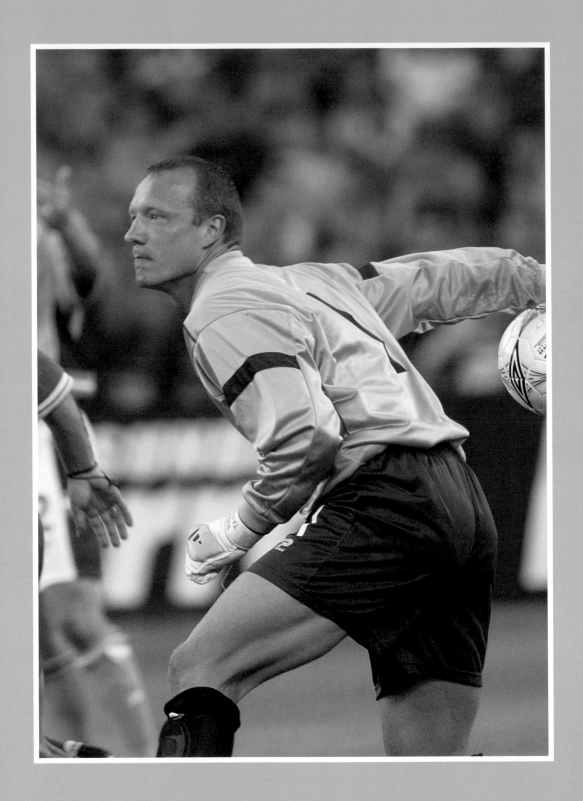

Maik Taylor

German-born goalkeeper Maik Taylor began his Football League career with Barnet, having signed for the Underhill club from non-League Farnborough, where he won a Beazer Homes League Championship medal, in the summer of 1995.

He created such an excellent impression with Barnet that their manager, former England keeper Ray Clemence, reckoned him to be the best in the Third Division. It wasn't long before Southampton paid £500,000 to take him to The Dell, where his displays between the posts contributed enormously to calming a nervous Saints' defence that ultimately avoided the drop from the Premiership. However, following the arrival of Paul Jones from Stockport, Taylor found himself out of the Southampton side and in November 1997 he moved to Fulham for a fee of £800,000.

A good shot stopper, he kept 12 clean sheets in 28 games, this form leading to him winning his first international honour as an over-age player for the Northern Ireland Under 21 side that beat Switzerland 2-1 in April 1998. The following season he helped Fulham win the Second Division Championship, making many brilliant saves in the unbeaten run of 15 games which saw just six goals conceded. This resulted in him gaining his first Northern Ireland caps, along with a well-deserved place in the PFA Division Two side. He continued to perform heroics for the Cottagers and in 2000-01 proved himself to be the best keeper in the First Division by recording a total of 19 clean sheets. He was rewarded by his fellow professionals with a place in the PFA First Division team.

Almost unbeatable in one-on-one situations, he lost his place in Fulham's Premiership side to Dutch international Edwin van der Saar, yet he remained first-choice for Northern Ireland. Taylor began the 2003-04 season on loan at Birmingham City but the move was such a success that a permanent transfer was eventually arranged. Capped 43 times by Northern Ireland, his double save at Manchester City in February 2004, when he seemingly clawed the ball out when it was behind him, was world class.

"We may be rivals for the jersey, but we're the best of friends and help each other whatever way we can."

- Maik Taylor on Roy Carroll

Personal File

Position: Goal Keeper
Born: Maik Stefan Taylor,
          Hildeshein, Germany
          4 September 1971
Clubs: Farnborough Town,
          Barnet,
          Southampton,
          Fulham,
          Birmingham City

NI Caps: 43

Games

Year	Opponent	Result	Score	G	Year	Opponent	Result	Score	G
1999	Germany	lost	0-3		2003	Cyprus	drew	0-0	
	Moldova	drew	0-0			Spain	lost	0-3	
	Canada	drew	1-1			Ukraine	drew	0-0	
	Republic					Finland	lost	0-1	
	of Ireland	won	1-0			Armenia	lost	0-1	
2000	France	lost	0-1			Greece	lost	0-2	
	Turkey	lost	0-3			Italy	lost	0-2	
	Germany	lost	0-4			Spain	drew	0-0	
	Finland	lost	1-4		2004	Ukraine	drew	0-0	
	Luxembourg	won	3-1			Armenia	lost	0-1	
	Malta	won	3-0			Greece	lost	0-1	
	Hungary	lost	0-1			Norway	lost	1-4	
2001	Yugoslavia	lost	1-2			Estonia	won	1-0	
	Norway	lost	0-4			Serbia &			
	Bulgaria	lost	0-1			Montenegro	drew	1-1	
	Czech					Barbados	drew	1-1	
	Republic	lost	1-3			St Kitts &			
2002	Denmark	drew	1-1			Nevis	won	2-0	
	Iceland	won	3-0			Trinidad &			
	Malta	won	1-0			Tobago	won	3-0	
	Poland	lost	1-4		2005	Poland	lost	0-3	
	Liechtenstein	drew	0-0			Wales	drew	2-2	
	Spain	lost	0-5			Azerbaijan	drew	0-0	
						Canada	lost	0-1	
						England	lost	0-4	

Sammy Todd

It was while representing Northern Ireland schoolboys that English clubs were soon alerted to Sammy Todd's potential. He was invited for trials with Leeds United but was not impressed and decided to stay in Ulster for a little longer, signing amateur forms for Glentoran.

In the summer of 1962, he was again persuaded to come to England, on this occasion by Burnley's Northern Ireland scout Alex Scott. This time he was not discouraged and soon signed professional forms for the Clarets in September 1962.

Todd made his Burnley debut in the last game of the 1963-64 season. It was a memorable occasion for the soft spoken Irishman as the Clarets crushed Spurs 7-2. Tall and flaxen-haired, Sammy Todd was equally at home in midfield or defence and was only 19 when he won the first of four Under 23 caps.

Then, still not quite 21, he made his full international debut alongside team-mates Alex Elder and Willie Irvine in Northern Ireland's 4-1 victory against Mexico at Windsor Park in June 1966.

With the arrival of Colin Waldron and Jim Thomson at Turf Moor, Todd's days in the Burnley side seemed numbered but in 1969-70 he won back his place and enjoyed his most consistent spell in the first team. Following the appointment of Jimmy Adamson as Burnley manager, replacing Harry Potts, Todd found himself surplus to requirements.

In May 1970 Todd left for Sheffield Wednesday, newly relegated to Division Two for £40,000. After making a promising start to his Hillsborough career, he began to struggle for consistency, although he won three more Irish caps to go with the eight he collected while at Turf Moor.

In February 1974 he assisted Mansfield Town for a brief loan spell and his half a dozen games for the Stags were his last in the Football League before being released by the Owls. He joined Great Harwood in the Lancashire Combination later playing and coaching at nearby Padiham.

Personal File

Position: Wing-half
Born: Samuel Todd,
Belfast
22 September 1945
Clubs: Leeds United,
Glentoran, Burnley,
Sheffield Wednesday,
Mansfield Town (loan),
Great Harwood,
Padiham

NI Caps: 11

Games

Year	Opponent	Result	Score	G
1966	Mexico	won	4-1	
1967	England	lost	0-2	
1968	Wales	lost	0-2	
1969	England	lost	1-3	
	Scotland	drew	1-1	
	Wales	drew	0-0	
1970	USSR	drew	0-0	
	Scotland	lost	0-1	
1971	Spain	lost	0-3	
	Cyprus	won	3-0	
	Cyprus	won	5-0	

Norman Uprichard

Goalkeeper Norman Uprichard began his career with Distillery before joining Arsenal in the summer of 1948. Unable to make the grade with the Gunners, he moved to Swindon Town in November 1949 and made his debut against Torquay United on Christmas Eve.

Despite being in goal when the Robins suffered some heavy defeats – notably 8-2 at Southend United and the club's record defeat of 9-0 at Torquay United, Uprichard won the first of 18 full international caps for Northern Ireland and it wasn't long before he was signed by First Division Portsmouth.

He marked his Pompey debut with an own goal against Spurs but had the last laugh as the south coast club won 2-1. His second game for Portsmouth against Sheffield Wednesday at Hillsborough was also dramatic in that with Pompey leading 4-3, Uprichard suffered smashed knuckles in a last minute unsighted clash with Derek Dooley. Happily he recovered and returned to the Portsmouth side by Christmas, wearing a special padded glove.

Although he was only a small keeper, Uprichard soon won over the Portsmouth crowd. Renowned for his bravery, he became famous for his one-on-one saves and also for punching the ball out among a crowd of players.

Known as 'Black Jake', his popularity was such that he needed his goalkeeper's cap to collect all the sweets thrown to him at warm-ups before games.

He appeared in the 1958 World Cup Finals in Sweden and it was in this competition in the match against Czechoslovakia that he played for 70 minutes with a broken hand, but still helped his side to a 2-1 win.

Despite suffering from a catalogue of injuries during his seven-year stay at Fratton Park, he appeared in 191 games for the club. Once, when he was not fit to keep goal, he appeared on the wing for the reserves and scored two goals! He left Portsmouth for Southend United in July 1959 and after short spells at Hastings and Ramsgate, took a pub in Sussex before returning to Ireland to run the bar at Queen's University.

Personal File

Position: Goalkeeper
Born: William Norman McCourt Uprichard,
Portadown
20 April 1928
Clubs: Distillery,
Arsenal,
Swindon Town,
Portsmouth,
Southend United,
Hastings, Ramsgate

NI Caps: 18

Games

Year	Opponent	Result	Score	G	Year	Opponent	Result	Score	G
1952	Scotland	lost	0-2		1955	Wales	lost	2-3	
	England	lost	0-2		1956	Scotland	won	2-1	
	Wales	lost	0-3			England	lost	0-3	
1953	England	drew	2-2			Wales	drew	1-1	
	Scotland	drew	1-1		1958	Scotland	drew	1-1	
	France	lost	1-3			Italy	lost	1-3	
	Wales	lost	2-3			Czechoslovakia	won	2-1	
1955	England	lost	0-2		1959	Spain	lost	2-6	
	Scotland	drew	2-2			Scotland	drew	2-2	

Norman Whiteside

Norman Whiteside stepped out to make his World Cup debut in 1982 with the confidence of a player who has been around and seen it all. Yet he was just 17 years and 41 days old and the youngest player ever to appear in a World Cup finals tournament.

He had made his League debut for Manchester United only a few weeks earlier, as a 16-year-old substitute in a 1-0 win over Brighton.

But Whiteside was always ahead of his time both in terms of skill and physical development. He scored a century of goals per season when playing schoolboy football. Whiteside was discovered by United's Belfast scout Rob Bishop and was signed by the Reds when he was 15. Ever since he was a boy, he had been tall and strongly built and his confidence to take on all-comers in passing, running, shooting or tackling earned him comparisons with George Best. But his vigorous and fearless style of play was more reminiscent of Joe Jordan, the Scotland international centre-forward. Whiteside deliberately modelled himself on Jordan's style after he joined Manchester United: 'I was made to feel wet behind the ears. It was then that I decided that nobody else was going to push me around.'

He demonstrated his keen scoring ability at the highest level in 1983 when he scored for United in the League Cup Final against Liverpool and in their 4-0 win over Brighton in the FA Cup Final replay.

In 1983 AC Milan offered Manchester United £1.5 million for Whiteside. Manager Ron Atkinson and chairman Martin Edwards agreed to the deal but Whiteside wanted to continue his career at Old Trafford. After that he became even more of a key man in the United set-up.

Originally a centre-forward, he now used his power and strength in midfield. He often outshone Bryan Robson and took over the captaincy when Robson was injured. It was from a position deep on the right that he found the space to set himself up to score the only goal in the 1985 FA Cup Final against Everton.

His performances for Northern Ireland were equally telling. He scored the goal in Ireland's astonishing defeat of West Germany in Hamburg in 1983 and laid the groundwork for Jimmy Quinn's goal in Bucharest, which gave Northern Ireland qualification at Romania's expense for the 1986 World Cup. When Whiteside went to Mexico, he became the youngest player ever to appear in two World Cup tournaments. Although Northern Ireland were eliminated in the first round, Whiteside scored in their 1-0 win over Algeria where he was by far the most effective man on the pitch.

Personal File

Position: Midfielder/Forward
Born: Norman Whiteside, Belfast
7 May 1965
Clubs: Manchester United, Everton

NI Caps: 38
NI Goals: 9

Games

Year	Opponent	Result	Score	G	Year	Opponent	Result	Score	G
1982	Yugoslavia	drew	0-0		1985	Spain	drew	0-0	
	Honduras	drew	1-1			Turkey	won	2-0	2
	Spain	won	1-0		1986	Romania	won	1-0	
	Austria	drew	2-2			England	drew	0-0	
	France	lost	1-4			France	drew	0-0	
1983	West					Denmark	drew	1-1	
	Germany	won	1-0			Morocco	won	2-1	
	Albania	drew	0-0			Algeria	drew	1-1	1
	Turkey	won	2-1			Spain	lost	1-2	
1984	Austria	won	3-1	1		Brazil	lost	0-3	
	Turkey	lost	0-1		1987	England	lost	0-3	
	West					Israel	drew	1-1	
	Germany	won	1-0	1		England	lost	0-2	
	Scotland	won	2-0	1		Yugoslavia	lost	1-2	
	England	lost	0-1		1988	Turkey	won	1-0	
	Wales	drew	1-1			Poland	drew	1-1	
	Finland	lost	0-1			France	drew	0-0	
1985	Romania	won	3-2	1	1990	Hungary	lost	1-2	1
	Israel	won	3-0	1		Republic			
	Finland	won	2-1			of Ireland	lost	0-3	
	England	lost	0-1						

Norman Whiteside

Whiteside began to lose his form and became increasingly upset by injuries. When Alex Ferguson took over as team manager and decided the team needed an overhaul, Whiteside's days at United were numbered. In the summer of 1989 with 67 goals in 272 League and Cup games to his name, Whiteside left Old Trafford and moved to Everton in the hope of putting sparkle back into his game.

Though his lack of pace often told against him, his ability to hold the ball and the vision of his flicks, led Billy Bingham to compare him with Kenny Dalglish.

His appearances at Goodison, however, were to be limited by injury and in 1992 he decided to call it a day and retire – still only in his mid-twenties. He was then a full-time student at Salford University where he qualified as a chiropodist. He also plays in occasional charity matches and undertakes after dinner speaking.

"He came at me like the Karate Kid."

- David O'Leary, Arsenal and Republic of Ireland

Left: Northern Ireland's Norman Whiteside (l) takes on Yugoslavia's Velimir Zajec (r)

Mark Williams

A commanding central defender with Shrewsbury Town, helping the Gay Meadow club win the Third Division Championship in 1993-94, Mark Williams had made 123 appearances before signing for John Duncan's Chesterfield for £50,000 in the summer of 1995.

Dangerous at set pieces with his heading ability, 'Bomber' soon won over the Spireites fans and in 1997-98 was voted the club's 'Player of the Year'. His rock-like performances for Chesterfield saw him rewarded with a call-up to the Northern Ireland 'B' squad and after impressing manager Lawrie McMenemy he became the first Chesterfield player to make a full international debut when starting the match against Germany in March 1999. Having been in discussion with the club over a new contract, Williams finally left Chesterfield under the Bosman ruling, joining Watford prior to the start of the 1999-2000 season. Settling down immediately, he formed a good understanding with Robert Page at the heart of the Hornets' defence and established himself as a regular in the Northern Ireland line-up.

Surprisingly he was allowed to leave Watford and join Wimbledon in July 2000. He continued to notch the occasional goal but was unlucky not to net a hat-trick in a 5-0 defeat of Queen's Park Rangers, scoring twice and having another effort cleared off the line. Voted the Dons' 'Player of the Year', he also scored his first-ever international goal against Bulgaria in March 2001. The following season he suffered a broken leg in the first game but played on for a couple of matches before this was diagnosed!

With his contract coming to an end he was allowed an early release to join Stoke City's ultimately successful bid for Division One survival. Even so, he didn't do enough to earn a longer contract and after playing in America for Columbus Crew, rejoined his former club Wimbledon, who by now had become the MK Dons.

Personal File

Position: Central defender
Born: Mark Stuart Williams, Stalybridge 28 September 1970
Clubs: Newtown, Shewsbury Town, Chesterfield, Watford, Wimbledon, Stoke City, Columbus Crew (America), MK Dons

NI Caps: 35
NI Goals: 1

Games

Year	Opponent	Result	Score	G	Year	Opponent	Result	Score	G
1999	Germany	lost	0-3		2002	Liechtenstein	drew	0-0	
	Moldova	drew	0-0			Spain	lost	0-5	
	Canada	drew	1-1		2003	Cyprus	drew	0-0	
	Republic of Ireland	won	1-0			Finland	lost	0-1	
2000	France	lost	0-1			Armenia	lost	0-1	
	Turkey	lost	0-3			Greece	lost	0-2	
	Germany	lost	0-4			Italy	lost	0-2	
	Finland	lost	1-4			Spain	drew	0-0	
	Luxembourg	won	3-1		2004	Norway	lost	1-4	
	Malta	won	3-0			Estonia	won	1-0	
	Hungary	lost	0-1			Serbia & Montenegro	drew	1-1	
2001	Yugoslavia	lost	1-2			Barbados	drew	1-1	
	Iceland	lost	0-1			Trinidad & Tobago	won	3-0	
	Norway	lost	0-4		2005	Switzerland	drew	0-0	
	Czech Republic	lost	0-1			Poland	lost	0-3	
	Bulgaria	lost	3-4	1		Wales	drew	2-2	
	Czech Republic	lost	1-3			Azerbaijan	drew	0-0	
						Austria	drew	3-3	

Danny Wilson

Midfielder Danny Wilson was on the books of his home-town club Wigan Athletic before joining Bury in the summer of 1977. However, following the Shakers' relegation to the Fourth Division, Wilson moved to Chesterfield, helping the Spireites to finish fifth in Division Three in his first season at Saltergate.

His impressive displays led to a transfer to Nottingham Forest but he was unable to hold down a regular place and after a loan spell with Scunthorpe United, he joined Brighton and Hove Albion.

Wilson scored twice on his debut as the Seagulls beat Cardiff City 3-1, going on to net 10 goals in 26 games. His midfield promptings helped Albion to finish sixth in Division Two in 1984-85 and the following season he had his best return in terms of goals scored with 16 in all competitions, including a hat-trick in a 5-2 League Cup win over Bradford City.

During the club's relegation season of 1986-87, Wilson won the first of 24 full international caps for Northern Ireland when he played in the goalless draw against Turkey at Izmir.

In the close season, Wilson who had scored 39 goals in 155 games, left to play for Luton Town. He netted 10 goals from midfield in his first season for the Hatters, as they finished ninth in Division One and helped the club win the League Cup, scoring one of the goals in a 3-2 defeat of Arsenal. The following season he was again the Hatters' leading scorer and played in another League Cup Final, but shortly afterwards he left to play for Sheffield Wednesday.

In his first season at Hillsborough, he helped the Owls win promotion to the top flight and in 1991-92 to third position in Division One. Surprisingly released in the summer of 1993, he moved to neighbours Barnsley, later becoming the Oakwell club's manager. He led the Tykes into the Premiership but lost his job after they were relegated. He then took charge of Sheffield Wednesday but was again sacked following the Owls' relegation. He then spent four years in charge of Bristol City before parting company with the club in the summer of 2004 after they had lost to one of his former clubs Brighton in the play-off final.

Personal File

Position: Midfielder
Born: Daniel Joseph Wilson,
Wigan
1 January 1960
Clubs: Wigan Athletic, Bury,
Chesterfield,
Nottingham Forest,
Scunthorpe United (loan),
Brighton and Hove Albion,
Luton Town,
Sheffield Wednesday,
Barnsley

NI Caps: 24
NI Goals: 1

Games

Year	Opponent	Result	Score	G	Year	Opponent	Result	Score	G
1987	Turkey	drew	0-0		1989	Malta	won	2-0	
	Israel	drew	1-1			Chile	lost	0-1	
	England	lost	0-2		1990	Hungary	lost	1-2	
1988	Yugoslavia	lost	0-3			Republic			
	Turkey	won	1-0			of Ireland	lost	0-3	
	Greece	lost	2-3			Norway	lost	2-3	
	Poland	drew	1-1	1		Uruguay	won	1-0	
	France	drew	0-0		1991	Yugoslavia	lost	0-2	
	Malta	won	3-0			Denmark	drew	1-1	
1989	Republic					Austria	drew	0-0	
	of Ireland	drew	0-0			Faroe Islands	drew	1-1	
	Hungary	lost	0-1		1992	Austria	won	2-1	
	Spain	lost	0-2			Scotland	lost	0-1	

Kevin Wilson

A sprightly striker, Kevin Wilson had trials with Sheffield United and Stoke City before Derby County gave him his chance in League football when they signed him from non-League Banbury United in December 1979.

Although he was Derby's leading scorer in 1981-82, his most prolific period was the start of Arthur Cox's first season in charge, when he scored four goals against Hartlepool United in a League Cup tie and a hat-trick against Bolton Wanderers before breaking an arm against Plymouth Argyle.

When he recovered he joined Ipswich Town for £150,000 and towards the end of his first season at Portman Road, netted a hat-trick in a 5-1 home win over Stoke City. With Ipswich, Wilson became a Northern Ireland international through a parental qualification and went on to earn 42 caps. One of his six goals at international level was the only goal of the game against the formidable Uruguayans in May 1990. He had scored 45 goals in 116 games for the East Anglian club when they sold him to Chelsea for £335,000 in the summer of 1987.

He continued to score on a regular basis for the Stamford Bridge club and in almost five seasons' football, he netted 47 goals in 172 first team outings before joining Notts County for £225,000 in March 1992.

There followed a loan spell at Bradford City before he left Meadow Lane to join Walsall on a free transfer. He helped the Saddlers gain promotion from Division Three before joining Northampton Town. Appointed the Cobblers' manager, he had three seasons in charge at the Sixfield Stadium before later managing a number of non-League clubs including Bedford Town, Aylesbury United and Kettering Town.

Personal File

Position: Forward
Born: Kevin James Wilson,
Banbury
18 April 1961
Clubs: Banbury United,
Derby County, Ipswich Town,
Chelsea, Notts County,
Bradford City (loan)
Walsall,
Northampton Town

NI Caps: 42
NI Goals: 6

Games

Year	Opponent	Result	Score	G	Year	Opponent	Result	Score	G
1987	Israel	drew	1-1		1992	Faroe Islands	won	5-0	1
	England	lost	0-2			Austria	won	2-1	
	Yugoslavia	lost	1-2			Denmark	lost	1-2	
1988	Yugoslavia	lost	0-3			Scotland	lost	0-1	
	Turkey	won	1-0			Lithuania	drew	2-2	1
	Greece	lost	2-3			Germany	drew	1-1	
	Poland	drew	1-1		1993	Albania	won	3-0	1
	France	drew	0-0			Spain	drew	0-0	
1989	Hungary	lost	0-1			Denmark	lost	0-1	
	Spain	lost	0-4			Spain	lost	1-3	1
	Spain	lost	0-2			Lithuania	won	1-0	
	Malta	won	2-0			Latvia	won	2-1	
	Chile	lost	0-1		1994	Latvia	won	2-0	
1990	Republic of Ireland	lost	0-3			Denmark	lost	0-1	
	Norway	lost	2-3	1		Republic of Ireland	drew	1-1	
	Uruguay	won	1-0	1		Romania	won	2-0	
1991	Yugoslavia	lost	0-2			Liechtenstein	won	4-1	
	Austria	drew	0-0			Colombia	lost	0-2	
	Poland	won	3-1			Mexico	lost	0-3	
	Yugoslavia	lost	1-4		1995	Republic of Ireland	lost	0-4	
	Faroe Islands	drew	1-1			Latvia	won	1-0	

Nigel Worthington

Nigel Worthington proved to be a most consistent performer after the then Notts County manager Jimmy Sirrel crossed the Irish Sea to sign him from Ballymena United, where he was 'Young Footballer of the Year' during the summer of 1981.

He soon established himself as a regular at Meadow Lane before in February 1984, his former manager at County, Howard Wilkinson brought him to Hillsborough to join Sheffield Wednesday in their successful promotion drive to the First Division.

At the end of that season, Worthington won his first cap for Northern Ireland against Wales in the penultimate match of the ill-fated Home Championships. After that he rarely missed a game at international level, including a visit to Mexico for the World Cup Finals in 1986. Worthington was one of the Owls' most consistent performers in a 10-year spell at Hillsborough and in 1990-91 assisted them to the top flight after their quite undeserved relegation the previous season. He was also a member of the team that carried a cup back to Hillsborough for the first time since 1935 – the League Cup, after a shock 10-0 victory over favourites Manchester United. He stood down for Phil King in the 1993 League Cup Final but was back on duty for the FA Cup Final, only to collect a losers' medal, following Arsenal's 2-1 victory in the replay.

Also that season he surpassed Ron Springett as Wednesday's most capped player while also being named Northern Ireland's 'Player of the Year'. He had appeared in 417 games for the Owls when in July 1994 he rejected new terms and opted to join his old boss Howard Wilkinson at Leeds United – the third time Wilkinson had signed him!

After being used as cover at both left-back and left-half, he became the target of the Elland Road boo-boys but he still managed to push his international appearances through the 60-cap barrier and in his final season often wore the skipper's armband for Northern Ireland.

After a spell with Stoke City, Worthington was appointed player-manager of Blackpool before hanging up his boots to concentrate on the management side of things. In January 2001, Worthington was appointed manager of Norwich City and in 2003-04 helped the Canaries win promotion to the Premiership.

Though they played some entertaining football in 2004-05, Worthington couldn't keep the Canaries in the top flight when with their fate in their own hands, they lost their last game 6-0 at Fulham!

Personal File

Position: Left-back/Midfielder
Born: Nigel Worthington,
Ballymena
4 November 1961
Clubs: Ballymena United,
Notts County,
Sheffield Wednesday,
Leeds United,
Stoke City,
Blackpool

NI Caps: 66

Games

Year	Opponent	Result	Score	G	Year	Opponent	Result	Score	G
1984	Wales	drew	1-1		1992	Scotland	lost	0-1	
	Finland	lost	0-1			Lithuania	drew	2-2	
1985	Israel	won	3-0			Germany	drew	1-1	
	Spain	drew	0-0		1993	Albania	won	3-0	
1986	Turkey	drew	0-0			Spain	drew	0-0	
	Romania	won	1-0			Denmark	lost	0-1	
	England	drew	0-0			Republic of Ireland	lost	0-3	
	Denmark	drew	1-1			Spain	lost	1-3	
	Algeria	drew	1-1			Lithuania	won	1-0	
	Spain	lost	1-2			Latvia	won	2-1	
1987	England	lost	0-3		1994	Latvia	won	2-0	
	Turkey	drew	0-0			Denmark	lost	0-1	
	Israel	drew	1-1			Republic of Ireland	drew	1-1	
	England	lost	0-2			Liechtenstein	won	4-1	
	Yugoslavia	lost	1-2			Colombia	lost	0-2	
1988	Yugoslavia	lost	0-3			Mexico	lost	0-3	
	Turkey	won	1-0		1995	Portugal	lost	1-2	
	Greece	lost	2-3			Austria	won	2-1	
	Poland	drew	1-1			Republic of Ireland	lost	0-4	
	France	drew	0-0			Republic of Ireland	drew	1-1	
	Malta	won	3-0			Latvia	won	1-0	
1989	Republic of Ireland	drew	0-0			Canada	lost	0-2	
	Hungary	lost	0-1			Chile	lost	1-2	
	Spain	lost	0-4			Latvia	lost	1-2	
	Malta	won	2-0		1996	Portugal	drew	1-1	
1990	Hungary	lost	1-2			Liechtenstein	won	4-0	
	Republic of Ireland	lost	0-3			Austria	won	5-3	
	Uruguay	won	1-0			Norway	lost	0-2	
1991	Yugoslavia	lost	0-2			Sweden	lost	1-2	
	Denmark	drew	1-1			Germany	drew	1-1	
	Austria	drew	0-0		1997	Italy	lost	0-2	
	Faroe Islands	drew	1-1			Belgium	won	3-0	
1992	Austria	won	2-1						
	Denmark	lost	1-2						

Tommy Wright

Goalkeeper Tommy Wright was discovered playing for the Irish League side Linfield and signed for Newcastle United at the beginning of 1988 as third choice keeper behind Gary Kelly and Martin Thomas. First team opportunities seemed even scarcer the following season when United parted with a large sum to purchase Wimbledon's Dave Beasant. But when he failed to settle in the north-east and was transferred to Chelsea early in 1989, Tommy Wright was finally given the chance to show what he was capable of. At the end of that season, he received his first international caps for Northern Ireland in a World Cup group tie in Malta and then at home to Chile in May. Over the next two seasons, with no outstanding keeper available, he lost out somewhat to Alan Fettis but in 1991-92 he came back to favour as manager Billy Bingham's preferred choice.

Following Newcastle's signing of John Burridge and Czech international Pavel Srnicek, he went on loan to Hull City. On his return to St James Park, he went 18 months without a first team appearance before winning back his place under the management of Ossie Ardilles. Again he lost out to Srnicek but after some erratic displays by the Czech, new manager Kevin Keegan recalled him to the side. Wright helped the Magpies win the First Division Championship and for Northern Ireland in February 1993 he saved a penalty in a 2-1 win in a World Cup qualifier in Albania. This was Northern Ireland's first away victory since September 1991.

Wright left Newcastle at the start of the 1993-94 season and though hampered by injuries at the City Ground, he was between the posts as Frank Clark guided Forest into the Premiership. There followed loan spells with Reading and Manchester City before he later joined the then Maine Road club on a permanent basis.

Sadly injuries again restricted his first team opportunities and following the rise of Nicky Weaver as City's No.1 keeper, Wright was loaned out to Wrexham. An injury crisis at Newcastle saw Wright brought back to Tyneside on a month's loan and then the following season he spent three months at Bolton Wanderers, again on loan. Still unable to make any headway at Manchester City, he returned to Ireland to continue his career at Ballymena United.

"Football is all about pressure. You have to learn to live with it."

- Tommy Wright

Personal File

Position: Goalkeeper
Born: Thomas James Wright,
Belfast
29 August 1963
Clubs: Linfield, Newcastle United,
Hull City (loan)
Nottingham Forest,
Reading (loan), Manchester City,
Wrexham (loan),
Newcastle United (loan),
Bolton Wanderers (loan),
Ballymena United

NI Caps: 31

Games

Year	Opponent	Result	Score	G	Year	Opponent	Result	Score	G
1989	Malta	won	2-0		1994	Latvia	won	2-0	
	Chile	lost	0-1			Denmark	lost	0-1	
1990	Hungary	lost	1-2			Republic			
	Uruguay	won	1-0			of Ireland	drew	1-1	
1992	Faroe Islands	won	5-0			Romania	won	2-0	
	Austria	won	2-1			Liechtenstein	won	4-1	
	Scotland	lost	0-1			Colombia	lost	0-2	
	Germany	drew	1-1			Mexico	lost	0-3	
1993	Albania	won	3-0		1997	Germany	drew	1-1	
	Spain	drew	0-0			Albania	won	2-0	
	Albania	won	2-1			Italy	lost	0-2	
	Republic					Belgium	won	3-0	
	of Ireland	lost	0-3			Portugal	drew	0-0	
	Spain	lost	1-3			Ukraine	lost	1-2	
	Lithuania	won	1-0		1998	Albania	lost	0-1	
	Latvia	won	2-1		1999	Canada	drew	1-1	
					2000	France	lost	0-1	

STATISTICS

Most Capped Players

1	Pat Jennings	119
2	Mal Donaghy	91
3	Sammy McIlroy	88
4	Jimmy Nicholl	73
5	Michael Hughes	71
6	David McCreery	67
7	Nigel Worthington	66
8	Martin O'Neill	64
9	Gerry Armstrong	63
10	Keith Gillespie	60
11=	Iain Dowie	59
	Terry Neill	59
13	Billy Bingham	56
	Danny Blanchflower	56
15	Jimmy McIlroy	55
16=	Allan Hunter	53
	John McClelland	53
18=	Alan McDonald	52
	Jim Magilton	52
20=	Sammy Nelson	51
	Chris Nicholl	51
	Gerry Taggart	51

Top Goal Scorers

1	David Healy	16
2	Colin Clarke	13
3=	Gerry Armstrong	12
	Iain Dowie	12
	Jimmy Quinn	12
6=	Billy Bingham	10
	Johnny Crossan	10
	Jimmy McIlroy	10
	Peter McParland	10
10=	George Best	9
	Norman Whiteside	9
12=	Derek Dougan	8
	Willie Irvine	8
	Martin O'Neill	8
15=	Billy McAdams	7
	Gerry Taggart	7
17=	Phil Gray	6
	Jimmy Nicholson	6
	Kevin Wilson	6
20=	Wilbur Cush	5
	Willie Hamilton	5
	Michael Hughes	5
	Sammy McIlroy	5
	Jimmy Magilton	5

Acknowledgements

The publisher wishes to thank the following for permission to reproduce work in copyright:

© Associated Sports Photography (pp 17, 18-19, 21, 22-23, 25, 28, 29, 37, 40, 44, 45, 46, 47, 48, 49, 51, 52, 54, 62, 64, 66, 67, 76, 77, 80, 81, 82, 84, 85, 92, 98, 99, 100, 101, 102, 103, 104, 105, 106, 107, 108, 109, 112, 120-121, 122, 123, 129, 130, 131, 135, 136, 137, 138, 139, 140, 141, 144, 146, 148, 149, 154, 166, 167, 170, 171, 172, 173, 174, 175, 177, 178, 180, 181, 184, 186, 188-189, 190, 193, 196, 200, 202, 207, 208, 209, 211, 214, 215, 218, 219, 220, 221, 222, 224, 225, 226, 227)

© EMPICS (pp 14, 26-27, 32-33, 34, 38, 56, 60, 72, 78, 86, 94-95, 96, 114, 116, 124, 126, 142, 152-153, 156-157, 158, 160, 162, 168, 194, 198, 216-217)

© Getty Images (pp 70, 132)

© Lancashire Evening Post (pp 16, 20, 24, 30, 31, 36, 41, 50, 63, 65, 68, 69, 74, 75, 83, 90, 93, 113, 118, 128, 134, 145, 150, 155, 176, 179, 182, 185, 187, 191, 192, 197, 201, 203, 204, 206, 230, 232)

© Pacemaker (pp 88, 210)

The publisher would also like to acknowledge the kind assistance of Lee Purcell.